Love and Friendship
in Plato and Aristotle

Love and Friendship in Plato and Aristotle

A. W. PRICE

CLARENDON PRESS · OXFORD

Oxford University Press, Walton Street, Oxford OX2 6DP

Oxford New York Toronto
Delhi Bombay Calcutta Madras Karachi
Petaling Jaya Singapore Hong Kong Tokyo
Nairobi Dar es Salaam Cape Town
Melbourne Auckland

and associated companies in
Berlin Ibadan

Published in the United States
by Oxford University Press, New York

First published 1989
First issued in paperback 1990
Reprinted 1991

British Library Cataloguing in Publication Data
Price, A. W.
Love and friendship in Plato and Aristotle.
1. Love. Theories of Aristotle & Plato,
384–322 B.C. 2. Friendship. Theories of
Aristotle & Plato, 384–322 B.C.
I. Title
152.4
ISBN 0–19–824899–7

Library of Congress Cataloging in Publication Data
Price, A. W.
Love and friendship in Plato and Aristotle/A. W. Price.
Bibliography: p. Includes index.
1. Love—History. 2. Friendship—History. 3. Plato.
4. Aristotle. I. Title.
BD436.P75   1988   177'.7—dc19   88-25279
ISBN 0–19–824899–7

Printed and bound in
Great Britain by Biddles Ltd.
Guildford and King's Lynn

In Memory of

Peter Price (1921–1967),

Mary Price (1897–1980),

Magda Minio-Paluello (1910–1987).

There is an element of pleasure even in mourning and lamentation: there is grief, indeed, at their loss, but pleasure in remembering, and in a manner seeing, both what they did and what sort of person they were (Aristotle, *Rhetoric* 1.11.1370b25–8).

ACKNOWLEDGEMENTS

Finishing one's first book as one reaches the age of 40 gives one the sense of all too many figures from one's past looking over one's shoulder; whether they are approving or disapproving one cannot tell, for they are out of eyeshot. To cite them gratefully is not to recruit them to one's side, but to acknowledge one's debts.

To my parents, of course, I owe everything, including this book. Yet what they have given me is much more than a matter of course: it is the active encouragement in being oneself that can make the child's home seem a world, and the adult's world a home. Richard Wollheim has written truly, 'Culturally we are heirs to our adolescence'; the richness of mine is a particular debt I owe to them. It is also they who supplied me with the best and (unpredictably) most congenial of godparents: Peter Price, Anthony Camps, and Alethea Hayter. All three of these have been a literary example to me; for two of them I can expect to be writing in time.

This book would be a pretence, and my life a poor thing, without a number of friendships which I hope I can pick out without disparaging the remainder. First and last, there is my brother Richard: though I do not know that they ever mention it, Plato and Aristotle implicitly hold that the relationship of identical twins at its best is the paradigm towards which other friendships aspire; rightly. To a series of institutions I owe a series of attachments nurtured within them, but matured outside: to John Scholes at Winchester, Walter Wenzel at York, Nigel Yandell at Wadham, and Peter Cockhill again at York. For me their invisible presences quicken 'these poor rude lines' with a life that is not their own. My best friend at Balliol, Ronald Knox, spoke at his wedding about the value of friendship, and had the right to do so: in the words of Montaigne, 'Even as he did excell me by an infinite distance in all other sufficiencies and vertues, so did he in all offices and duties of friendship.' Colleagues can be another matter; but not Ian Ker, Anna Baldwin, Marie McGinn, or David Mabberley. One can feel ambivalently about one's friends' partners; Mark Rowe and Naomi Saxl have been enhancing.

I owe my classical education especially to L. A. Wilding at the Dragon School, John Stow (clearest of heads) and Francis King (noblest of hearts) at Winchester, and Jasper and Miriam Griffin (brightest and kindest of tutors) at Oxford. I had the good fortune there to have two contrasted models in ancient philosophy: Anthony Kenny, who showed me how enjoyable it can be, and John Ackrill, who taught me how difficult it remains. No doubt my greatest intellectual debt is to Richard Hare, who trained me in moral philosophy and influenced my ideas greatly, and yet has always been at his most appreciative when they diverge, constructively or critically, from his own. A recent stimulus has been Martha Nussbaum; despite inevitable disagreements in detail, she has refreshed my conviction that the role of scholarship is to illumine, and not to eliminate, a personal response to texts.

Life is long, but so is the writing of books. Most of the first draft of this was written during three years spent on leave from the University of York as a Lecturer in Philosophy at Wadham (which at least, of course, freed me from lecturing). The friendliness of the Fellows made that a very happy time. The second draft was written during a sabbatical term from York, which came just as I was in need of it. Responses from Martha Nussbaum and David Walker removed a few of the mistakes; an anonymous reader of two sample chapters made useful comments about presentation. Among the pleasures of publishing philosophy with Oxford University Press is dealing with their philosophy editor, Angela Blackburn.

Kensington, London   A.W.P.
December 1987

CONTENTS

NOTE TO THE READER

The writer on classical texts has to live with the fact that their relative dating, which with modern texts is an initial datum, is a matter of speculation; chronology becomes, indeed, a very focus of controversy. There are two contrasted ways of escaping from this predicament: to take an author's works one at a time, or to treat them as parts of a single work.[1] My sympathies tend to the second policy: whether or not we are willing to say with Proust, 'The great men of letters have always only created a single work',[2] the best commentary on any given work must be other works by the same author. Taking texts singly is liable to leave too many of the ideas to be found in them inchoate and deficient. Of course such commentary will be constrained by whatever lines of development one thinks one can make out, and it must always be subject to the qualification that there may be changes of mind that are escaping us. Moreover, one may at any time make it into an issue whether two works are at one or at odds; it then becomes question-begging to retain a presumption in favour of reconciling interpretations. In preparing this book, for instance, I have tried to reflect upon the *Symposium* and *Phaedrus* separately, in order to avoid the circularity of coming to the view that they are somewhat more akin than is generally thought through using the one to interpret the other.

For my purposes, it is a major turning-point in Plato when in *Republic* Book 4, with an explicitness that conveys novelty, he accommodates conflict of desire within the soul by dividing it into parts. This development does clearly differentiate the *Symposium* (in which all desires derive from a unitary desire for the good) from the *Phaedrus* (which represents the tripartite soul by the famous simile of the chariot). Of course that has restricted my syncretism. I have been less restrained by a different line of thought: if we stress the character of Platonic dialogues as literary artefacts, we may be struck by the

---

[1] Preference here must be partly a matter of temperament: I well remember sermons on the Trinity by the admirable Dean of Balliol in my time, the Revd Frank McCarthy-Willis-Bund, in which he distinguished natural 'lumpers' from 'splitters'; the same division applies to ancient philosophers.

[2] *A la recherche du temps perdu* (Paris, 1954), iii. 375.

possibilities of irony that the form permits; instead of taking the figure of Socrates as a mouthpiece of Platonic doctrine, we may then examine points of presentation for indications that Plato may be distancing himself from what Socrates says (or from his silence). I have been conscious of the charms of such an approach ever since I heard Wolfgang Wieland lecturing in Marburg in 1966. There are two reasons why it has scarcely influenced this book, one general and one particular: in general, literary interpretation of Plato is even more insecure than philosophical, and better functions as an appendage than a foundation; in particular, I happen to believe that the Socrates of the *Symposium*, *Republic* (after Book 1), and *Phaedrus* (unlike, say, that of the *Parmenides* or *Theaetetus*) is expressing, if never definitively, Plato's own views.[3]

Aristotle does not pose us that problem, since what survives of his work is not dialogues but lecture-notes. However, the student of his moral philosophy faces a different complication. We possess not one but two Aristotelian *Ethics*, the *Nicomachean* and the *Eudemian*, or rather almost two *Ethics*: Books 5–7 of the *Nicomachean* (as they appear in most but not all manuscripts) are to be supplied to form Books 4–6 of the *Eudemian*. Where they really belong is therefore debatable. Anthony Kenny has recently argued, mostly on stylometric grounds, for placing them unqualifiedly within the *Eudemian Ethics*.[4] I have to admit to finding this issue more intriguing than important, for two reasons. Firstly, I incline to suppose (I believe like D. J. Allan) that the two *Ethics* were written quite close in time and differ for the most part not in containing different theories, but in presenting the same theories for different audiences (the *Nicomachean* being more popular, the *Eudemian* more esoteric).[5] Secondly, it must support syncretism in practice that the common books are needed within both *Ethics*: a self-denying policy of looking exclusively at what remains, within either *Ethics*, would be more scrupulous than fruitful. On the topic of friendship, I shall draw

---

3 There are the qualifications in respect of the *Phaedrus* that Socrates' first speech is explicitly a piece of devil's advocacy, while his second is partly mythical in a way that puts indeterminate limits on its seriousness. Further, I suspect the psychology of the *Symposium* of being deliberately retrogressive, for it is more Socratic than that of the *Phaedo*.

4 *The Aristotelian Ethics* (Oxford, 1978). I shall refer to the common books as if they are *Nicomachean*, but only for ease of reference, not because I am competent to disagree with Kenny.

5 Admittedly, the distinction between a new theory, and a new presentation of a theory, is a vague one.

attention to certain divergences which may or may not represent actual changes of mind;[6] but most often I shall draw on both *Ethics* to illustrate the same points.

I fear that one omission may trouble non-classicists: although I am writing about topics close to everyday life, I shall say little about the historical background, of which my knowledge is that of an amateur. I have always kept within reach two invaluable books by Sir Kenneth Dover: *Greek Popular Morality in the Time of Plato and Aristotle* (Oxford, 1974), and *Greek Homosexuality* (London, 1978); I would advise the reader to do the same.

In quotations I use the following translations, with modifications: of Plato's *Laws* by T. J. Saunders (Harmondsworth, 1970), of the *Phaedo* by David Gallop (Oxford, 1975), of the *Phaedrus* by C. J. Rowe (Warminster, 1986), of the *Republic* by Paul Shorey (London, 1935) and Desmond Lee (Harmondsworth, 1974), and of the *Theaetetus* by John McDowell (Oxford, 1973); of Aristotle the Revised Oxford Translation, ed. Jonathan Barnes (2 vols.; Princeton, 1984), except for the *Eudemian Ethics* Books 1, 2, and 8 by Michael Woods (Oxford, 1982).[7] I also refer to these translations: of the *Laws* by A. E. Taylor (London, 1934), and of the *Symposium* by Benjamin Jowett (Oxford, 1892) and Léon Robin (Paris, 1929); of the *Eudemian Ethics* by J. Solomon (Oxford, 1925), of the *Nicomachean Ethics* by W. D. Ross (Oxford, 1925) and Terence Irwin (Indianapolis, 1985), and of the *Politics* by T. A. Sinclair and T. J. Saunders (Harmondsworth, 1981).

The 'list of modern works cited' at the end of the book is precisely that, and not an eccentric attempt at a bibliography; it includes a fraction of what I have relevantly read, and a proportion of what I have admired.

---

[6] I tentatively think that these divergences support a further supposition of mine, that the *Nicomachean Ethics* was written with the benefit of the *Eudemian*, and not vice versa.

[7] I was particularly fortunate in being able to take over, at a late stage, Rowe's admirably faithful translation of the *Phaedrus*; I shall signal most of my few departures from that.

ABBREVIATIONS

PLATO
(* perhaps spurious)

Apol	*Apology*
Charm	*Charmides*
Crat	*Cratylus*
Critias	
Euthyd	*Euthydemus*
Gorg	*Gorgias*
*Hippias Major	
Ion	
Laches	
Laws	
Lysis	
Menex	*Menexenus*
Meno	
Pdo	*Phaedo*
Phdr	*Phaedrus*
Phil	*Philebus*
Pol	*Politicus*
Prot	*Protagoras*
Rep	*Republic*
*7th Letter	*Seventh Letter*
Soph	*Sophist*
Symp	*Symposium*
Theaet	*Theaetetus*
Tim	*Timaeus*

ARISTOTLE
(* almost certainly spurious)

Cat	*Categories*
De an	*De anima*
De gen an	*De generatione animalium*
De gen corr	*De generatione et corruptione*
EE	*Eudemian Ethics*

Hist an	*Historia animalium*
Magna moralia	
Met	*Metaphysics*
Meteor	*Meteorologica*
NE	*Nicomachean Ethics*
Phys	*Physics*
Poetics	
Pol	*Politics*
Pr Anal	*Prior Analytics*
Problemata	
Rhet	*Rhetoric*
Top	*Topics*

K. J. DOVER

GH	*Greek Homosexuality*
GPM	*Greek Popular Morality in the Time of Plato and Aristotle*

I

FRIENDSHIP AND DESIRE IN THE
LYSIS

I

What is the topic of the *Lysis*, and what is its conclusion? As typically of those Platonic dialogues that may be presumed closest to the manner and method of the historical Socrates, there are apparently simple answers. The topic is friendship (*philiā*), and the conclusion failure: Socrates opens the main body of the discussion by remarking, 'I do not even know how one person becomes the friend of another' (212a5–6); he closes the whole dialogue by admitting, 'We have not yet been able to discover what a friend is' (223b7–8). And yet, to a closer scrutiny, the subject-matter is Protean, constantly changing and eluding our grasp, and its treatment, though inconclusive, already distinctive and suggestive in ways that intimate what kind of theory Socrates, or rather Plato, is after. In certain respects this turns out to be rather different from how we tend to talk abstractly about friendship; it rapidly becomes an issue, long before any theory has been achieved, whether, if friendship is their topic, they are approaching it rightly. If they are not, neither is Aristotle. In his two surviving treatments, in the *Nicomachean* and *Eudemian Ethics*, Aristotle effectively takes the *Lysis* as his starting-point; with no other Platonic dialogue does he show such a detailed, yet implicit, familiarity.[1] He takes over from it not only points of detail, but general presuppositions that locate his own conclusions, which are not aporetic, in the same conceptual region. If Socrates' failure in the *Lysis* is wholly misconceived, so is Aristotle's success in his *Ethics*. My aim in this book is to display that their approach is reflective and fertile, well-conceived in theory and pregnant in practice; to respond to it briskly with the clichés of modern thought is to prefer the pleasures of the parrot to the pains of the philosopher.

---

[1] Comparable are only his explicit criticisms of the *Republic* and the *Laws* in *Politics* 2.1–6.

FRIENDSHIP AND DESIRE IN THE *LYSIS*

One deservedly influential scholar, who has brought my topic to life in ways without which this book would be not so much different as inconceivable, has not altogether escaped the danger of opposing to Greek theoretical assumptions what remain, until *they* have been explicated, mere modern moralistic commonplaces. Gregory Vlastos, in a well-known essay, has paid Plato the tribute not of faded reverence, but of lively disparagement. He casts him as the champion of a 'spiritualized egocentrism', a man 'scarcely aware of kindness, tenderness, compassion, concern for the freedom, respect for the integrity of the beloved, as essential ingredients of the highest type of interpersonal love', who could not allow 'that the ultimate purpose of the creative act should be to enrich the lives of persons who are themselves worthy of love for their own sake'.[2] Vlastos takes a definite view of the topic of the *Lysis*, and a positive view of its conclusions, as his phrase 'the theory of *philiā* in the *Lysis*' simultaneously indicates (ibid. 9, n. 20). According to this theory, as he articulates it, a proper object of affection must be useful (cf. 210c5–d4), that is useful to the subject of the affection (cf. 213e3 ff., especially 215a8–b1). A crucial notion is that of need: the good man, as such, is self-sufficient, and needing nothing will love no one (215a6–b2); whereas the invalid will love the doctor for the sake of a cure, and the pauper the rich man for the sake of assistance (d4–6). Vlastos concludes with a moral complaint: 'The lover Socrates has in view seems positively incapable of loving others for their own sake, else why must he feel no affection for anyone whose good-producing qualities *he* did not happen to need?' (op. cit. 8–9). Does this criticism treat the *Lysis* fairly, or is it a typical instance of moralism setting up its own target?

Vlastos starts by placing weight upon an initial argument in which Socrates forces upon Lysis the conclusion that no one loves him so far as he is useless—which, as he is a young boy, means that no one loves him much (207d5–210d4). The basis of the argument is a triple equation between loving another (207d6), wishing him to fare well or be happy (*eudaimōn*, e4), and letting him do what he wishes (e6). Socrates leads Lysis through a well-graded series of examples: being allowed less liberty than a servant (208a6) or a slave (b6), over his parents' property (b7–8) or his own person (c1–2), not only by his father in respect of his father's property (a2) or his own person (d1–

---

[2] 'The Individual as Object of Love in Plato', in *Platonic Studies* (Princeton, 1981), 30–1. In fairness to Vlastos, it must be said that he is not unaware that such phrases call for interpretation (ibid. 10, n. 24).

2), but even by his mother in respect of her property (d3–7). The implication is that, since his parents allow him a free hand only in matters about which he is trained (209a7–c2), they love him only to the extent that he is accomplished and useful (210c5–d4). Socrates thus succeeds in demonstrating to Hippothales, an older boy at once absurdly and vulnerably in love with Lysis, how one ought to speak to one's favourite, humbling and checking him, not puffing him up and turning his head (210e2–5). Ostensibly, he achieves that by proving to Lysis that he lacks the affection even of the father by whose name he is still called (204e3–5). But that conclusion can hardly stand: it contradicts not only what they agreed in the first place ('I suppose, Lysis, that your father loves you very much, and your mother too', 'Certainly', 207d5–6), but also what Socrates will assume again ('Sometimes a father treasures his son before all his other possessions', 219d6–7—if that is a common case of parental devotion, and not an investment in a young Mozart). Moreover, still stranger claims have preceded: from the unremarkable observation that Lysis's parents allow him licence with stylus and plectrum (209b2–7), Socrates inferred that, on the day his father thinks Lysis wiser than himself, he will entrust to him his person and his property (c4–6); to make the absurdity blatant, he added the same of Lysis's neighbour (c6–d3), the Athenians (d4–5), and even the King of Persia himself (210a5–7). It must be evident to everyone that Lysis has been bamboozled; that, perhaps, is his real humiliation. So far, then, nothing serious has been said to merit solemn strictures; I shall return to Vlastos's complaint later.[3]

Lysis is relieved by Menexenus, a close friend of the same age. In tribute to their relationship, Socrates at last seizes upon a topic: how one person becomes another's friend (*philos*, 212a5–6). The question can only so be understood; but what follows exploits the various sense of *philos* so confusingly that the topic comes apart in their hands. Three senses, or perhaps usages, of *philos* are in play:

(i) Reciprocal, and equivalent to our 'friend'; usually conveyed by a pair of correlative pronouns (212a6, c8), once by a conjunction of

---

[3] Cf. D. B. Robinson, 'Plato's *Lysis*: The Structural Problem', *Illinois Classical Studies* 11 (1986), 69, n. 15. (To this article, which supersedes everything known to me previously published on the *Lysis*, I shall be shamelessly indebted; unless I say otherwise, I shall be referring to it when I refer to him.) No doubt the trouble lies in the equation of loving someone, or wishing him happiness, and letting him do what he wishes; but sorting that out requires at least a distinction between ends and means, which has still to come.

the active and passive moods of the verb *philein* (213a6–7), and once simply by the plural 'the *philoi*' (213a7).

(ii) Neuter and passive, meaning 'dear'; often followed by a personal dative (most explicitly at 212e6), and introduced by a list of *philo-* compounds (for instance, 'horse-lover', 'dog-lover', 212d5–7).

(iii) Masculine and active, meaning 'fond'; often followed by a genitive (most explicitly at 213b5–6).[4]

Since Socrates interweaves the three usages instead of disentangling them, he naturally forces Menexenus into the quandary that none of them catches *the* meaning of *philos* (213c5–9); the upshot is, ostensibly, failure.

Is that how the reader is intended to take it? Aristotle responds constructively by conjoining the three usages: 'A man becomes a friend whenever being loved he loves in return' (*EE* 7.2.1236a14–15). Was Plato already envisaging that? D. B. Robinson is sceptical (71–2, 80–2), noting persuasively,

Each paraphrase is rejected because another sense of *philos* can be produced which this paraphrase does not represent. The only reason for this can be an assumption that *philos* has some one basic meaning. If one is setting oneself the aim of obtaining one single equivalent of *philos* in all its senses, then none of these suggestions will do and a negative conclusion is justified. This is certainly Plato's ostensible aim here; and I think it may also be his real aim (ibid. 72).

Plato may even have welcomed a failure to achieve a nominal definition as turning us to the search for a real definition of the nature of friendship (ibid. 81); he may have conceived Socrates as escaping from a shallow quagmire of verbal frivolity (cf. *Euthyd* 278b2–7) onto the terra firma of psychological reflection. The upshot is a change of aim, away from the pursuit of a paraphrase towards an investigation of the grounds of friendship (as the form of the question put to Menexenus already anticipated, 212a5–6). If Socrates values winning a friend above all else (211e2–8), that is not because he would place

---

[4] Cf. Robinson, 65–8. Transition from (i) into (ii) is eased by a switch from a masculine *philos* to a neuter *philon* which is initially generalizing (as is idiomatic in Greek), and then passive (cf. 212d4 and e6); transition from (ii) into (iii) is then prepared by a return from the neuter to the masculine (213a4 ff.). The grammatical distinctions are sacrificed now and then by attaching *philos* to a dative (meaning 'friend to') in contexts permitting 'fond of' (or 'desiring the *philiā* of') but not 'dear to' (215d5, 217a2, 6, 218a1, 221d4). In his 'Plato's *Lysis*', B.Litt. thesis (Oxford, 1961), 24, Robinson emphasized that Plato is extending the uses of *philos* and *philein* far beyond what was normal in Greek prose, thus connecting *philos*, in the sense of 'friend', with other uses of *philos* and *philein*; his aim, as I shall be locating it, is to suit his programme of placing friendship within a theory of desire.

friendship upon an ideal pinnacle soaring high above human nature, but because he regards it as a fulfilment of fundamental human needs and desires. His ensuing failure to identify these is a stumbling upon real obstacles, which will have to be cleared to make way for a philosophical understanding.

2

Following his new path, Socrates first has recourse to poets (214a1) and natural philosophers (b4–5) who testify that like is dear to like.[5] He questions this as a sufficient condition of friendship by appeal to another commonplace, that bad men are unfriendly to one another (b7–c2, cf. *Gorg* 507e3–6, *Phdr* 255b1–2). He states two grounds: that they wrong one another (c2–3, cf. *Rep* 1.351c7–352d2), and that they are at odds even with themselves (c7–d3). That they are 'never like even to themselves' (c8) must mean that they are of two minds even at the same time (cf. *Rep* 1.352a7, anticipating the account of internal justice at 4.443c9–e2), though the epithets 'impulsive' and 'unstable' (214d1) also convey that they change their minds over time. However, that makes bad men only alike verbally in being 'bad': in reality, they are unlike both to themselves and to one another. Hence it can still be maintained that like is friend to like, so long as this is understood as a 'riddling' way of saying that the good alone are friends (d4–6). If the alike and the good form a single class, is it *qua* being alike or *qua* being good that they are friends? Both possibilities are problematic. To the extent that two men are similar, neither can do anything to benefit the other that each could not do on his own; and if neither can assist the other, how can they cherish one another (214e3–215a2)? While to the extent that a man is good, he is self-sufficient, in need of nothing, and so will cherish and love no one (a6–b2). Neither missing one another when absent, nor having any use for one another when present, good men will not be friends (b3–c1).[6]

[5] An 'ancient' saying (*Symp* 195b5, cf. *Gorg* 510b2–4), already put to ironical use at *Odyssey* 17.218.

[6] Socrates says nothing to make precise or plausible the premiss that good men are self-sufficient. One idea that may underlie it, shared by Xenophon's Socrates (*Memorabilia* 1.2.14, 1.6.10) and Democritus (Diels-Kranz fr. 282), is that material simplicity and austerity aid the satisfaction of one's desires by reducing their scope. Another, recurrent in Plato (*Menex* 247e6–248a7, *Rep* 3.387d11–e7), is that it is better to depend on one's own resources, and not on luck, for achieving *eudaimoniā*; the ideal could then be to make of goodness an unconditional disposition to be *eudaimōn*, so that *eudaimoniā* would come to manifest a purely internal state. The contingencies of love and friendship would then become an irrelevance.

Socrates finally confirms that like is not dear to like by invoking Hesiod: 'Potter is angry with potter, bard with bard, and beggar with beggar' (215c8–9). Similarity is not only insufficient for friendship, but a ground of enmity; therefore, 'it is necessary that especially things most similar to one another should be filled with enmity, strife, and hatred' (d2–4). Why this should be so is not explained, and Hesiod in effect simply helps a transition to another suggestion, that 'things most dissimilar' to one another are filled 'with friendship' (d4). Examples serve first to support this (the poor and the rich, the weak and the strong, the invalid and the doctor, the ignorant and the informed, d5–7), then gently to mock it (not only the moist and the dry, the hot and the cold, but even the sharp and the blunt, e5–8), and finally to refute it (the just and the unjust, the good and the bad, even friend and enemy, 216b1–8). In a way, this is a weaker refutation (cf. Robinson, 'Plato's *Lysis*', 37): whereas before it was argued that the absence of similarity is *necessary* for friendship, here it is merely illustrated by example that the presence of dissimilarity is not *sufficient*. However, it may be that Plato did not see it quite like that. In his rejection of certain kinds of explanation in the *Phaedo*, he seems to exclude as paradoxical that one and the same thing should be the cause (that is, we might say, the salient cause) of opposite effects, as the accruing of two both of the relative largeness of ten and of the relative smallness of eight (96e2–4). So Socrates may be thinking here (in a way precisely analogous to his application of Hesiod) that, since dissimilarity is sometimes a ground of enmity, it can never in itself be a ground of friendship; it cannot be that one and the same consideration should tell now for, now against, a single upshot. If so, and friendship is indeed a single *explanandum*, dissimilarity cannot help explain the possibility of friendship.

That opposites should be friends was never plausible in the first place except as an anticipation of a somewhat different thought. The poor man, for instance, needs to be *philos* to the rich man for the sake of assistance (215d4–6). 'Be *philos* to' must be equivalent to 'cultivate the *philiā* of'; but why the rich man should respond is mysterious. In effect, any hope of explaining reciprocity falls away, and an impersonal goal becomes the focus. This emerges all the more clearly in expansion of Socrates' next proposal: that which is neither good nor bad becomes *philos* to the good (216e7–217a2). The previous instance of invalid and doctor (215d6) reappears: the invalid is compelled, because of illness, to be *philos* to the doctor (217a5–7). A body is not, as such, either good or evil (b2–3); it can be affected by illness like hair daubed with ceruse (d1–6) in such a way that it does not become malignant (any more than the hair really becomes white), but tends towards recovery. In the case of knowledge, the distinction is between complete ignorance, and a partial ignorance that at least knows itself and allows room for a desire to know (218a2–b1); in the case of goodness in general, it is between complacent badness, and a partial badness that accommodates a desire to be good (217e4–9). Such examples make desire the focus rather than friendship; *philos* in the sense of 'dear' (passive) or 'fond' (active) has taken over from *philos* in the sense of 'friend'. Thus the term 'desire' (*epithūmiā*) twice accompanies the term *philiā*, as if it made little difference which we used (217e8–9, 221e4). That goes with an increasingly impersonal presentation of subject and object. It cannot signify much that the invalid tends to make way as subject for the body (217a4–5, b3, 219a1): talk of his body as 'welcoming and loving' (217b4) is equivalent to talk of the invalid *qua* invalid, for it is persons who are the subjects of desire. More significant is the depersonalization of the object: the doctor (a6) is followed by the art of medicine (b4, 219a3), whose goal is health (217a6, 219a3–4). This confirms the evolution of the topic, as Robinson observes:

One cannot be 'friends with' health because only persons can be friends and health is not a person. This should be enough to warn us that though Plato is still discussing relationships which can be described in terms of the word *philos*, he is no longer describing relationships which are themselves friend-ships even if it is thought to be implied that they lead to friendships (74).

Moreover, what now takes up attention is not (as we might have expected) the relation between desire and friendship, but that between means and ends. Here truth familiar to us rapidly makes way for overstatement: that one thing may be dear for the sake of something else which is dear leads to the conclusion that there must be a single starting-point, a 'first dear' (*prōton philon*) for the sake of which 'all the other things' are dear (219c5–d2), and the retraction that it alone is truly dear, while the other things, which we call dear for its sake, are deceptive images of it (d2–5). It must surprise us equally that the starting-point must be single, and that it must have a monopoly on being dear.[7] The

---

[7] It may well be that 'all the other things that we say are dear for its sake' (219d2–3) are not all means to *any* good, but all the means to whatever is the final good of health, with the word 'we' signalling not a new generalization, but the initial remark 'The medical art, we say, is dear for the sake of health' (c1); but at least 220b1–3 must be assuming that there is a unique point from which all chains of things dear derive.

argument seems both shrewd and disappointing: Socrates is right to reject any comparison of value between end and means (e5–7), which would be, in effect, to count the same value twice over; but his inference that, properly speaking, the means are without value is tautological if 'value' means intrinsic value, but not innocuous in divorcing valuing from preferring (for a valueless means to a great good will be preferred to a minor intrinsic good, cf. 219d5–e4).[8] Socrates does not state explicitly what he takes the 'first dear' to be; no doubt it is one's own faring well or *eudaimoniā*.[9] The one suggestion that follows (after some further speculative enquiry which we may ignore) is that it is what one lacks or needs, and thus what one is deprived of, or 'one's own' (*oikeion*); that is proposed as the goal at once of 'love' (*erōs*), friendship, and desire (221d6–e4). Thus the goal of loving or *philein* turns out to be both impersonal and egocentric; friendship proper seems forgotten.

And then it suddenly returns: addressing Lysis and Menexenus, Socrates ostensibly infers,

Therefore if you are *philoi* to each other, you are by nature somehow *oikeioi* to one another. And so if anyone desires anyone else, or is in love with him, he would never have conceived his desire, or love, or friendship if he had not happened to be somehow *oikeios* to the beloved either in mind or in some mental character, disposition, or kind (221e5–222a3).

There is even a further twist to please Hippothales: true love must be reciprocated (a6–7). This makes explicit the logical feature that being *oikeios* is now a symmetrical relation (if A is *oikeios* to B, so is B to A); but this in turn confirms the sleight of hand, for possessing and losing are usually asymmetrical. In fact, there is a conscious play on two senses of *oikeios* (cf. Robinson, 76): that of which one is deprived is *one's own* (a sense shared by *philos* itself), while congenial friends tend to be *akin* (a commonplace about friendship). This new suggestion comes on the scene abruptly, and departs in failure: it might mean that like is friend to like, or (if the *oikeion* is the good) that the good are friends; but both those possibilities have already been refuted (b3–d8). Whence the final aporia.

---

[8] We meet the same overstatement of the subordination of means to ends in the *Laches* (185d5–7), and even, to inconsistent effect, in the *Gorgias* (contrast 468b8–c1 with c2–5). Rather than distance Socrates from Plato here, we should remind ourselves that these were first steps in the logic of preference, promising of a more assured stride to come (as already at *Rep* 2.357c5–d2).

[9] Cf. *Euthyd* 278e3–282a6, *Meno* 77b6–78b2, though they also indicate, despite 220b7–8 here, that Plato tends to count as truly 'good' not *eudaimoniā* itself but what reliably yields or produces it (cf. Robinson, 75, n. 19).

3

Uncertain what to make of all this, we may first look to see how Aristotle exploits it. Firstly, the *Lysis* provides, or confirms, many of the commonplaces that form the background to his own discussion. On behalf of the theme that like loves like he follows Plato in quoting Homer (214a6; *EE* 7.1.1235a7, cf. *NE* 8.1.1155a34), and citing natural philosophers (214b2–5, *Gorg* 510b2–4; *NE* 1155b6–8, *EE* 1235a10–13); against it, both quote Hesiod (215c7–d1; *NE* 1155a35–b1, *EE* 1235a17–18). On the attraction of opposites both again have natural philosophy in mind (215e5–9; *NE* 1155b1–6, *EE* 1235a13–16), though they indicate the irrelevance to their interests of physical speculations (Plato by guying them, 215e6–8, cf. *Symp* 186d6–7; Aristotle explicitly, *NE* 1155b8–9, *EE* 1235a29–31). Closer to those interests is the theme that only good men can be friends (214b6–7, d5–e1, 215a4–5; *EE* 1234b26–7, 1235a31–3, cf. *NE* 1155b11–12). This is linked to the love of like for like by being supported by a claim that bad men not only wrong one another (214b8–c3; *EE* 1234b24–5, 7.2.1236b13–14), but are not similar even to themselves (214c7–d3; *NE* 9.4, *EE* 7.6); it is opposed by the thought that the good are self-sufficient (215a6–c1; *NE* 9.9.1169b3–8, *EE* 7.12.1244b1–15).[10] Secondly, Plato's failure in the *Lysis* to define friendship in relation to the various uses of *philos* (212a8–213c9) inspires Aristotle's success (already quoted): 'A man becomes a friend whenever being loved he loves in return' (*EE* 7.2.1236a14–15, cf. *NE* 8.2.1155b27–8).[11] Thirdly, and perhaps most significantly, Aristotle's success does not separate him from one of the assumptions that is causing Plato trouble (cf. Robinson, 77–9). Plato assumes a close connection between *philos* in the senses of 'friend' and of 'dear'; indeed, he fails to distinguish them, and so, to our eyes, wambles in and out of discussion of friendship in a way that

---

[10] Verbally, the *Eudemian Ethics* is here slightly closer to the *Lysis* than the *Nicomachean*: note 'impulsive' (*emplēktos*, 214d1, *EE* 7.6.1240b17), and 'sufficient to himself' (*hikanos hautō(i)*, 215a7, *EE* 7.12.1244b7).

[11] Especially close verbally are 212e6 and *Eudemian Ethics* 7.2.1236b3–4, both with a neuter *philoumenon* that is generalizing, not impersonal, and so related to the *Nicomachean* masculine *philoumenos* (8.3.1156a16, 18, 8.5.1157b32). A genuinely neuter *philoumenon* occurs in the *Eudemian Ethics* (7.1.1235b19, 22), but not in the *Nicomachean*, which prefers the gerundive *philēton* (first at 8.2.1155b17–27), already occasional in the *Eudemian Ethics* (7.2.1236b35, 7.4.1239a35, *pace* Robinson, 78, n. 24).

threatens to dissolve the topic. Aristotle keeps the senses apart, but does not discard Plato's attention to things, as well as persons, that are dear. Indeed, he grounds, and classifies, kinds of friendship by reference to different categories of things that are loved: just as inanimate objects can be loved as being good, pleasant, or useful, so can men (*EE* 7.2.1236a10–14); just as the good, pleasant, and useful differ in kind, so do lovings and friendships (*NE* 8.3.1156a6–8). Hence both Plato and Aristotle view friendship against the general background of the structure of human desire. Aristotle's more developed analogue to Plato's 'first dear' (219d1) came earlier (*NE* 1.2.1094a18–22, *EE* 1.8.1218b9–12); but for him the problem about how the good man can need friends reduces to the question how friends can contribute to his own final good or *eudaimoniā* (cf. *NE* 9.9.1169b3–4, *EE* 7.12.1244b5).

Yet Vlastos finds a clear contrast between 'the lover Socrates has in mind' in the *Lysis*, who 'seems positively incapable of loving others for their own sake' ('The Individual as Object of Love in Plato', 8–9), and Aristotle's formula for perfect friendship, 'wishing another's good for his sake, not for yours' (as at *Rhet* 2.4.1380b36–7, *NE* 9.4.1166a2–4), which Vlastos locates as 'still far from the Kantian conception of treating persons as "ends in themselves" ', and yet 'the closest any philosopher comes to it in classical antiquity' (op. cit. 10, n. 24). Deferential mention of Kant in this context is always useful as an indication that the author subscribes to what Richard Wollheim has called 'the phantasy that morality marks the spot where human beings discard human nature'.[12] Whether Aristotle also adopts that phantasy we shall see later on (I think not); does the *Lysis*, even in its unsuccess, imply a theory that conflicts with his formula? I have already dismissed Vlastos's appeal to the preliminary piece of reasoning between Socrates and Lysis (207d5–210d8). Yet he finds worse to come:

> Socrates goes on to argue (213e3 ff.) that if *A* loves *B*, he does so because of some benefit *he* needs from *B* and for the sake of just that benefit: the sick man loves his doctor for the sake of health (218e4); the poor love the affluent and the weak the strong for the sake of aid (215d6) . . . No reason is offered why we could love anyone except for what we could get out of him (op. cit. 8).

The complaint is a specific one: that, in preference, one loves those whom one finds it rewarding to love is hardly a fact to which they are

---

[12] 'The Sheep and the Ceremony' (Cambridge, 1979), 38.

likely to object; what Vlastos is identifying is 'straightforward utility-love' (ibid.), motivated by the ulterior end of contingent convenience, and inspired by those 'good-producing qualities' that one may '*happen to need*' (ibid. 9, my italics). Hence he infers that Plato is subsuming all love of persons under that love of the useful to which (as we shall see) Aristotle does not apply the altruistic formula. Is this fair? It is initially important to note, not to settle the question but to place it correctly, that we must not be surprised to be presented with cases of *philiā* that we would never dignify with the title of 'friendship'.[13] Greek *philiā* extends more widely than our friendship in two directions: it includes 'the very strongest affective relationships that human beings form', such as family relations and even love-affairs;[14] but it also includes 'casual but agreeable acquaintance'.[15] 'Utility-friendship' is to us a paradox; 'utility-*philiā*' will be one of Aristotle's categories. *Philiā* is a relation of mutual benefit and trust which generates special obligations and sometimes affection; but its goals may be restricted, and its motivations not distinctive. Hence Plato's example of the doctor and his patient (215d6) must not surprise us; what we have to consider is whether he views cases of *philiā* that are also cases of friendship in the same light. All, I think, that might suggest that he does is that he is trying out the attraction of opposites as the basis of *all* friendship, clearly on the assumption that friendship has a single nature (which is why the proposal comes to grief over a few cases where dissimilarity makes for enmity); but of course, as Vlastos bizarrely overlooks, the attempt fails. It is unsurprising that, in making it, he concentrates on cases of utility-friendship. Aristotle makes the same connection, borrowing his examples from the *Lysis* itself (215d4–7): 'Friendship because of utility seems especially to arise from contraries, e.g. between poor and rich, ignorant and learned' (*NE* 8.8.1159b12–14, cf. *EE* 7.5.1239b23–7). So far, a contrast between an egoistic Plato and an altruistic Aristotle is imported, not discovered; I hope that it will become evident in the course of this book that it can nowhere be made out. To set the final, tentative and unsuccessful, proposals in the *Lysis* in illuminating opposition to approaches alien to Plato we shall do better to look first within Plato

[13] I shall discuss this most fully at the end of Chapter 5.
[14] Martha Nussbaum, *The Fragility of Goodness* (Cambridge, 1986), 354; though she may be exaggerating when she nicely remarks, 'We can say that two people are "just friends"; no such thing could be said with *philiā*' (ibid. 328 n.), even a *philiā* contrasted with *erōs* can be indistinguishable from it up to a point (cf. *Phdr* 255e1–2).
[15] K. J. Dover, *GH*, 49.

himself, at the speech that he gives to Aristophanes in the *Symposium*, and then at modern attitudes (already evidenced in Vlastos) that find that speech more congenial than anything that Plato will assert himself through the mouth of Socrates.

4

For all its ostensible failure, the *Lysis* ends its investigation of the grounds of desire (before it abruptly returns to friendship) with two suggestions that Plato was not later to take back: the object of desire is that which one lacks, and that which one lacks is that which one is deprived of (221d7–e3). Desire presupposes need, and the origin of need is loss. The goal of life is therefore to retrieve the place where one began; we shall meet again 'the archaeology of love taken up in its teleology'.[16] Unresolved in the *Lysis* is how to relate this conception to the notions of the similar and of the good, and how to incorporate it within an account of mutual friendship; it remains unexplained how the end of each man's desire may involve another individual, and how two individuals can benefit one another. For a phantasy that offers a fictional answer to these questions, one turns to Aristophanes' invention in the *Symposium* of pairs of human beings each originating from a single double creature that Zeus divided into two like Siamese twins (189d5 ff.). Whether similar or dissimilar, good or bad, identical or different in gender, the separated halves relate like tallies, needing to be rejoined if they are to recover their lost integrity. It need not be debated whether this is the best of 'Just So' stories, or a mythical adaptation of a deep aspect of human experience; for it may be both.[17] What it captures, and renders unparadoxical, is the thought that a pair of individuals who have never met may, in consequence of a universal human desire (recast as the demand for integrity), have for one another a need that nobody else could satisfy. The drawback is not merely that the diagnosis is not fact but fiction. It is also that it really explains nothing: why should integrity, so explicated, be desirable? A remark that Socrates ostensibly reports from Diotima is a fair objection to Aristophanes (who rightly takes his own speech as its

[16] I quote from L. A. Kosman, 'Platonic Love', in W. H. Werkmeister (ed.) *Facets of Plato's Philosophy* (Assen, 1976), 65.

[17] Cf. Dover, 'Aristophanes' Speech in Plato's *Symposium*', *Journal of Hellenic Studies* 86 (1966); Nussbaum, *The Fragility of Goodness*, 171–6.

object, 212c4–6): no one values even a part of himself unless he believes it to be a good (205e1–206a1). Aristophanes has succeeded imaginatively in accommodating the notions of loss, need, individuality, and mutuality, and in circumventing queries about similarity and dissimilarity; but his failure to find a role for the good is also a failure to make sense of desire.[18]

Love as reinvented by Aristophanes is grounded on egocentricity: each lover values the other as his own other half. Plato (through the mouths of Socrates and Diotima) objects that that omits goodness; others may object that it excludes loving the other in virtue not of one's *Ur*-self, but of the person that *he* is. Can we demythologize Aristophanes in a way that simultaneously removes that possible complaint? Certainly we can express a pertinent thought: what answers in another to my desire may be not his qualities, but his haecceity.[19] The thought appeals, but is it explanatory? If it aims to account for love by deriving it from a special kind of need, I think that it creates a mystery out of a confusion: the individual *qua* individual may indeed be the *object* of love, but his haecceity cannot be its *ground* (that is, what it is in him that one needs). That what one needs should be a particular in its particularity may not be excluded by the logic of 'need', but it belongs within no conceivable theory of human nature (not even Aristophanes'). If, alternatively, the role of the thought is not to make the individual the ground of love as well as its object, but to exclude the giving of grounds, at least in terms of the subject's needs, as inevitably implying that all loving is for the sake of oneself and not of its object, then the thought expresses a moral obscurantism that creates (to borrow some wording from Wollheim) 'a phenomenon that may excite our reverence but certainly eludes our understanding' ('The Sheep and the Ceremony', 38). To value friendship highly without relating it to the needs of *both* parties is to invent values in a vacuum created by the expulsion of motivation.[20]

---

[18] In the medieval tag, 'whatever is desired is desired under the aspect of the good'. (From the time of the *Republic*, Plato will qualify that in respect of the appetites, cf. 4.438a1–5.)

[19] Cf. Montaigne: 'If a man urged me to tell wherefore I loved him, I feel it cannot be expressed, but by answering; Because it was he, because it was my selfe' ('On Friendship', *Essays* 1.27). This apparently goes even further, grounding my desire in my haecceity as well as in his.

[20] If the thought does appeal, this is surely because it constitutes part not of an explanation of object-choice in terms of need, nor of a rejection of any such explanation, but of the phenomenology of love once it has already come into being. Cf. Roland Barthes on the theme of the 'atopos', *Fragments d'un discours amoureux* (Paris, 1977),

Plato was an idealist who (it may be fair to speculate) could only respect human nature because he took an extraordinary view of its potentialities; but he was a philosopher foremost, and a moralist only in consequence. Despite its failure either to define or to explain friendship, the *Lysis* succeeds in setting the scene for a genuine understanding; as Plato no doubt intended, it therefore constitutes a limited achievement under the guise of a fiasco. Even those who are less sympathetic than I to the theories that Plato, and Aristotle, were subsequently to develop are wise to accept the *Lysis* as a point of departure, and foolish to reject it as a false start. In this way, of all Plato's investigations into love and friendship it is the *Lysis* that is the least dispensable.

43–5. Particularly illuminating is his description of how, seeing in the other's eyes a total innocence (Barthes alludes to Maeterlinck's Mélisande) of the suffering that he causes me, I place him as it were outside himself and his own character. In happier cases of being in love, and in cases of friendship, the innocence will rather be not of his failings in my regard, but of his merits.

2

LOVE IN THE *SYMPOSIUM*

I

What is love (*erōs*)? The answer that Socrates reports to the company at Agathon's dinner-party from the priestess Diotima is far from Feste's ('What is love? 'tis not hereafter', and so on): 'Love is for possessing the good oneself for ever', or (more literally) 'for the good to belong to oneself always' (206a11–12). The definition is extended and stipulative (cf. 205a5–d8); it is, in effect, a statement of the final goal of all desire.[1] Diotima offers a disarming analogy: all makers are 'poets' (from *poiein*, 'to make'), though only some are so called (205b8–c9). However, what lends the definition point is less that analogy than its application in defining what is idiomatically called 'love'. Diotima defines its characteristic activity as generation, mental or physical, in beauty (206b7–8). It is not elementary to work out how the two definitions relate.

There are clearly two ways in which the 'beautiful' (*kalos*) is integral to love: within generic eros, the lover desires to possess beauty (which is love's *goal*); within specific eros, the lover is inspired by someone else who already possesses beauty (and is love's *occasion*). Within the definition of specific eros, there are two possible senses of the phrase 'generation in beauty': it might mean begetting upon a beauty, or else bearing or bringing to birth in the presence of beauty. Bearing is indicated by the recurrent description of the lover as 'pregnant' (first at 206c1), and by the mention of a personified Beauty as a goddess of childbirth and not conception (206d2–3). Yet it is inescapable that begetting, and indeed impregnating, is man's role in sexual procreation; Plato will touch on that as quickly and vaguely as he can (208e1–3), blurring the distinction by effectively subsuming begetting under bearing, as if sperm were a kind of foetus, and orgasm

---

[1] The extension was doubtless helped by poetic usage, cf. Jürgen Wippern, 'Eros und Unsterblichkeit in der Diotima-Rede des *Symposions*', in Helmut Flashar and Konrad Gaiser (eds.) *Synusia* (Pfullingen, 1965), 148, n. 41; also by a verbal fashion in Socrates' circle passing from the playful into the habitual, cf. K. J. Dover, *GH*, 156–7.

a release from birth-pangs (cf. 206d7–e1). We shall find him exploiting the ambiguity in the case that most interests him, that of sowing seed through personal contact in another's mind (209b7–c7).

The truism that love is of beauty (first taken over by Socrates, 201a9–10, from Agathon, 197b5, but now corrected, 206e2–5) has been developed, through an association between love and desire (200a2–3), and a propositional expansion of the goal of desire (204d5–7), in order to define the lover's goal. As terms for what it is his goal to possess, 'good' (*agathos*) and 'beautiful' (*kalos*) are interchangeable (204e1–4) but not synonymous: a shift from 'beautiful' to 'good' is twice needed to prepare for the thought that the final end of desire is happiness or *eudaimoniā* (202c6–11, 204e1–7). Both the difference and the equivalence between them are well captured by K. J. Dover's pithy differentiation: 'Anything which is *kalon*, i.e. which looks or sounds good (or is good to contemplate), is also *agathon*, i.e. it serves a desirable purpose or performs a desirable function, and vice versa.'[2] The *kalon* is what presents itself appealingly (though not only to the senses); the *agathon* is good for someone in some way (though not only instrumentally); the *kalon* draws us and the *agathon* helps us. To spell out their equivalence: whatever attracts us also benefits us (if only in its contemplation); while, so long as our judgement colours the way things strike us, whatever serves us well is likely to create in us a favourable impression. Plato can alternate between the two notions, at will but not indifferently: they capture connected but distinct aspects of things. Thus, in a wide sense, the goal of love is indeed beautiful. Yet Socrates cannot be acquitted of some deft footwork: that love is of beauty is truistic not of the goal of love but of its occasion or object, and to the effect not merely that its object appeals, but that it appeals in a special way of which at least the paradigm is the attraction of physical beauty. Even when the 'generation in beauty' is mental and not physical, Socrates will require that its object have a more or less beautiful body (compare 209b4–7 with 210b6–c1); but his reason is not made clear. In the case of physical procreation, beautiful women are no more fertile than plain ones; it is not, one would think, for the sake of procreation that the former are preferred. Socrates merely takes from Diotima the thought that, since generation is immortal and so divine, it is fitting that it should take place in beauty rather than in ugliness (206c6–d2, cf. 209b4–5). That appeal

---

[2] *Plato: Symposium* (Cambridge, 1980), ad 201c2; cf. *GPM*, 69–73.

to the divine seems extraneous, and sophistical: why must something that is divine in one way (being linked to immortality) be divine in another (being linked to beauty)? The *Symposium* only contains a partial answer in a limited case: if the generation is mental, and the occasion is brought within the goal in that it becomes recipient as well as inspirer, so that the generation is at once a bearing and a begetting within another (with the loved one taking on the lover's ideas), then the object of love must have the beauty of mental promise. However, Diotima may well be assuming that most women are beautiful, to an extent, to the lover of women (cf., of pederasty, *Rep* 5.474d4–475a2); a total lack of attractiveness would not cause sterility in the woman, but it might cause impotence in the man.

Beauty as the goal of love also needs clarification. That love is of a beauty it lacks (200e8–201a10) might have suggested, in view of Agathon's own ideal of smoothness (195c7, 196a1), that what the lover is after is a course of skin care. That cannot be both the kind of beauty and the kind of possession (cf. 201b6) that are meant. Most familiar would be the thought that the lover wants to possess 'a beauty' in the sense of his (and no one else's) making love to him or her. In fact, that will turn out to be part of what Socrates does envisage, even if the procreation is mental—if we can count doing philosophy with a beautiful boy as a Platonic way of making love to him. But the route thither is less direct: it is beauty in its wide sense that is involved in the lover's goal, and as an aspect of acquiring the good for ever. Central here is neither beauty, nor ownership, nor immortality, but goodness. Ownership alone is no ground of love, unless, perhaps, one uses the phrase 'one's own' (*oikeios*) as a label for the good (205e1–206a1). Immortality is more tricky. The notion is slipped in deftly: that it is always that men want to possess good things (to capture in awkward English an ambiguity easy in Greek) meant that men always want to possess them (205a7–8) before it meant that they want to possess them always (206a11–12). No doubt we are not now to understand that men have two goals, to be happy and to be immortal, at least if that would imply that Tithonus would always be better alive than dead (which would contradict *Euthyd* 289a7–b2). Nor is it clear that Socrates is *inferring* from a desire for happiness a desire not only to be happy so long as one is alive (consider 'And they lived happily ever after'), but also that one's happiness should never cease: he says that 'always' is to be *added* to wishing to possess the good (206a10). He may just be taking over from Diotima an assumption that happy men never want to die. In the form of a desire for an ersatz survival, that will cease to be an assumption: we *see* men and animals at work sacrificing everything else in order to leave behind a family or a name (cf. 207a7–c9, 208c2–e1). What we shall need to explore is how he can regard ersatz survival as a kind of survival. He has to take that view if he is to subsume a desire for 'generation in beauty' within a more general desire to achieve one's own eternal happiness; otherwise death would simply have to be accepted as a dead end.

What is the condition of the lover who wants, somehow, to acquire beauty through generating in beauty? Socrates argues against Agathon that, since desire presupposes lack (200a5–b2), love of beauty cannot already be beautiful itself. On the face of it, that fits taking the goal of love to be cosmetic. But the point can be restated: the man who wants to be happy cannot be happy already. However, Socrates himself allows a desire to retain in the future what one already enjoys in the present (d3–6); so the man who is happy now can still have a desire for future happiness. Why should the fact (which is a logical necessity) that he is not *yet* happy *in the future* be supposed to constitute any kind of present defect? There is an answer to that: Plato argues that I cannot desire to have now what I already have, upon the ground that I have it willy-nilly (c3–5); so he should also suppose that I cannot desire to have in the future what the future holds for me *of necessity* (to my belief, we must add); hence the lover cannot already be knowingly *such as to be* happy in the future, and that is a state, if rather a sophisticated one, of present deficiency.[3] We may think that this is more serious as an objection to Agathon (who was presumably describing the essential nature of the god Love when he poured complimentary epithets upon him) than as a disparagement of the human lover (who may not expect to have the future in his pocket); but Plato, at any rate, would certainly see it as an imperfection that, for humans, future happiness is at the mercy of future contingencies.

We may still suspect a fallacy. I would object that, in assuming that I cannot want what I have already, or can already depend upon, Plato is forgetting that I can already have what I want. That saying 'I want *x*' does commonly imply both 'I lack *x*' and 'I cannot depend upon

---

[3] I owe this point to Michael Stokes, *Plato's Socratic Conversations* (London, 1986), 128–9. It invites the reply that, while an attitude towards the present must be idle, a desire about the future may, in context, guarantee its own fulfilment: being such as to become in a certain state in the future may itself be, or involve, a state of desire. Yet, in making sense of Plato, the point remains helpful.

having *x*' is a matter of conversational implicature, and not of logical entailment: the implication can be cancelled by a special context of utterance (say, being asked of one's possessions, 'Do you want them all?'), and it does not accompany the verb 'want' itself in all sentential contexts (for instance, not in 'I have what I want'). Others have objected otherwise, I think less justly. R. E. Allen once complained that Agathon's personification of love leaves behind a trail of confusion: 'Love is a relation. As such, it lacks nothing and desires nothing. It implies, however, privation or lack in the lover.'[4] But that, I believe, grants Socrates all that he intends. Socrates' love lacks beauty just as Paul's charity is not puffed up; that is, whoever loves lacks beauty, just as whoever is charitable is not conceited.[5] More precisely (for there may be a residuum of pride even in exemplars of charity), we should say that being humble is part of being charitable, or that the charitable are humble *qua* charitable; similarly, the lover is without beauty *qua* lover. Compare the adage 'Love is blind': that ascribes not total myopia to a state of mind (whatever that could mean), but blindness to the lover to the extent that he is in love. A refinement on the same point answers another, and widely accepted, objection. Why should lacking *enough* beauty to be a lover be lacking *all* beauty? Why should desiring *anything* presuppose lacking *everything*?[6] Such questions ascribe to Socrates this principle:

For all *x*, if I desire *x*, then, for all *y*, I lack *y*.

But we should rather simply understand this:

For all *x*, if I desire *x*, then I lack *x*.

Just as lovers are in lack *qua* lovers, so the lover who desires *a* is in lack *qua* desiring *a*; that is, he lacks *a*. It need not be forgotten that, since desire requires not only lack but awareness of lack, desiring *a* may presuppose possessing *b*: when we come finally to the Platonic ascent we shall find that the succession of new desires and felt deficiencies is also a succession, always one stage behind, of fresh possessions and achievements. Nor need it be an objection to what is meant (though it

---

[4] 'A Note on the Elenchus of Agathon: *Symposium* 199c–201c', *Monist* 50 (1966), 460.
[5] Here, of course, I am indebted to Gregory Vlastos; cf., for instance, 'The Unity of the Virtues in the *Protagoras*', in *Platonic Studies*, § 3. Allen was writing at about the time when the phrase 'Pauline predication' was being coined (by Sandra Peterson Wallace, ibid. 254, n. 88).
[6] Cf., for instance, Dover, *Plato: Symposium*, ad 201b6.

is a correction to what has been said) that the loving may itself be beautiful in a way, so that, after all, the lover has some beauty *qua* lover.[7] Socrates' thesis is that possession always restricts the scope of love (though it may at the same time, by making possible new desires, give it new scope); it is precisely in respect of the things he does or can desire that the lover is lacking. *In relation to its object*, lacking is part of loving. It is the task of allegory to make points, not qualifications; allegorically, Love is a pauper (cf. 203c6–d3).[8]

A pauper, but not a loser. He is 'portionless in beautiful and good things' (202d5) in that none of them is his stable possession, but not to the extent that they always elude him. He is the son of Resource as well as of Poverty (203c5), at once desirous of skill and inventive of it (d6–7), now living now perishing, now knowing now unknowing, in a manner that may reflect the intermissions of genital sexuality (e1–4). Both to illustrate and to specify his intermediacy Diotima exploits the non-exhaustive contrast between knowledge and ignorance. Confusingly, what lies between them is defined differently in the illustration (202a2–10) and in the specification (203e5–204b5): in the illustration the intermediary is true opinion, inferior to knowledge in that it lacks an account, superior to ignorance in that it matches reality; in the specification it is rather distinctive of ignorance that it mistakes itself for wisdom.[9] The descriptions are not inconsistent, but they are different. Clearly what fits the case of Love is not complacent

---

[7] So Dover, ibid., ad 201b1–4.

[8] I believe that what I have said also makes unnecessary an interesting attempt to rescue Socrates' logic by Martha Nussbaum: 'Socrates' argument depends on a strong hidden assumption: that all beauty, *qua* beauty, is uniform, the same in kind. All manifestations of the *kalon* must be sufficiently like one another that if you lack one kind it is natural to conclude that you lack them all' (*The Fragility of Goodness*, 179). I cannot see that this works: even if all beauties are homogeneous, I might want some beauty not because I lack all beauty but because I want some more. (If we deny this, while retaining the connection between desire and lack, and without stringently restricting the argument to the lover *qua* lover, we make the assumption of homogeneity refutable by any instance of having one beauty and wanting another; then it could not possibly survive the ascent-passage, let alone experience.) So we still need to make my point, that 'Love is destitute' signifies 'Whatever I love I lack', and not 'If I love anything I lack everything'; then there is nothing here to indicate homogeneity. I discuss the issue further in Appendix 1.

[9] The *Lysis* (218a2–b1) makes the same distinction as *Symposium* 203e5–204b5, though it labels it differently. The *Symposium* distinguishes from knowledge and ignorance an unnamed state that is the cognitive aspect or presupposition of the love of wisdom (*philosophiā*); the *Lysis* distinguishes two ways of lacking understanding, of which one makes the person himself foolish, the other not. In both passages the contrast is between not knowing while recognizing that one does not know (*Lys* 218b1), and being ignorant while supposing that one is perfectly well off (*Symp* 204a4–6).

correctness, but dissatisfied ignorance. This confirms, in its implications, my reading of Love's destitution: a proper sense of dissatisfaction makes the best of an unideal situation (and so is not altogether without its own beauty), and it demands some understanding of that situation (so that it presupposes a certain awareness). Desire is presented as a state at once of insecurity (I do not desire what I am bound to gain or to retain), and of capacity (I do not desire what I am bound to miss or to lose). Both features fit the kind of immortality that Diotima is about to explicate: it is a contingency, neither guaranteed nor excluded by the sort of creatures that men are.

2

Diotima's strategy, as Socrates reports it and Plato records it, is to make plausible a kind of survival beyond death that requires no real entity to maintain strict identity by alleging the same kind of survival within a lifetime. If that were the only kind that life offers, and what life offers fully satisfies us, the prospect would open of an achievable and fully desirable immortality. So a *radical* interpretation, according to which Plato is equating such survival with personal identity over time, should have point in context, as well as current interest for us. However, such a reading is unlikely to accommodate the quite different immortality which Plato deduces from the essence of the soul in other dialogues. After working out a form of the radical interpretation, I shall mention indications in favour of a *modest* interpretation which should be more compatible with familiar Platonic doctrine elsewhere.

Diotima first comes to focus upon physical survival over a lifetime. We speak, she concedes, of an individual creature's living and being the same from infancy to old age (207d4–6). But though we call him the same, the fact of the matter is that he never retains the same constituents; rather, he is always being renewed in respect of every part of his body (d6–e1). We cannot say that he remains the same creature because he retains the same body: strictly speaking, he does not. What then is a body? We are not to view it, conservatively, as a structured complex constituted by, or made up of, parts with which it is not identical; for that conception would have the effect of reconciling strict identity over time with a gradual replacement of parts. Nor,

more radically, can we view it as a temporal sequence of bodily stages
linked, say, in that each stage is a structured and functioning set of
elements each of which preserves or replaces some element of the
previous set; for that sequence does not exist at any time but takes
place over a period of time—it does not change, but unfolds. Rather, a
body is a functioning set or bundle of corporal parts, and strictly
ceases to exist if any part is replaced. Hence a body, strictly speaking,
is a very transient thing. Bodily survival is a matter not of strict
identity over time, but of a sequence of successors. If we want to talk
strictly of identity, we need a new concept, say that of a 'superbody'
which survives as long as the sequence continues. Such an entity
would be a logical construction, arriving on the scene only on the coat-
tails of a set of suitably related bodies, with its identity tied to that of
the first member of the set (not to the whole set, if it can be envisaged
that the superbody might have enjoyed a different history). At this
stage we have an option about how to treat ordinary talk of bodily
identity as something that does last through a lifetime: we can attach it
to the natural concept of a body and call it loose, or we can attach it to
the artificial concept of a superbody and call it notional. In either case
Diotima will be claiming (on this line of interpretation) that there is
no *real* bodily identity over time.

    An analogous story should apply to the mind. Its contents or
elements form a medley: 'ways, habits, opinions, desires, pleasures,
pains, fears' (207e2–3), then also 'knowings' (*epistēmai*, e5). Of these
mental states, pleasures and pains are most easily taken to be *episodes*;
the rest are only or more easily taken to be *dispositions*. That 'of these
none remains the same to each man, but some come into being, and
others are lost' (e3–4) comes to something different in the two cases.
An episode ceases as it is displaced by another; its return may require
no change in the subject other than the reactivation of a disposition.
By contrast, the departure of a disposition is a change which a process
or activity is needed to undo. Diotima speaks of knowings as dispositions: 'What is called rehearsing exists because knowing goes out of
us; for forgetting is an exit of knowledge, and rehearsal by implanting
anew a new memory in place of the departing one preserves the
knowing, so that it seems to be the same' (208a3–7). This is a curious
passage. That the knowing is preserved is precisely what is being
strictly denied: 'preserves the knowing so that it seems the same' is
self-contradictory, if (as I presume) 'seems' here excludes 'is'. Further, if the knowing has already departed it is too late to rehearse it; if

it is just on the point of departing it is surely preserved and not replaced by a rehearsal which reinforces it, for a rehearsal is an exercise of a knowing. Diotima specifies that 'each single knowing suffers the same' (a3); about dispositions (in contrast to episodes) this is an exaggeration analogous to the earlier claim that every bodily part is replaced (207e1). The two pieces of exaggeration taken together preclude identifying body or mind with some element that does endure (which would be a more or less artificial way out of the argument). On a radical interpretation, what general picture of the mind emerges? The mind is a bundle of episodes and dispositions, and so strictly as transient as the most transient of them.[10] However, there are sequences of such bundles (or mental stages) linked, say, in that vaguely *enough* of each bundle preserves or replaces elements of its predecessor.[11] We may then say that what lives through such a sequence of mental bundles is a 'supermind', which survives a lifetime (at least). A supermind is, in effect, the subject of a mental life; but, like a superbody, it is an invented entity, and supports no more than a notional identity over time.

Such an interpretation is new only in detail.[12] It makes Plato anticipate recent theories at once heterodox and hard to escape (one thinks of David Hume, and Derek Parfit). It will make him at the next stage, when the topic becomes survival beyond death, extend such theories in a way that, depending on one's sympathies, one may find either a liberation or a *reductio ad absurdum*. But there is evidence within, or relating to, the passage that indicates, perhaps not decisively, a more modest reading. An initial point is that there is nothing novel in the materials that Plato is placing at Diotima's disposal.[13] The body flows and is destroyed (*Pdo* 87d9, 91d7); it is in a condition of influx and efflux (*Tim* 43a5–6). Fleeting in the soul too are opinions (*Meno* 98a1–2), knowledge (*Pdo* 75d10–11), wisdom

---

[10] Cf. Paul Auster: 'Our lives carry us along in ways we cannot control, and almost nothing stays with us. It dies when we do, and death is something that happens to us every day'; *The New York Trilogy* (London, 1987), 199. And yet he can only be thinking of dispositions, for a day is a long time.

[11] Such a theory usually neglects dispositions, no doubt because, more clearly than episodes (redescribable impersonally as events), they surely need a home; cf. Richard Wollheim, *The Thread of Life* (Cambridge, 1984), 17.

[12] Cf. Léon Robin, *Platon: Le Banquet* (Paris, 1929), p. lxxxvii; I. M. Crombie, *An Examination of Plato's Doctrines* (London, 1962), i. 361–3; Martin Warner, 'Love, Self, and Plato's *Symposium*', *Philosophical Quarterly* 29 (1979), 336; my 'Loving Persons Platonically', *Phronesis* 26 (1981), 27, 31.

[13] I owe the details to Wippern, op. cit. 150, n. 62.

(*Laws* 5.732b8–9), and memory (*Phil* 33e3).[14] Hence it would be surprising if Plato were seriously using the same materials here to construct a most un-Platonic model of the soul. A second point is that the radical interpretation appears to be operating with a poorer ontological repertory than the passage displays. It replaces a man by a dualist conjunction of superbody and supermind, which are factitious subjects and not agents. Indeed, there is no room here for a non-reductive notion of agency: a bodily movement will count, reductively, as an 'action' if (too crudely) it matches the content of some mental state that causes it. Yet Plato seems to be assuming that at least the cognitive elements of the mental sequence are subject to the control of an agent. 'Rehearsal' (208a5) is a way of preserving or replacing knowledge; it is an intentional mental activity which produces a certain episode (one of recollecting) as a way of reinforcing some disposition (cf. *Theaet* 153b9–10, *Phdr* 228b6). The subject of this activity is presumably a man or his soul, manipulating his cognitive states like the limbs of a puppet.[15] (Of course, such subjects can also be vulnerable to a reductivist account; but none is indicated here.)

Moreover, there appears to be a significant contrast between the ways in which Diotima speaks of soul and body that the radical interpreter is overlooking. Denial of the constancy of hair, flesh, and bones goes with an imputation that an animal (207d4), which is a compound of mind and body, is only *called* the same over time.[16] So Diotima is asserting a very close relation between the elements of a body and the body itself: strict bodily identity is a simple function of the identity of bodily parts. By contrast, it is not said that a soul is called the same over time, while really its contents are constantly being replaced. On the identity of the soul as the renewer of its own

---

[14] The *Meno* contrasts opinion with knowledge, probably because the fleeting of opinion is not an involuntary forgetting but a voluntary discarding (cf. *Rep* 3.412e10–413c4).

[15] The *Phaedo* makes the soul also the agent of bodily renewal, reweaving the body as it is worn thin (87e1). Here it is 'mortal nature' (207d1) which 'always leaves behind something new and different in place of the old', within both mind and body (207d1–3); but that can only mean, rather loosely, that it is in the nature of psycho-physical structures that their elements are replaced rather than preserved—which leaves the issue of agency open. If Plato had made Diotima ascribe this role to the soul, that would have complicated her later dichotomy between pregnancy in soul and in body (208e1 ff.); but we shall see that her theory has more force if bodily changes as well as mental ones constitute the soul at work.

[16] Loss and replacement apply to the body *as a whole* (e1).

contents no such conditions are imposed; rather, the active term 'rehearsal' (208a5) intimates that such mental continuities as there may be are subject to the activity of a soul whose own identity rides free.[17] What Diotima needs to emphasize, in preparation for talk of a kind of survival beyond death, is that, when one looks at a single bodily or mental life in abstraction from the liver, one finds its elements being replaced rather than preserved; the identity of a soul as a subject of life is most likely no more an issue for her than it is elsewhere for Plato.

So it seems best, less radically, to distinguish the soul itself, as the controller at least of its own cognitive states, from the physical and mental history that together constitute incarnate life. It is of this that we have been given a fuller view, according to which it hangs together in two kinds of ways: firstly, in the identity of the soul whose life, for a time, it is; and secondly, in the repetition and renewal of its elements. So long as we maintain a distinction between the subject of a life, and the life it leads, we can hope to do justice to what Plato is saying about lives here without putting it in conflict with what he says about souls as mental substances elsewhere.

3

After defining eros in an extended sense as a desire to possess the good oneself for ever (206a11–12), Diotima raised the question of how that goal is pursued by eros in the more idiomatic sense (b1–3). Her answer was 'generation in beauty' (e5). She has now to explain how that subserves immortality, of a kind. However, in multiplying examples of quasi-immortality she at times loses sight of eros in any familiar sense, so that we are left with the impression of hearing a more or less persuasive account of we know not exactly what.

It was baldly stated before that generation may be physical or mental (206b7–8). Physical procreation is described first among dumb beasts (207a7–c1), and then among human beings (208e1–5). Animals are subject to overriding desires to conceive offspring, to nurture them, and if necessary to die for them. These desires come naturally upon them (the metaphor is of illness, 207a9), and cannot be

---

[17] Cf. a remark by Wollheim (*The Thread of Life*, 20): 'It will come to seem that such interrelatedness as is to be found between the events that make up a single life is something that comes about through the way in which persons lead their lives.'

rationalized away (b6–7). Equally, of course, animals cannot speak to
define the goal of such activities; nor, if it is of Diotima's kind, are
they likely to have an individual conception of it. However, since we
share an animal nature with them, we can draw on universal human
desires that are communicable in order to interpret their behaviour by
an unconscious teleology. Humans actually suppose that they will
achieve a kind of immortality through their descendants (208e3–5);
their mutual awareness of this provides evidence of a teleology common to all 'mortal nature' (207d1).

At a first glance, associating a desire to copulate with a desire to
reproduce suits Diotima well. Sexual reproduction is a process of
renewal within a family comparable to that within an individual (cf.
207d6–e1). A body counts loosely as surviving through a lifetime by
means of processes comparable to those by which a family survives
through generations; seen in a wide perspective, the death of an
individual animal is not more salient than the passing of a stage in his
life. So an animal's instinctive struggle to survive evidences a wider
motive equally present in his wish to reproduce (which is why it will
come naturally to him to die for his offspring, 207b3–5). Such physical survival as alone is possible stops at no individual frontiers; the
enemy is not death, but sterility. Yet we have to ask more precisely
how a line of descendants can contribute to one's own possession of
the good. About how others' lives can count as 'one's own' I shall
reflect later; how does prolonging one's family tree relate to possessing the good? If one has no ground to value even the members of one's
own immediate body unless they are good (205e3–5), why should one
value one's offspring as such? If they are to turn out good, they need to
be educated; but that is mental and not physical generation. So there
is a danger after all, if physical procreation is itself desirable, that
immortality will turn into a goal independent of goodness.[18] Diotima
describes those who have children as 'providing for themselves for all
time to come immortality and memory and happiness, as they suppose' (208e4–5). It may be that the clause 'as they suppose' conveys
that Plato is aware that sexual reproduction cannot of itself ensure that
one's descendants live well and remember their ancestors. However,
most likely the word 'ensure' is too demanding: no kind of generation,
mental or physical, can do that. The self-perpetuation of a family at

---

[18] Cf. Ferdinand Horn, *Platonstudien* (Vienna, 1893), 279–80.

least maintains a genetic capacity to lead a worthwhile human life, and to respect one's forebears.

Of mental generation Diotima offers three kinds of example, variously adequate for her purpose: reputation, educative pederasty, and poetry or legislation. The first and the third have the effect of dissolving the topic. Purporting to report Diotima, Socrates takes over from Phaedrus two erotic examples of dying for love, Alcestis and Achilles (179b5–d2, e1–180b5); he presents them as dying for love not of another person but of posthumous glory (208c2–e1). Their motive would seem to be eros in the wide sense (desire to possess the good for ever), to which eros in the narrow sense (love of Admetus or Patroclus) is incidental; it confirms this that they are joined by Codrus, who died not for a loved one, but to hand on his kingdom to his children (208d4–6). The same problem is raised by the 'descendants' of Homer and Hesiod, that is the poems that by their immortality have brought them immortal glory (209d2–4), and the 'children' of Lycurgus and Solon, that is the laws through which they have generated all kinds of virtue (d4–e3). Are these instances of generation in beauty? If so, what was the beauty? If not, it must be false that procreation needs beauty as a midwife (*pace* 206c4–5, d2–3, 209b3–4). Dover suggests that 'the beautiful medium . . . can only be the virtuous character of the societies for which Homer sang and Solon legislated' (*Plato: Symposium*, 151–2). It may not be right to object that Solon *made* his society virtuous, for Plato may have viewed the achievements of Lycurgus and Solon as conservative rather than radical; but the result would still be artificial. What is worse, generation in beauty was intended to define eros commonly so called (206b1–e5); in that, it would turn out to have failed. Also unsatisfactory about these examples is that they are not set out in order to illustrate what ought to follow on 207e1–208b2, which is an account of a kind of mental generation that stands to individual mental renewal as sexual reproduction stands to individual physical renewal. Perhaps it could be made out that legislators who 'beget all kinds of virtue' (209e2–3) are each passing on his own character, and that poets bequeath parts of their own mental life. But Plato needed to distinguish between the different roles of Achilles and Homer. Through writing the *Iliad*, Homer may have been handing on memories in a way analogous, on Diotima's account, to recreating one's own. The role of rehearsal suits this extension: telling oneself things over again is broadly the same kind of activity as telling others of them for the first time (think how conversation and correspondence so often serve the two purposes simultaneously). The knowledge I create in others stands to my past life in the same kind of way as the memory I refresh in myself: both my future memory and theirs can be viewed as inheritors of my present memory, so that one vein in their lives becomes an extension of my life. But that does not apply to Achilles: he is the subject and (it is being supposed) original of Homer's narrative, but he was not its original narrator. He did nothing to pass on his own memories, which perished without replacement even if Homer's account correlates well enough with them; so his immortal fame is the continuation of his mental life only in a loose sense that should have been superseded.

More to the point is educative pederasty (209a8–d1); this will become, in effect, Diotima's topic. Men who are more pregnant in soul than in body prefer boys to women. It is supposed, but not explained, that they still need the stimulus of beautiful bodies (b4–5); but they also need a beautiful soul to educate (b6–7). The boy's role is complex: like Socrates (*Theaet* 150b6–9), he is a midwife to another's labour; he is also a parent, real or adoptive, who *shares* his lover's children.[19] The lover's potential ideas and virtues are to become actual as part of the mental life of both lover and beloved. We need to interpret this in the light of the preceding account of the unity of a mental life (207e1–208a7). By bearing and nurturing his mental progeny together with the boy, the man grants it a double life, within both of their minds. To apply and extend the notion of a rehearsal, we may think of the man as speaking and acting in ways that simultaneously renew and develop his qualities in himself, and bestow the same on the other. The implication must be that virtues are preserved and transmitted in ways more similar than dissimilar: the boy's future state will stand to the man's present potentialities in the same kind of way as will the man's own future state. So long as the boy lives, and does not deteriorate, the man's virtues will be alive in him. By a virtue here we must mean not merely a type (independently

---

[19] The root *koino-* appears three times within four lines (c4–7). The ambiguity of terms like *tokos* and *gennēsis* between begetting and bearing (cf. Dover, *Plato: Symposium*, 147) is here notably exploited rather than resolved: it fits begetting that the man 'lays hold of the beautiful person and has intercourse with him' (c2–3); it fits bearing that the lover is already pregnant (b3, c3), and 'brings up what has been generated together with him', as if the other becomes an adoptive parent of a newly born child.

realizable in strangers), nor strictly a token (since tokens are transient, even within a single life), but rather a set of tokens causally linked to form a single, if branching, history. So interpreted, the 'children' (c5, 8) that they share are the virtues and their manifestations that the boy acquires, and the man develops, through their life in common.

That the man's potential qualities become the actual qualities of both fits one reading of a clause in itself ambiguous: in contact with the boy the man brings to birth what he has long been bearing, literally 'both in his presence and in his absence remembering' (209c3–4). What is the lover remembering? Dover supposes it to be the boy, translating 'in his presence and remembering him in absence' (op. cit. ad loc.). This implies that it is the lover's mental life alone that changes: even if a visual memory of the boy could inspire like the sight of him, it would make of him a midwife but not an adoptive parent; for *he* cannot receive virtue from the lover at a distance. But I find this reading unlikely: it does not fit the emphasis here on their sharing the children; and it requires of Plato a striking change of mind before the *Phaedrus*, where memory is good for the spirits (251d6–7), but only actual seeing can release what longing in absence (*pothos*) bottled inside (e2–4). Hence I prefer Léon Robin's construal of the phrase (in his translation) as 'calling it to mind close to and far away', where 'it' signifies the progeny; by transmitting his way of life to the boy, the man can find himself at a distance from it (more strictly, from one branch of it) when the boy is absent. To apply a phrase of Aristotle's, the virtue of each is 'in a sense the same thing, though in separate individuals' (*NE* 8.12.1161b33); what the boy's mental life owes to the man is both a branch of the man's life and distinct from that branch of which the man remains the subject.

What is not made explicit, now or later, is how such branching offers the lover a hope of immortality. So here, where talk of 'generation in beauty' is at last apposite (but for the failure to explain the relevance of physical beauty), talk of possessing the good for ever is as yet unjustified. However, it was doubtless easy for Plato, within his culture, to assume a sequence of loves whereby, as the boy grows into a man, he becomes a lover of boys in his turn. Hence every branching should be followed by another within an unending tree of a family of minds.[20]

---

[20] This will become explicit in the *Phaedrus* (276e5–277a4).

4

Diotima has been describing an immortality open to what is mortal. After explaining how, even within a single life, survival is matter of renewal rather than of preservation, she concludes as follows:

In this way everything mortal is preserved, not by being always together the same like the divine, but by what is departing and being lost through age leaving a substitute of the same kind. By this means . . . the mortal partakes of immortality, both the body and everything else; but the immortal in another way (208a7–b4).

This contrasts a kind of survival through replacement with a divine immortality through identity. Yet familiar in other dialogues are proofs that even human souls are immortal.[21] That need not be contradicted here: souls may fall not under 'everything mortal' and 'the body and everything else' (sc. that is mortal), but 'the immortal';[22] yet Diotima may well appear to be setting aside immortality as an essential property in favour of survival as a contingent achievement. But must these different conceptions be in competition, or can they coexist? Should we, in respect of them, be compatibilists, or incompatibilists?[23] A presumption in favour of consistency is confirmed by the coexistence in later dialogues of the two conceptions. The *Phaedrus* both argues that the soul is essentially immortal (245c5–246a2), and links a kind of immortality to sowing seed in other minds (276e5–277a4); while the *Laws* both ascribes to every man every desire for immortality, whether by leaving a name or leaving descendants (4.721b7–c6), and gives an account of the soul's essential nature close to that in the *Phaedrus* (10.895e10–896e2).[24] But how is a compatibilist construal to be made out? The distinction that it needs to exploit is, I propose, precisely that sketched earlier within the 'modest' interpretation of 207c9–208b2. The surviving of death by a soul that, while incarnate, leads a physical and mental life is one thing; another is the continuation of that life, or aspects of it, within a life led by another soul. There are two ways in which one might try to

---

[21] Cf. *Pdo* 102a10–107a1, *Rep* 10.608d3–611a3.

[22] So Dover, op. cit. 149.

[23] One forthright incompatibilist, among others, is R. Hackforth, 'Immortality in Plato's *Symposium*', *Classical Review* 64 (1950).

[24] Cf. Richard Kraut, 'Egoism, Love, and Political Office in Plato', *Philosophical Review* 82 (1973), 342; Harold Cherniss, Letter to the *Classical Review* NS 3 (1953), 131.

identify a life: (1) by reference to the identity of a single soul that leads it; (2) by reference to continuities and causal connections not defined by the identity of any subject. (1) must be doubly unsatisfactory for Plato: it can yield no sufficient condition, if metempsychosis effects a succession of lives (as it surely must if it even crosses the barriers between species);[25] nor any necessary condition, if lives can branch taking on new subjects. So (2) must be intended (ideally alongside a claim that the unity that constitutes a single life, simple or branching, is a creation of the activity of a subject or subjects). The immortality that Plato proves elsewhere is a property of the soul as subject; the quasi-immortality that Diotima offers attaches to lives individuated independently of subjects.

Plato's redescription of survival in terms of replacement must put us in mind of modern discussions of personal identity (even before we have clarified his meaning partly in their language). The branching of lives has become a leitmotiv within the work of the most ingenious and radical investigator, Derek Parfit. He tells one story not wholly dissimilar to Plato's: a Scanner records the exact states of my brain and body and transmits this information to a Replicator which then creates, out of new matter, a brain and body exactly like mine. He then raises the question: is it me?[26] What most differentiates Plato's picture from this are two features: Plato, perhaps unlike Parfit, believes that self-reduplication can actually occur, not (of course) to the extent that Parfit is phantasizing, but still sufficiently to justify talk of a kind of survival; but Plato, on the more modest interpretation, thinks that what can thus be transferred is not a person (if we identify our 'person' with his 'soul'), but a life.

Notoriously, one immediate upshot is a problem about identity. This need not arise from Parfit's first version of his story, in which the Scanner destroys the body and brain that the Replicator will recreate; but his New Scanner leaves the original body and brain intact, so that the upshot is a duplication. Of the resultant pair of persons each can remark, pointing at the other, 'If I am here, I cannot also be there.' Each might view himself as merely part of a divided person; but the division may be too drastic (across two planets, as Parfit tells the story) for that to be at all plausible. Analogously, within Plato's picture, the parent might say of the infant, 'If my corporeal life is taking place here, it cannot also be taking place there'; for their lives

[25] Cf. *Pdo* 81d6–82b8, *Phdr* 249b1–5, *Tim* 90e3–92c3.
[26] *Reasons and Persons* (Oxford, 1984), 199–200.

have no present physiological link. Perhaps our uncertainties here are less acute: once we start to think of lives independently of subjects, our intuitions fail rapidly; the term 'person' has more staying power. Do I survive Parfit's process? Parfit urges, surely rightly, that it would be artificial to count me as surviving in his first version (without duplication), while denying this of the second version in order to avoid the question which body and brain I subsequently am: how can a double success be a failure? His conclusion is that it is continuity that matters for survival, not identity. Plato is less explicit, but the indications are in the same direction. Even if we feel more freedom with lives than with persons to distinguish parts within wholes in whatever ways are logically convenient, we shall be cutting the cloak of identities to match the cloth of continuities; the latter will seem the reality, the former a way of speaking that may or may not get us into trouble. Most indicatively, Diotima is clearly carefree about a multitude of progeny, physical or mental; it comes out in her ranking of legislators even above heroes and lovers (if 209c7–e4 is climactic) that she assumes that anyone would choose to transmit his life to as many people as possible.

In another way the logic of identity is equally inapt for Plato as for Parfit. A life held together over time by causal connections and continuities will always hold together more or less; but the logic of identity is all or nothing. Diotima contrasts mortal survival with that divine immortality which involves being 'altogether the same' (208a8). We might suppose that being an offspring is an all-or-nothing affair; but Diotima implicitly makes the reality a matter of degree by subsuming it under the rubric 'leaving a replacement such as it was itself' (b2–3). What Bernard Bosanquet calls 'spiritual kin-ship'[27] certainly comes in degrees: love and legislation more or less transform the lives of others. Plato is happy to provide Diotima with parallels which exemplify only fragmentary inheritances: memories of the heroism of Alcestis or Achilles, poems by Homer or Hesiod. Those cases may appear to raise no problems about the individuation of lives, but they only differ in degree from cases, however unlikely to be realized, that do. Parfit describes a 'psychological spectrum' that captures the situation aptly: at one extreme, I lose a few of my memories and character-traits, and gain a few of Napoleon's; at the other, I lose all my memories and character-traits, and gain a

---

[27] *The Principle of Individuality and Value* (London, 1912), 283.

complete set of Napoleon's (op. cit. 231). At what point along the spectrum do I cease to exist? Here a transition from talk of persons to one of lives does nothing to help answer the question; what it does do is to reduce our intuition that there ought to be an answer. The implication must be that how much psychological influence one must have over another to count as passing on one's mental life to him is not a question with a determinate, or even a useful, answer. The only formulable line would seem to be a wildly generous one: exerting a single piece of influence might count as annexing the whole life to whose parts it stands in a relation of contiguity. But that would be artificial: what we want and value is a matter of degree. In this respect, even talk of survival fails to mirror the reality.

We face a more local problem: how closely is Plato respecting his earlier definition of the goal of generic eros as possessing the good oneself for ever (206a11–12)? Here we can see the internal advantage, to the *Symposium* taken in isolation from Plato's other writings, of the radical interpretation: if the activity of specific eros, which is generation in beauty, is fully to achieve the generic goal, it ought to be *myself* that I replicate physically or mentally; while the modest interpretation has it that what I replicate, more or less richly, is merely *my life*. Such a corollary of the radical interpretation would seem finally to break down the barriers between persons; that might be taken as liberating, or self-evidently absurd. It is true that personal immortality becomes possible only in a manner of speaking: even survival through a lifetime was only offered to 'superminds' and 'superbodies', which were purely factitious entities. But the inference would remain that, if we are fully satisfied by what life offers us, even though longevity be notional and only ephemerality real, then there are options after death even in this world to satisfy us equally. However, it is clear from elsewhere, and (I suggested) even implicit here, that Plato does not wish to transform subjects of experience into fictions. The question becomes how best to characterize an immortality within mortality whose achievement is desirable even for souls that are themselves fully immortal.

Various interpreters offer a variety of turns of phrase (I shall quote them in italics) that, for all their felicity, seem rather to sheathe the problem than to bate it. R. Hackforth takes Diotima to be asserting that 'any mortal creature . . . can survive only *vicariously*, by leaving behind another like itself' (op. cit. 43). Richard Kraut allows that an achievable goal that is a '*second best*' may become a '*substitute*' for an

unachievable one (op. cit. 340–1). Terence Irwin equates a desire to
propagate what we value with 'a desire to do the *second best* to
ensuring our own immortality in possession of what we value, if we
can ensure its possession by others'.[28] However attractive, such
remarks seem close to a bare assertion that giving is a satisfactory
alternative to receiving (as is blatant in Irwin); but why, in general,
should causing another to benefit be nearly as good as benefiting
oneself?[29] Plato, regrettably, leaves it to us to speculate about an
answer. I speculate as follows. A human being engrossed in the life he
is leading, and not too self-conscious in his role as its subject, naturally comes to value it for its own sake, that is, if the abstraction is
possible, independently of its relation to himself. His life is, after all,
constantly an object of his attention; he himself is always the subject
of that attention, but only at times its explicit object. If Diotima is
right, a life is indeed to be abstracted from a liver, in such a way that
causal continuities can preserve it, or an aspect of it, across a change of
subjects. If the life, or aspect of a life, continues to flourish, any of its
past subjects may count that as contributing to his own success, where
'his own' expresses not a direct relation of ownership, but an indirect
relation that is accompanied by an attitude of identification.[30] Integral
to this proposal is that lives should be lived in a manner that generates
this attitude. Diotima's descriptions only capture that in part.
'Rehearsal', as an activity of the subject, should attach him to the
knowings that he thereby preserves or replaces (208a5–6). Procreation, sexual (208e1–5), tutorly (209a8–c7), poetic (d1–4), or legisla-
tive (d4–e4), all involves deliberate activity. But life within the body
(cf. 207d6–e1) and the non-cognitive mind (e2–5) is described as
happening, and not as being led; its subject is rather passive than
active. It is plausible that a passive relation of a subject to a life would
not inspire the same sense of identification; if so, Plato needs to

---

[28] *Plato's Moral Theory* (Oxford, 1977), 241.

[29] Kraut has something to say: 'To care about my future self is already to care about
things other than the habits, beliefs, and desires I now have, for these habits, beliefs,
and desires will not exist far into the future. There is therefore not as great a difference
as one might have thought between creating virtue in my future self and creating virtue
in someone whom I love and who will survive me' (op. cit. 341). But this replaces the
persisting self with temporal selves, which (contrary to Kraut's intention) is not
compatible with Plato elsewhere.

[30] Of course this much modifies the sense in which one is possessing the good *oneself*.
That price has got to be paid (as Hackforth, Kraut, and Irwin all confirm); and it is a
real one (which can only buy immortality of a kind, cf. 207d1). The problem is to define
just what one is paying for what.

redescribe the relation on Diotima's behalf.[31] It is true that, so long as the subject is active in procreation, he will always make his life actively his own at the moment of passing it on to another, which is minimally sufficient for her purpose; but the force of her train of thought (notably from 207a6–b6 on sexual reproduction, to c9–e1 on corporeal renewal, linked by b6–c9) is that living one's life and transmitting it are processes similar in kind. Plato could better her in making that out.[32]

5

In discussing Diotima's named exemplars of mental procreation (Alcestis, Achilles, Codrus, Homer, Hesiod, Lycurgus, Solon) I found it obscure how they all generated in *beauty*. Only Alcestis and Achilles were lovers in a strict sense, and that, on her account of their motivation, only incidentally. So her topic, which was to be erotic love as a species within generic eros (206b1–3), is in danger of having dissolved. If so, Socrates is a poor symposiast, who has hijacked the topic that Phaedrus inspired Eryximachus to propose and they all welcomed (177a2–d7), retaining only the title of the original destination. However, Diotima's more developed cases, which mentioned no names, fitted topic and definition much better: the lover of women is attracted to physical beauty and generates in it children of the flesh, while the lover of boys is attracted to physical and mental beauty and generates in it mental children. Even here there was a local failure of match, between the content of the goal, and the physical beauty of its occasion: physical beauty (unlike the beauty of mental promise) is not connected with fertility; and even if the woman needs to attract the man physically to save him from impotence, why should an analogue be true of the boy? This last question will receive no answer in the *Symposium*; but at least the emphasis of Diotima's exposition was on the right topic.

Yet when we come to the ascent-passage, the topic threatens to dissolve anew. The lover is described as advancing from a single beautiful body to all beautiful bodies, to the beauty of practices, to the

---

[31] As I noted, the *Phaedo* makes the soul the agent in renewing the body (87e1); that is what is needed here.

[32] So also could Aristotle, in his own metaphysical terms; cf. his account of beneficence in *NE* 9.7 (which I shall exploit in Chapter 4).

beauty of the sciences, and so to the Form of Beauty itself (211b7–d1). If we take his ascent to be strictly a *scala amoris*, through a succession of objects with which he is literally in love, then familiarity should not blind us to its boldness, nay bizarrerie. Loving Beauty itself is perhaps all right because it is a mystery (illumined dimly by a sexual metaphor at 212a2). And loving a single beautiful body, which sounds wrong to us (what one loves, however physically, is persons, not mere bodies), becomes all right once we bear in mind that the Platonic body is not, when alive, unconscious and Cartesian: it is not only a *sine qua non* (*Pdo* 65a7), but also a partaker (83d6–7, 94b7–e4), of pleasures, passions, even opinions, of a kind. But then loving all beautiful bodies, not just one, looks like Don Juanism. To quote Da Ponte: 'It's all love. He who is faithful to one is cruel to the others; I, who have an abundance of sentiment, wish them all well.' While loving practices and sciences seems just not on. In illustration, consider the erotic symptoms of *Phaedrus* 251 (comparable to Sappho's at the wedding feast): if these are not to be discarded (which would be a loss), are they to be transferred, in abstract yet alluring phantasies, to the contemplation, say, of the Lycurgan constitution?

Two ways of avoiding the absurdities of an impersonal eroticism, while denying any erotic losses to be set against intellectual gains, ought to be these: one might try either to personalize the later stages, or to de-eroticize the starting-point. As it happens, both ways have already been put forward, by Walter Pater and J. M. E. Moravcsik, respectively. We may begin by regretting that as a general account neither promises well. It will follow that we need a less uniform interpretation that may accommodate the heterogeneities of Plato's material.

Pater's conception is implicit in his general reconstrual of the world of Forms:

The lover is become a lover of the invisible, but still a lover, and therefore, literally, a seer, of it, carrying an elaborate cultivation of the bodily senses, of eye and ear, into the world of intellectual abstractions, as if now at last the mind were veritably dealing with living people there, living people who play upon us through the affinities, the repulsion and attraction, of *persons* towards one another, all the magnetism, as we call it, of actual human friendship or love.[33]

It is in connection with this that Pater finds a special role for the Form of Beauty:

<hr>

[33] *Plato and Platonism* (London, 1893), 139–40, slightly abbreviated; cf. 134, 146.

Abstract ideas themselves become animated, living persons, almost corporeal, as if with hands and eyes. And it is as a consequence, but partly also as a secondary reinforcing cause, of this mental condition, that the idea of Beauty becomes for Plato the central idea; the permanently typical instance of what an idea means (ibid. 170).

Thus Beauty itself becomes an object of personal affection. (In one shameless sentence, Pater goes so far as to suppose that a young man's longing for the Forms may be reciprocated; ibid. 184.) As for the intervening stages, even the beauty of practices and laws might be appreciated in the person of a morally educated individual (as, in the case of the Spartan Helots, by 'the young servitor' who displays 'a sort of bodily worship' of the 'gallantry of his youthful lords', ibid. 217). I quote Pater's self-indulgence not because it is risible, but because it is illuminating: he shows sensitivity to a real problem of interpretation. However, he was too little of a philosopher, and too regretful an ascetic, to be faithful to Plato.[34] It is having things both ways to call the lover 'literally, a seer' of 'the invisible'; and, as 'invisible' implicitly concedes, it cannot be right to interpret Forms as 'almost corporeal, as if with hands and eyes' (even with the more typically Paterian evasions of 'almost' and 'as if') when Plato tells us not to imagine Beauty as 'a face or hands or anything else of which a body partakes' (211a6–7). Pater is alive to the erotic aspect of the end as of the beginning of the ascent (cf. d3–e4); but it is a limitation that he will not take seriously Plato's aesthetic preference for what is 'pure, clear, unalloyed, not full of human flesh and hues and much other mortal trash' (e1–2). The Form of Beauty can offer nothing (to borrow an earlier phrase of Pater's) like the face of one's friend.

Alternatively, one might intellectualize the ascent from its beginnings. This is proposed by Moravcsik.[35] In his view, even at its starting-point (210a7) love 'is not mere sexual desire; rather, it is the love of bodies for the sake of bodily beauty that can be abstracted and contemplated on a general level' (op. cit. 291). This implies that 'the move from mere sexual interest to some sort of aspiration, presumably aesthetic, is made before the ascent is begun' (ibid.). Moravcsik takes eros here to be 'aspiration': it is 'any over-all desire or wish for what is taken to be good', or 'the wish or desire . . . for things deemed

---

[34] Richard Jenkyns's uninhibited attack is one-sided, but not refutable: *The Victorians and Ancient Greece* (Oxford, 1980), 253–61.

[35] 'Reason and Eros in the "Ascent"-passage of the *Symposium*', in J. P. Anton and G. L. Kustas (eds.) *Essays in Ancient Greek Philosophy* (Albany, 1971).

on account of their nature to be worthy of having their attainment
become a man's ultimate goal' (ibid. 290). That fits Diotima's definition of the genus (206a11–12); and it is at most a minor slip that his
description of the first step, which is particular (210a7), already looks
forward to the second one, which is generalizing (a9–b1). Yet I
believe his approach to be misguided, in two related ways. Firstly, it is
not an accident that he brackets sex and passion together (thus
'asexual' and 'passionless' occur equivalently, op. cit. 290); he is
operating with a dichotomy between rational desire on the one hand,
and sexual appetite on the other.[36] But that is unfair to passion; it is
even unfair to sex, which Diotima has not contrasted with reason but
subsumed under it, most unexpectedly when even an animal's desire
to copulate (207b1–2) was related to hopes of immortality. Secondly,
justice is not being done to the intensity of the feelings directed both at
beauties and at Beauty (211d3–e4). They are clearly of the same
family as the more concrete symptoms of *Phaedrus* 251, which,
though inspired by an implicit memory of Beauty itself, are impas-
sioned in a quite particular way: they register an effusion of desire
(c7) in the presence of an object of infatuation, and not just the
conception of an aspiration. This passionate eros, ignored or devalued
by Moravcsik, provides for Plato the impetus to the ascent; and it is
only when a still greater intensity of feeling is achieved that the ascent
is complete (211d9–e4). Plato's linking of the intellectual and the
erotic may not be to everyone's taste; but by overlooking it Moravcsik
shows himself, as W. K. C. Guthrie comments with uncharacteristic
tartness, 'curiously out of touch'.[37]

Ideally, we must prefer a less one-sided interpretation that, taking
as the material of the ascent both generic and idiomatic eros, may
hope to accommodate them in all their aspects, personal and ascetic,
emotional and intellectual.

6

I begin with a structured translation of Diotima's programme,
intended to facilitate discussion without prejudging it:

---

[36] In this way he anticipates the bicameral psychology of Socrates' first speech in the
Phaedrus (cf. 237d3–c4), with the contrast that he ascribes eros to reason and not to
appetite.

[37] *A History of Greek Philosophy* (Cambridge, 1962–81), iv. 393, n. 3.

A1   (210a7) He must love one body,

A2   (a7–8) and generate there beautiful discourse,

A3   (a8–b3) and then realize that the beauty of any one body is closely akin to that of any other, and that, if one must pursue beauty of appearance, it is great folly not to consider the beauty of all bodies one and the same;

A4   (b4–6) having realized this he must become a lover of all beautiful bodies, and slacken his intense love of the one, disdaining it and thinking little of it;

B1   (b6–c1) after this he must think beauty in souls more honourable than that in the body, with the result that, if someone was capable in his soul and had even a little bloom, that would suffice for his loving and caring for him

B2   (c1–3) and bringing forth such discourse as will improve young men,

B3   (c3–5) in order that he may now be forced to look upon the beauty in practices and laws and see that it is all akin itself to itself,

B4   (c5–6) in order that he may think the surface beauty of the body a little thing;

C1   (c6–7) after practices he must be led to sciences, so that he may now see the beauty of these,

C2   (c7–d4) and looking towards beauty already in its width he may no longer be base and mean-spirited in his slavery to the beauty of one (loving, in a menial way, the beauty of a certain boy or man, or of a single practice), but having turned to the wide sea of beauty and contemplating it

C3   (d4–6) he may bring forth much beautiful and fine discourse and thoughts in unlimited philosophy,

D   (d6–e1) until, strengthened and nourished there, he catches sight of a certain science which is single and such as to be of the following beauty.[38]

There are two processes at work in the ascent, generalization and ascension, displaying two directions of displacement of interest, horizontal and vertical. Generalization takes place *within* levels: the steps

[38] There are a few points to be made about text or translation. b8: *tis* is probably a more or less exclusive 'someone' rather than a promiscuous 'anyone' (cf. d2, 7). d1: I have followed Schleiermacher in reading *tō(i)* for the MSS and papyrus *to*. d1–3: I have translated between brackets words that M. D. Reeve elegantly deletes, in 'Eleven Notes', *Classical Review* NS 21 (1971), 326. (One ground which he gives, that *oiketēs* is a weak companion to *douleuōn*, seems tenuous; cf. *Theaet* 172d1.)

A3, B3 and C2 are all generalizing steps, and A, B, and C are three levels.[39] Within level B, to love a soul is to love a person for his mental qualities in a way that then invites generalization, just as, within level A, loving a body is loving a person for his physical qualities in a way that then invites generalization. B3 stands to B1 pretty well as A3 to A1. It is not a deep contrast that, while the beauty of bodies is 'closely akin' (*adelphon*), that of souls, practices, and laws should only be 'akin' (*sungenes*): these last three are different categories, though the beauty of each is interdefinable with that of the others. The generalization arises from reflection (which is what is precluded by 'folly' or 'want of understanding', *anoia* b2) issuing in a realization (a8, b4), or figurative perception (c4), that the beauty instantiated in one body or soul is equally present in other bodies or souls.[40] Generalization serves two further purposes. Firstly, it confirms a reduced valuation of, and commitment to, an inferior object, whether individual physical beauty (b5–6), physical beauty in general (c5–6), or any individual beauty (d1–3). B4 might seem a mere repetition of the start of B1 (b6–7); but it is only once beauty of mind has been grasped as a unity that it can be set on the scales against beauty of body, just as that, grasped as a unity (b1–3), could be weighed as a whole against individual beauty. We may call this role of generalization *consolidation*. Secondly, by yielding a grasp of universals (the single beauty of bodies, or the interrelated beauties of souls, practices, and laws), generalization paves the way for a grasp of the Form of which all beautiful things partake.[41] This role of generalization may be called *intimation*.

Ascension takes place *between* levels.[42] Generalization arises out of reflection; it is less clear what gives rise to ascension. Perhaps it is essential here that the lover be led by a wiser guide, whether up to level A (210a6–7), or up to level C (c6–7); it must be her influence (if

[39] It would be a mistake to divide level B between B2 and B3, as Robin well observes (*Platon: Le Banquet*, p. xciii). This is confirmed by the absence of any separate reference to B1 in the later summary (211c2–7); also 'in order to' (*hina*) is properly used of consequent steps within levels (with 210c3, cf. c5 and 211c8).

[40] Given that the lover is set on procreating mental but not physical beauty, there is the difference that what matters is the actual beauty of bodies, but the potential beauty of souls.

[41] Robin writes well, at level A, of 'a sort of disindividualization of physical love, which will serve to forward ascension towards spirituality' (op. cit. p. xciii).

[42] The metaphor of ascending is first explicit in the recapitulation (211c2–3); it is already implicit in the metaphor of 'the wide sea of beauty' (210d4), clearly imagined as being viewed from a newly gained height.

we take the guide to be female, like Diotima), and not the lover's understanding (which comes later, c5–6), that persuades him at the start of level B (b6–7) that mental beauty is 'more honourable' than physical. Yet that assigns only a superficial motivation (deference towards the guide), and provides no justification. Another partial explanation is that the lover capable of the ascent is predisposed to develop a pregnancy in soul; that must be why, right at the start, he is persuadable to seek out a boy to inspire beautiful discourse (a7–8), rather than a woman to carry on his family tree. But it is not easy to decide how far he can be motivated simply by a preference for mental offspring. With what procreating does he begin? The 'beautiful discourse' of A2 (210a8) must be taken in proper order: it must be such as to facilitate the next step (A3), which is generalization from particular to universal beauty of body. It is supremely, I suggest, a kind of love poetry (praising the boy as lovely rather than as temperate).[43] Because any description must ascribe shareable qualities, this is an aid towards aesthetic generalization.[44] The force of 'there' (*entautha*, a7) must be not that the lover makes the boy into a poeticizing Narcissus, but that his own poetry is inspired by the boy's presence.[45] No doubt it will also be presented to the boy, who will ideally commit it to his memory. Such verbal offspring offer a kind of immortality, so long as they are read or remembered, by their object or by others; but this is a restricted immortality, affecting other men's lives to a marginal extent (and only compensatingly many others if the poetry is exceptional). So there is clear point (at least if one is not 'the excellent Sappho, or the skilled Anacreon', *Phdr* 235c3–4), in ascending to level B: one can then propagate capacities (like the virtues of 209b7–c2) whose exercise constitutes a more significant part of a life. Yet here we may be stopped short: why should the lover ascend any further? Of course, in Plato's own opinion virtues need to be backed by knowledge, which ultimately means knowledge of the Forms, if

---

43 Robin, again, gets it right: 'His impressions [sc. of the boy's physical beauty] will translate themselves into enthusiastic speeches' (op. cit. p. xciii). Less correct is Werner Jaeger's gloss: 'speeches characterized by a feeling for higher things, for noble ideals and honourable aspirations'; *Paideia* (Oxford, 1939–45), ii. 194. That fits what we read earlier (at 209b7–c2), but here anticipates the discourse of B2, which is 'such as will improve young men' (210c2–3).

44 Cf. Moravcsik, op. cit. 293.

45 For a similar use of 'in' (*en*) signifying the personal occasion and not the precise location of an activity, cf. *Phdr* 228e4.

they are never to lead a man wrong (this is implicit at 212a3–6); but why should vicarious survival be better served by propagating virtue with knowledge than without? The *Symposium* itself contains no answer, and this, I think, is a major omission.[46]

Irwin offers a different explanation: 'The progress is elenctic. At each stage the pupil tests his aspirations against his present objects of admiration, and though he was not previously aware of it, finds the objects inadequate to the aspiration' (op. cit. 170). This is wholly plausible, if we supplement it a little: the lover must be not just indeterminately predisposed to develop pregnancy in soul, but fresh from a prenatal apprehension of the Forms (cf. *Meno* 98a4); this will make him at once capable of the ascent, and dissatisfied until he has completed it. It is not a large objection that nothing is said here about recollection: Socrates' time is short, and Plato is never willing to bring on the pre-existence of the soul and its memory of the Forms for a brief appearance. It is more of an obstacle that Diotima in fact presents the ascent as a series of attractions, not dissatisfactions: each step up, prompted by the guide, is justified by the appreciation that follows of a new kind of beauty; nothing is said to indicate that attraction by the new is preceded, and motivated, by dissatisfaction with the old. Irwin's description may be welcomed, but only as a supplement. A modest alternative to explanation is retrospective justification: Plato may be supposing that each stage justifies *itself* once the guide has prompted its achievement: to perceive the new beauty is to appreciate it. Bad desires may cloud one's perception and hence one's appreciation, and good desires be needed to open one's eyes; but no appeal to desire (or to dissatisfaction) is needed to prove that open eyes are desirable. Love may be the best helper (*sunergon*, 212b3–4) not because it provides reasons, but because, in a promising soul well prompted, it is receptive of, and responsive to, the opening of new vistas. To anyone who doubted the point of the ascent Plato might simply have replied, 'Expertus potest credere.'[47]

---

[46] It is true that Plato had an early answer to fall back on: Socrates teaches in the *Meno* that true opinion is fleeting, and only knowledge is stable (97e6–98a8); hence reliable transmission proves knowledge (99e5–100a2). It need not exclude some version of that contrast that, as we saw, even knowledge, *mirabile dictu*, needs to be renewed by rehearsal (207e5–208a7).

[47] 'Experience is belief'; this may be part of the force of the recurrent visual metaphors (210c3, 4, 7, d7; let alone e4, 211b6, d2, 3, e1, 4, 212a2, 3).

7

How widely or narrowly are we to understand the lover's interest in beauty? There are two issues here: we must try to determine how it relates to a concern for other values, and whether it is monopolized, at each stage, by the latest beauty that he has seen.

The ascent-passage mentions only one Form, that of Beauty, and yet supposes that a grasp of it will yield 'true virtue' (212a5–6), which must include both justice and wisdom.[48] We do find a Form of Goodness playing a unifying and overarching role in *Republic* 5–6; but I noted that, for Plato, 'good' and 'beautiful' have the same extension but not the same sense, since the good is good for one, while the beautiful is good to contemplate. Is there a way of understanding the unique place of Beauty within the ascent that accords with that? I think so. To be beautiful, in some way, is to be an appropriate object of a correlative kind of love; so Forms are objects of love *qua* partaking of Beauty.[49] In effect, the Form of Beauty constitutes the world of Forms *qua* objects of love. Lesser beauties are Form-revealing, or Form-transparent; anything that partakes of a Form is beautiful to the extent that the contemplation of it can be an intimation of Forms. It is this aspect of beautiful things that brings together love and philosophy in the *Symposium*, and makes the metaphysical ascent at the same time a *scala amoris*. Thus the uniqueness of the Form of Beauty at its apex answers to the singleness of its topic, love.[50]

As the lover advances, horizontally and vertically, what happens to the old objects of devotion as new ones come into view? Are they discarded, or just demoted? We have to decide between an *exclusive*, and an *inclusive*, reading. An exclusive reading could take two Forms: strongly, it could claim that, until it reaches its apex,

---

[48] It will be a Platonic thought that Beauty achieves this by reminding the lover of companion Forms (cf. *Phdr* 254b6–7); how that relates to what I am about to propose is indeterminate.

[49] Despite the phrase 'everything else' (211b2), this must even hold of Beauty itself: if it is to gratify the lover in a manner analogous to beautiful sights (d3–e4), it must itself, supremely, be beautiful to contemplate. Nowhere else does 'self-predication' (or better, self-participation) have such clear point.

[50] I complained earlier that Diotima assumes that physical beauty is relevant to mental procreation without explaining why. If the lover is to ascend towards Forms, we can supply a reason: even the austere *Phaedo* says that sense-perception is needed to remind us of the Forms (75a5–b2); it is, above all, visual beauty that can remind the lover of Beauty itself, and of the Forms *qua* objects of love.

the ascent is a series of deceptions and disillusionments, as the lover has repeatedly to realize that what he loved before has only a pretence of beauty; weakly, it could admit that the old beauties were indeed beauties, but claim that an interest in the old will always be overridden by an interest in the new. The strong form of the exclusive reading is clearly contrary to the text: Diotima's theme is that Beauty itself is supremely beautiful, and not that the lesser beauties are no beauties at all. Even the weak form is slightly curious: who is to say that there will *always* be instances of the latest kind of beauty available to divert the lover from returning to its predecessors? In fact, a dichotomy between strong inclusivity (with the lover often returning to them) and strict exclusivity (with him never turning back) neglects too much middle ground. Strong evidence for a more than minimal inclusivity, allowing the lover to retain some interest in lower objects, and not just when higher ones fail him, comes within C2: it describes the domain of his interest as 'beauty already in its width' (210d1) or 'the wide sea of beauty' (d4), which are not phrases to convey a narrow absorption in his latest project (here the sciences). Further, what C2 rejects is an exclusive devotion to some particular instances of beauty, and not a liberal attachment to all kinds and instances of beauty; if we retain what I translated as a parenthesis ('loving, in a menial way, the beauty of a certain boy or man, or of a single practice', d2–3), it is explicit that what is to be discarded is myopic attachments within levels, and not each previous level as a whole. Against that, there is the term 'disdaining' (*kataphronēsanta*, b5–6), which is the attitude of the generalizing lover of bodies towards any single body. However, that may be weaker than it sounds: within Alcibiades' later speech, taking *no* interest in physical beauty (216d8) and thinking it of *no* account (e3) go with 'disdaining' it 'to an almost incredible degree' (d8–e1); an unintensified 'disdaining' (more literally, 'looking down upon') need amount to no more than 'dishonouring' (compare 219c4 with d4), that is putting in its place, not turning out of doors. Further, 'disdaining' is associated with 'thinking little of' (210b6, c5–6), within which 'little' cannot easily mean 'nothing' when in 210b8 it must signify not nothing but enough for the purpose (cf. 'suffice', c1).[51]

---

[51] My translation of 210b8–c1 ('if someone . . . had even a little bloom, that would suffice for his loving and caring for him') follows Benjamin Jowett, and is, I hope, precisely right where Robin's emphasis is precisely wrong ('a body whose flower has no lustre at all'): physical beauty is still needed, but now a little is enough (cf. Pausanias at 182d7, and *Rep* 3.402d10–e1).

So textual details confirm a reading to some degree inclusive, without defining the degree. A more general point raised earlier is that the peculiar intensity of specifically erotic responses, which is valued highly enough to be transferred to the Form of Beauty (211d8–212a2), would have been lost long before if bodies were entirely supplanted as objects of interest by souls (supposing we exclude a cerebral eroticism); a generous and not grudging inclusivity would spare the lover erotic losses to be set against intellectual gains, and put him in a better position to respond to Beauty itself, when the time comes, in a way that does justice at once to its divine and his human nature. Quite false to the text, on the other hand, would be an *additive* reading which had the ascent multiply one's interests without reducing any; yet the scale of the reduction is not specified. That should not disappoint us: albeit in his own style, Socrates is giving an encomium of love at a party, and not a course in practical ethics.

8

Usually subsumed under the option between an inclusive and an exclusive reading is a question that I believe to be separate, and not less important: what happens to the individual as object of love? There are two roles that the loved one may play. Firstly, he may already possess instances of certain types of beauty, and so have a share (if only a small one) in the appeal of beauties of those kinds. Secondly, he may now receive new types of beauty from the lover, so that the lover's life flows, more or less richly, through him.[52] If we keep these roles apart, we can recognize that an individual may be important to the lover in the second way however little interest the lover takes in the beauty (other than that of promise) that he possesses already, and however narrow an interest the lover takes in forms of beauty. So one possibility is to interpret the ascent, whether on an inclusive or an exclusive reading, as an account of how lover and beloved mutually develop their interests in beauties that are more universal (by advancing horizontally) and more high-flown (by advancing vertically). In this way even an exclusive reading could

[52] If the beloved starts *too* well endowed in the first way, it may be impossible for him to play the second role; he had better be young enough that a lack of development is no defect.

accommodate even an exclusive devotion (in a sense) of the lover to a single beloved.

I shall now set out an interpretation intended to reconcile personal love with developing interests.[53] (For convenience, 'I' will signify the lover.)

A1   I prize a boy's body.

A2   I praise his body to him.

A3   I realize that what I admire in his body is shared by other bodies.

A4   I prize the beauty of bodies in general more than his particular beauty. (At this point I am at least unfaithful to him, and may desert him altogether.)

B1   I prize some boy's soul more than his body. (This could be the same boy as within A1–3, but may well be a new one.)

B2   I praise his soul to him. This praise would make *any* youth better; if bruited abroad, it will also make *other* youths better. (This implies some diversion of concern, but no discarding of my devotion to him.)

B3   I realize that what I admire in his soul, actual or potential, may be shared by other souls, trained by the same or similar practices and laws.

B4   (This stands to A4 as B1 stood to A1.) Just as I prize his soul more than his body, so I prize the mental qualities he may share with others more than the physical qualities he does share with them.

C1   I turn my and his attention and admiration to the sciences.

C2   A recapitulation in metaphor (note 'already', d1), covering A3, B3, and C1.

C3   In part a further recapitulation. 'Much beautiful and fine discourse' looks back to what was implicit in A3 and B3; 'thoughts in unlimited philosophy' describes the discourse (or rather dialogue) that now ensues on C1.

D   I turn my and his attention and admiration to the science of Beauty itself.

As I see it, there is a difference between the effects of generalization within levels A and B. At level A, appreciation of others leaves little

---

[53] Here I exploit, but modify, my earlier attempt in 'Loving Persons Platonically', 29.

ground for fidelity. What is envisaged is not precisely sexual promiscuity: the lover was aim-inhibited (as Freud would say) from the beginning, for his attachment to one body only produced *words* (210a7–8). Hence the only Don Juanism in question is one of attraction, not of gratification. For some idea of what it might come to, consider Socrates' susceptibility as described by Alcibiades: 'You see that Socrates is erotically disposed towards beautiful persons and always hanging around them and out of his mind about them' (216d2–3). Elsewhere, Socrates himself finds common a still greater indiscriminacy: *all* adolescents, he says, are electrifying (literally, 'biting') to the lover of boys, however different in profile or complexion (*Rep* 5.474d4–475a2). Such a generosity of response should inspire in a man pregnant in soul a non-particularized love-poetry inspired by, and intended for, ingenuous youth in general.[54] If this is the right way to interpret level A, then the single individual as the object of a focused attachment returns only at level B. There, though the lover's admiration is directed at virtue in general, his procreative activity takes the form not just of circulating verses but of instilling character, which must require a close personal relationship. This contrast between levels A and B was anticipated in the earlier description of educative pederasty: there (209b4–c2) the lover welcomes beautiful bodies in general before he attaches himself to a single boy beautiful in mind as in body. We may think of the lover within level A as only achieving an unstable state in which his inability to focus his attention is matched by the superficiality of the influence he exercises. It is true

---

[54] It is a possible suggestion that even indiscriminate love-making might be justified as an escape from myopic particularity. So Nussbaum: 'Ironically, loveless sex could be a useful form of training for Platonic love'; 'Plato on Commensurability and Desire', *Proceedings of the Aristotelian Society* Supp. Vol. 58 (1984), 70. However, liberation from the particular has point only in aiding a grasp of the universal, and making love is not, in itself, a contemplative activity. The flavour of the physical attraction that survives through the ascent (on an inclusive reading) is most subtly, but equivocally, conveyed in a later phrase: 'face and hands or anything else of which a body partakes' (211a6–7). It was perceptive of Ulrich von Wilamowitz-Möllendorf to be struck by the special mention of hands as well as face, and to suspect here a disclosure of Plato's own sensibility; *Platon* (Berlin, 1919), i. 385, n. 1. One may propose one (or both) of two possible and contrasted causes: a partial failure of sublimation, whereby (in Freudian terms) the displaced sexual interest regresses a short way back from the face towards the genitals; or a preference for those parts of the body that best reveal the soul. The second cause is suggested in a remark by Novalis containing a phrase quite close to Plato's: 'The more brilliant and educated a man is, the more personal his limbs are, e.g. his eyes, his hand, his fingers, etc.' (*Fragmente und Studien*, 'Die Enzyklopädie' § 6); *Werke und Briefe* (Munich, 1962), 509–10. Even young hands can convey an impression of mental gifts.

that, even within level B, there is a element of diversion: the lover's discourses will also inspire and influence young men in general (210c2–3). But in this context general broadcasting must be more of a spin-off than a distraction: nothing in the Socratic dialogues, or Plato's moral philosophy, allows that virtue could be effectively imparted so casually. Legislators are another case, and have the privilege of setting the background conditions for individual relation-ships; but at this stage the lover might at most be devoted to a small clan of young friends.[55] The same will be true of the later levels: dialectic, especially, is an exercise of the seminar or tutorial, and not of the lecture-theatre.

Is an interpretation of this kind helped or hindered by the remainder of Socrates'-speech (from 210e1)? It must be helped by one later sentence: 'Whenever someone, ascending from these things through loving boys rightly (*dia to orthōs paiderastein*) begins to see that Beauty, he would almost be touching the goal' (211b5–7). This implies that right up at least to the beginning of the end of his ascent the lover is still, in a manner, loving a boy.[56] Yet the strongest ground in favour of interpreting the ascent as an exercise of personal love is its relation to what precedes: if it is to bear out Diotima's original

---

[55] One may think, historically, of Stefan George's circle (preferably not forgetting that George had a Maximin with whom to be more particularly in love).

[56] So Dover sees in the word *paiderastein* 'a reminder that Diotima is not speaking of solitary mysticism, but of the "right" use . . . of the emotional relationships about which Phaedrus and Pausanias were talking' (*Plato: Symposium*, ad loc., cf. *GH*, 164). George Grote attempted to disarm the sentence by paraphrasing it as follows: 'Herein we have the climax or consummation of that erotic aspiration which first shows itself in the form of virtuous attachment to youth'; *Plato, and the Other Companions of Sokrates* (London, 1867), ii. 213. But the word 'first' is his addition, and it would be odd to ascribe unqualifiedly to rightly loving boys what comes more immediately of ceasing to love them. Dover appears further to imply that the relationship between the lover and his mentor is erotic; for he writes of 210c6–e1, 'It is the guide, the older partner, who must "lead (sc. the younger) to the sciences"', referring, presumably *à propos*, to his notes to 211b5–c1. Robin, perhaps to similar effect, refers back to 'the erotic pedagogy' of 210e2–3, where the lover was 'led by instruction' towards the objects of his love (op. cit. ad 211b5–6). This still relates the whole of the ascent to personal love, but in a slightly different way: of such love the protagonist remains an object, even if (as 211b5–7 will now permit) he ceases to be a subject. However, I think that this can be excluded quite simply: the subject of *paiderastein* must be the same as that of the 'whenever'-clause (211b5–6), where 'someone' means pupil, not guide. Just how their relationship is to be understood is left obscure: it must involve mental procreation, but perhaps not in beauty in an erotic sense (at least when the pupil is Socrates, or the guide a priestess). As I suggested in an earlier note, the lover may need a beautiful face to inspire a recollection of the Forms; but his psychagogue is already wise, and may or may not need a pretty pupil as a continuing inspiration.

definition of love in the specific sense as aiming at immortality through generation in beauty, it must have the task of completing the mental procreation, and in particular the educative pederasty, described in the so-called lesser mysteries of 209. Though it is only the discourse of 210c1 that is specified as being educative (c2–3), the emphasis upon discourse at every level (a7–8, c1–3, d4–6) confirms that communication is always the goal (cf. 209b7–c2).[57] If the ascent-passage has standardly been read as describing a discarding of persons for the sake of Forms, that is, if I am right, the result of two connected mistakes (whose effect is only slightly mitigated by an inclusive reading): confusing the loved one's role as an object of contemplation (in which he is soon largely superseded) with his role as a recipient of thought, and taking the passage out of context.

9

And yet it is possible that, at the moment that Diotima stands with Socrates behind her at the apex of the ascent, vicarious immortality is forgotten and a better immortality preferred. That would not establish the traditional interpretation, when the implications of 209 before are remembered in the mention of pederasty afterwards (211b5–7); but it would complicate the situation. We need to look closely at Diotima's closing sentences as Socrates reports them:

Do you think, she said, that it will be a poor life that a man leads who looks thither and views that [sc. Beauty itself] with that by which it has to be viewed, and has intercourse with it? Or do you not reflect that there alone he will succeed, seeing Beauty with that to which it is visible, in generating not images of virtue but true virtue, inasmuch as he is laying hold not of an image but of the truth? And that, generating and nurturing true virtue, he will have the privilege of becoming dear to the gods and, if any man can, immortal himself also (211e4–212a7)?

Questions that arise are: what kind of virtue is generated by the completion of the ascent, and in whom is it generated, only in the

---

[57] The ascent is introduced as 'the final mystery, for the sake of which also these things are' (210a1–2), that is, the generation of fame and virtue. This itself indicates that vicarious immortality, and intellectual initiation, must be brought together. What the ascent-passage valuably adds is an account of how the lover acquires his intellectual interests; it is no longer baldly asserted that he has long been pregnant in soul (as at 209c3).

lover or also in a loved one? Taking these lines out of context (as is proposed), we shall not find it easy to give an answer. In fact I shall end by arguing that their very ambiguity leaves us with no option but to read them in the context of the ascent itself, and that it is the impossibility of relating the previous stages of the ascent to any but a vicarious immortality that compels us, if we are to avoid a final acute discontinuity, to understand its upshot in the same way.

Perhaps general reflection might supply an answer in advance of any special scrutiny. Take this thought of Guthrie's: 'God, and the soul that has attained divinity, can presumably no longer feel *erōs* at all, for that is the intermediate state of one who has not yet fully attained.'[58] It might be said that the soul that has attained union (note the sexual metaphor in 212a2) with Beauty itself could retain no interest in any lesser object, and no desire for any goal yet to be achieved; even its own happiness would no longer be striven for (though it might now be secure). One might compare the state that Aristophanes' lovers will end in if Hephaestus consents to weld them together: in Nussbaum's words, 'Wrapped in each other's arms, there they lie, for the rest of their lives and on into death, welded into one, immobile' (*The Fragility of Goodness*, 176). However, even the life of the gods may not be all quite like that. Within *Symposium* 212a itself, if the phrase 'dear to the gods' (a6) is serious and not clichéd (as it must be if the final words 'immortal himself also', a7, are to mean immortal like the gods, and not, bathetically, as much as any other man), it invites the following expansion by Robin: 'When love disappears as a *tendency* towards that of which it is still deprived, it survives all the same, in reversion, as a benevolent *effusion*, as a granted favour, as a condescending act of grace' (op. cit. p. xcvii). No doubt, in its full explicitness, this is less close to Plato than to Proclus (cf. *Ad Alcibiaden I* 30–3); but the implications of the phrase 'dear to the gods' are to undermine Guthrie's thought, and to throw open the question whether union with the Forms is to be understood as issuing only in ecstatic contemplation, or also in active philanthropy.[59]

---

[58] 'Plato's Views on the Nature of the Soul', in Vlastos (ed.), *Plato II* (New York, 1971), 241; cf. Vlastos, 'The Individual as Object of Love in Plato', 32–3.

[59] That Love is not a god, since he is 'portionless in beautiful and good things' (202d5), whereas all gods are happy and beautiful (c6–7), does not imply that gods cannot love. Even gods are lovers to the extent that they desire future goods that are not guaranteed; benefiting mortal men through unpredictable intermediaries (202e8–203a8) is just such a good. Gods differ from men in never being at risk of counting as less than happy.

On the one side, one might cite the blissful inaction of the soul in the *Phaedo* that 'alone by itself' contemplates the Forms: 'Then it has ceased from its wandering and, when it is about those objects, it is always constant and unvarying, because of its contact with things of a similar kind' (79d4–6).⁶⁰ There is also the *Timaeus* (90b6–d7), where 'laying hold of truth' (c1–2, virtually the same phrase as at *Symp* 212a5), and achieving such immortality as is possible for human nature (c2–3), go with cultivating the divine by a contemplation of the divine motions (c6–d1). Yet it is sometimes made quite clear that union with, and even assimilation to, the divine is realized also in action, as in the *Theaetetus*: 'One must try to flee from here to there as quickly as possible. And flight is assimilation (*homoiōsis*) to god as far as is possible; and assimilation is becoming just and pious together with wisdom' (176a8–b3, cf. *Rep* 10.613a7–b1). Striking here is that flight from the world is equated with playing one's part rightly within it. Similarly, in the *Laws* (10.904c6–e3), the effect of intercourse with divine virtue (a sexual metaphor, d6) is to become outstandingly virtuous (d7), and unlike the unjust (c10). Thus to 'lay hold of' Justice, say, is not only to think just thoughts, but to be just, that is to act justly. Contemplating (*Symp* 210d4) and looking (212a2) cannot be self-contained activities when their objects are the moral, or practical, Forms. In respect of them Plato would have agreed with a maxim of M. Guyau's: 'Thought without action is incomplete thought.'⁶¹

On the whole, therefore, it is not to be presumed or even supposed that union with Forms means indifference to other people. When we look in the *Symposium* at 212a, we find that intercourse with Beauty generates (the sexual metaphor is maintained) true and not ersatz virtue. The contrast must be with the propagation of 'manifold virtue' ascribed to legislators at the end of the lesser mysteries (209e2–3). True virtue evidently requires underpinning by knowledge of the Forms; it requires progression from the level of laws and practices to the apex of the ascent. Within the more developed doctrine of the *Republic*, it is the virtue of the guardians, whose intellects are drilled in dialectic, in contrast to that of the auxiliaries and artisans, whose characters are trained through 'music' and habituation.⁶² So the lover does not finish up in exclusive devotion to the beatific vision; social

⁶⁰ Note the last clause, containing the same verb (*ephaptesthai*) as at *Symposium* 212a4, 5.
⁶¹ *Esquisse d'une morale sans obligation ni sanction* (Paris, 1896), 108.
⁶² Cf. Vlastos, 'Justice and Happiness in the *Republic*', in *Platonic Studies*, § 8.

virtue is a criterion even of the highest understanding. Yet saying this still leaves a large question open: is the culmination of virtue generated only in the lover, or also in a loved one? It is clear that the lover remains an agent; unclear is whether his agency involves not only a social sphere of activity, but personal influence within a relationship.

Different interpretations may appeal to different parallels. Closest in detail, though without mention of immortality, is a passage in the *Republic* (6.490a8–b7): there too we read of 'laying hold' of the nature of each thing 'with the appropriate part of the soul' (b3–4); also of 'mingling' with reality (b5; cf. 'intercourse', 212a2), of 'bringing forth intelligence and truth' (b5–6; cf. 212a5–6), and so of escaping from 'birth-pangs' (b7; cf. 206e1). The achievement is not wholly intellectual, for from it flows 'a sound and just character, which is accompanied by temperance' (c5–6); but it is an achievement for oneself, not for another. By contrast, the guardians who have looked upon 'that which gives light to all' are to 'use it as a pattern for the right ordering of the state and the citizens and themselves throughout the remainder of their lives' (7.540a4–b1); they are to mould others, and not just themselves. Clearly there is no change of mind between *Republic* 6 and 7; it can only be an accident of exposition that language close to that of the *Symposium* is used at a point where self-education is relevant and not the education of others. Certainly that language itself tells neither way. A nearer parallel is within the *Symposium* itself (209c2–7): we meet similar sexual language (compare 'consorting', 209c2, with 'having intercourse', 212a2), similar procreative language ('generate', *tiktein*, 209c3, 212a3, 5), and even similar terms for post-natal care (compare 'brings up together', 209c4, with 'nurtures', 212a6); we meet there a comparative 'more immortal' (209c7) to set beside 'if any man can, immortal' here (212a6–7). Yet there is a great difference between the role of the boy's beauty in 209c, and that of the sequence of beauties in 210: at each stage of the ascent the lover owes to the beauty in which he generates not only release from pregnancy, but the very character of his offspring; beauty has become less midwife than only begetter. Ideal Beauty has now inspired in him ideal virtue, and whatever gratitude he may owe it, he can do nothing to improve *its* nature. Whether he now improves anyone but himself looks an open question.

To settle the issue we have, after all, to view the apex of the ascent in the context of the ascent itself. It is a peculiar feature of the final stage that, assimilated to the ideal and divine, the lover may be called 'immortal' himself through winning for his soul a character which is as inalienable a personal possession as its own existence. This is an immortality not vicarious, but proprietary; achieving it may count as generation in beauty for the sake of immortality, but to entirely new effect. However, at all the previous stages of the ascent, where the immediate product was verbal communication and there was no new kind of immortality, a recipient was needed to offer the lover vicarious survival through assimilating aspects of his mental life. That point was explicit in talk of propagating virtue in others within level B (210c2–3); any suggestion that an interest in another person fades out after that is not only arbitrary, but forgetful of the fact that the goal of generation in beauty was always immortality (206e7–207a4), and not just the joys of self-creation. If, at the final stage, the heady charms of ideal Beauty put the lover out of mind of his original purpose, two will suffer: the lover, who throws away the chance of a double immortality (vicarious as well as proprietary), and the loved one, who is suddenly jettisoned with a once generous but now incomplete inheritance. It would seem strange to withdraw from identification with another person at the point when one's mental life most merits transmission. Union with the Forms should be enlightening, not entangling; why should achieving it exact so heavy a price?

I conclude that an individual is retained as an object of love throughout the later stages of the ascent, though the kind of life that the lover, under guidance, achieves for him and for himself changes very considerably. In one way, the ascent returns full circle. The beauty of laws, practices, and sciences is a corollary of their excellence; it makes them good objects of study, but not sources of wonder. By contrast, contemplation of Beauty itself offers the lover an intensity of experience that at once refreshes and eclipses the experience with which he began: gazing upon the Form of Beauty is even more, incomparably more, ravishing than looking at the forms of boys (211d1–e4). As I remarked at the start, this is a mystery; yet it helps to remove any suspicion that Diotima, in introducing philosophy as the summit of the lover's activity, has in fact quietly changed the subject, and is now praising not love but something different. Plato's theories of love, here and in the *Phaedrus*, contain much that is unfamiliar to us, including many things that we would expect to find under another heading; but even here his topic emerges in the end as the one that we thought, only so transfigured that what had seemed only one aspect of life, dominant perhaps only at one time of life, turns out, fully developed and understood, to amount to the best life. And this paradigm essentially involves an intimate relationship with another here on earth as well as an ascent towards the Platonic heaven. Personal love, of a kind, is thereby not supplanted, but glorified.

3
LOVE IN THE *PHAEDRUS*

As an account of love, Socrates's contribution to the *Symposium* has deficiencies to make one glad that it does not constitute Plato's final word. It invites supplementation in a number of respects.

It is distinctive of *being* in love that it stands much closer to *feeling* in love than loving stands to feeling love (if 'loving' means an affection that amounts to a particularized altruism). It would be possible, if unlikely, to love someone without ever feeling affectionate (though not without appropriate feelings, for instance of sympathy), but not to be in love without ever, indeed frequently, feeling in love. Feelings are part of the essence of being in love; they are a corollary of loving in the case of creatures with relevant feelings. An impassible god can love, but not be in love. To be in love without having the concept is to be confused by one's feelings (like Cherubino); even if I am a creature of feeling, I can love without having the concept and yet lack any feelings that confuse me. Hence, as Socrates reports Diotima, it half distances her from his ostensible topic that she shows so little interest in the phenomenology of love. The mythical description of Eros has its graphic moments: at one point, it seems to reflect the rhythm of genital sexuality (203e1–4); more specifically, we meet the *topos* of *thuraulia*, of the lover waiting outside the door (203d2–3, cf. 183a6, *Phdr* 252a6–7). Yet even those details were only inserted to illustrate an a priori principle that love, as a kind of desire, arises from a state of lack and poverty that it is constantly trying to escape. Only, I think, in the ascent-passage are we offered glimpses through the eyes of the lover himself (e.g. 210c7–8, d3–4, d7, 211d8–e4), and those in very general terms. Plato wishes rather to characterize certain roles in an abstract way than to convey what it is like for a subject to fill them. Even the object of love is cut to the measure of the argument: it is presented as 'beautiful and delicate and perfect and blessed' (204c4–5) not as a product of idealization, but as the formal complement of the lover's poverty. The results are illuminating, but always schematic. We are told that erotic enchantment marks both the beginning and the end of the ascent (211d5–e4); but the analysis focuses on the contents of a series of desires, and not on the distinctive feel of any mental state.

Moreover, the distance from felt experience was achieved not only by a restriction of focus, but by a too simplified and sanguine psychology. The sole goal of love is beauty (201a9–10), or else goodness (205e7–8). Its foundation is the desire to be *eudaimōn* (204e6–205a3); indeed, generic love simply *is* the desire for the good and *eudaimoniā* (205d1–3). Hence all a man's desires will automatically fall in line behind the successive evaluations of the ascent: there is no room for a conflict between reason and desire. It does not follow that there will be no conflicting considerations. Men who are pregnant both in soul and in body (cf. 209a1–2) may have to make certain hard choices; so may those, on the inclusive interpretation, who acquire new enthusiasms through the ascent, for it is not specified that, say, any higher good is always to be preferred to any lower one, irrespective of quantity. Even within one kind of project there may be losses and gains to balance, and not always uninteresting ones. Yet, while dilemmas remain possible, the difficulties will be ones of judgement and not of self-control. Similarly, Socrates is in a position to recognize some of the tensions that help to constitute love as a human condition: for example, a typical contrast between an identificatory attitude towards the other's mind, and a spectatorial attitude towards his body. This shows up in the different ways in which the loved one, unless he is a narcissist, will respond to the 'beautiful discourse' (that is, I suggested, physical praise) of 210a8, and the 'thoughts contained in abundant philosophy' of d5–6, adopting the latter but merely accepting the former. However, there is no room for a coarser conflict between non-evaluative responses (notably sexual) and responses that derive from the selection of a way of life. The result is a certain unreality which undermines one's confidence in the triumphalism of the ascent-passage.

There still seemed little ground to suppose that Socrates might be quietly changing the subject. The Form of Beauty could occupy the apex of the ascent precisely because, albeit mysteriously, it is the object of the most intense erotic response (211d1–e4); and it seemed intended, though not always explicit, that the ascent should involve three people (guide, lover, and beloved) within all its stages, and so constitute a model at once of intellectual development and of interpersonal relations. However, this amalgam of love and philosophy was not worked out wholly satisfactorily. Philosophy (literally, love of wisdom) was first ascribed to Eros just as one aspect of his intermediacy between deprivation and abundance (204b2–7). It next appeared as a species of generic eros co-ordinate with specific eros (205d5). That it later looms larger than the love of money or of physical exercise (d4–5) seems to have everything to do with the nature of reality, and little with the nature of eros. Little, not nothing, because of the attraction of the Form of Beauty; but the tastes of a merchant or athlete would seem as transmissible to a loved one as those of a philosopher.

If it is largely unclear why specific eros should point to philosophy, it is equally unclear why philosophy should need the support of eros: given at once the appeal of the Forms and the prudence of vicarious immortality, why should begetting *in* beauty be more desirable or achievable than begetting an appreciation *of* Beauty in any receptive soul? Why, for instance, should the guide, if not in love, be any less motivated than the lover to impregnate another soul? (*Pace* 209b4–5, the mere mention of pregnancy is no help.) An answer would need to bring out the relation of physical beauty at once to the Forms, and to the lover's psychology. Socrates implied that there was more to be said, simply by the role he assigned to appreciating bodies at the start of the ascent; but he did not say it.

If in one way Socrates' descriptions of love and of philosophy were made for one another, both were in that way defective. Aristophanes had imagined pairs of lovers each seeking for his or her other half, and for no one else (though willing to find consolation in others of the right sex, 191d6–192a1); that overstatement, which could apply literally only among the immediate products of the initial splitting, continues to charm us. Socrates follows Diotima to the opposite extreme: just as the goal of the ascent is to grasp each aspect of reality in the single way in which each can be grasped, so individuals as objects of love fall into just two categories (within tne rather wide class of those who have some physical allure, 210b8–9): either they can share a full grasp of reality, or they cannot. It would have fitted the analogy with sexual reproduction that mental procreation should be a function of the idiosyncrasies of the partners; but that point was not made within 209, and is alien to 210. Both lover and beloved have become in origin blank tablets (cf. the imagery of *Theaet* 194c4 ff.) that either can, or cannot, receive and retain the impress of knowledge. That there should be different styles of loving within the same levels is no more envisaged than that there should be different ways of grasping and appreciating the same strata of reality. Socrates presents the varieties of cognition, and of affection, with a consistent over-simplicity.

It goes with this that his lovers soon discard any personal interest in one another. The older has nothing to learn from the younger, and all the younger has to gain from the older is a perspective upon the nature of things that, being as transparent and featureless as a clear pane of glass, yields no insight into any distinctive feature of *his* nature. It is part of the concept of the ascent that beauty now creates not only the fact but the content of their discourse; but the beauty is external, or, if internal, unidiosyncratic. Neither has any reason to look into the other's eyes. The result fits a certain model of friendship, in which one forgets not only oneself but also one's friend: 'In this kind of love, as Emerson said, *Do you love me?* means *Do you see the same truth?*'; 'We picture lovers face to face but Friends side by side; their eyes look ahead'; 'Love does not consist in gazing at each other but in looking together in the same direction.'[1] The model has an austere charm; but it avoids sentimentality by not even being in danger of it. A world of personal sentiment, and of a kind of mutual interest and understanding that only sentiment can inspire, is left outside.

We cannot tell to what extent the deficiencies arose from a simplicity of thought, or a simplification of presentation. It is too easy a suggestion that we ascribe to brevity whatever omissions could be remedied without any inconsistency: that would be at once too generous (as if stating nothing but the truth implies that one knows the whole truth), and too mean (every lecturer knows that a time-limit affects what one says as well as what one does not say). But of course I have drawn these complaints not just from a modern repertory (which, except for chauvinists, might undermine them), but from what we read in Plato elsewhere; that is to say, from the *Phaedrus*.

2

Socrates' first speech is the victim and later the beneficiary of a double peripetia. It opens with the pretension to better Lysias (235c5–6) by a

---

[1] The first two quotations come from C. S. Lewis, *The Four Loves* (London, 1960), 78–9; the third I met ascribed in a book of aphorisms to Saint-Exupéry.

more systematic procedure: it will define love before investigating its effect for good or ill (237c8–d3). It is then condemned by Socrates himself as 'foolish and somewhat impious' (242d7), 'saying nothing healthy or true' (e5–243a1, cf. 262d2). Finally it is commended for identifying and censuring, within the genus of madness, 'a love called "left-hand"' (266a5).[2]

Like Lysias (230e6–234c5), Socrates is arguing against a boy's granting his favours to anyone who is in love with him (237b5–6). He imaginatively puts his speech into the mouth of a dissembler who is in love with a beautiful boy but has persuaded him that he is not in love (237b3–5). The significance of this has been variously interpreted.[3] I incline to understand it quite simply: we may suppose that the superiority of Socrates' speech to Lysias's is being tactfully mirrored in its ascription to a suitor who, being actually in love,[4] is motivated to take greater pains over his seductive argument (cf. Aristotle *NE* 7.6.1149b15–18). So the implication is, 'This will be better', that is, better and more persuasive rhetoric; not necessarily truer, nor falser, in content. The later endorsement of the speech as defining 'a love called "left-hand"' (266a5) will follow an argument that essentially contested concepts lend themselves to deceptive use by the orator who knows the similarities between things that are different (261e6–262b9, 263a2–c5).[5] In endorsing the speech Socrates reconstrues as a correct locating of one kind of love (such as effective rhetoric presupposes) what its supposed speaker intended as a deceptive extension of it over the whole field of love (such as constitutes effective rhetoric). Thus, in retrospect, Socrates' first speech will represent a blend of truth and falsity that can show up differently in different lights. But that is to come; initially, the speech is not introduced in any way that regiments our responses.

The modern reader (especially if he proceeds straight from the schematic idealizations of the *Symposium*) is likely to be struck by a sudden breath of actuality. Some of the speech's themes may even strike us as Proustian (so far has Proust annexed, if not invented,

---

[2] I prefer 'left-hand' to C. J. Rowe's 'left-handed': it is confusing if Plato is picturing this love as both 'on the left-hand side' (a3) and left-handed.

[3] Cf. Léon Robin, *Platon: Phèdre* (Paris, 1933), p. xxxii; R. Hackforth, *Plato's Phaedrus* (Cambridge, 1952), 40.

[4] No doubt to be glossed popularly: cf. Prodicus's definition of love as 'desire doubled' (B7), cited by K. J. Dover (*GH*, 43).

[5] It might suit Plato's realism better to call the concepts not essentially but naturally contested; that is, as a result of human nature and not their own.

them). A theme taken over from Lysias (232c4–d4) which is recurrent in Socrates' first speech (239a7, 240a5, 241c2, cf. 243c6), and denied in his second (247a7, 253b7—except, significantly, as a cause of falling from heaven, 248a8–b2), is that of envy (*phthonos*). Socrates' statement of it here is simple and rationalizing: he presents it as arising from the lover's self-interest in keeping his beloved so far as possible dependent upon himself. Also vivid to us (and also taken over from Lysias, cf. 231d4–6) is the theme of 'I am quite myself again' (241a4–b3), which grounds (a7) as well as causes the ex-lover's breaking promises that he made when in love. Again, the theme is presented here rather restrictedly. The thought that the ex-lover is no longer the same person (241a4, 7) is derived from the claim that he has now come to his senses (a2–4, 8–9); and it is indeed *this* claim that could alone plausibly justify the breaking of oaths and promises. However, that falling in or out of love is assuming or discarding a special personality is a theme that need not carry with it any disparaging of love. Later, Socrates will present a love that demands a reversal of the evaluative comparison here: there (256e4–6) the good sense that is contrasted with madness is a merely 'mortal' quality, 'dispensing miserly benefits of a mortal kind'. Common to both comparative evaluations is that falling in or out of love so transforms one's attitudes that it becomes difficult to identify with oneself across the transmutation that it effects. Such themes, even in a commonplace form, valuably indicate that Plato's idealism was not generated by a blind eye for reality.

The conceptual kernel of the speech is its definition of eros. After an initial emphatic statement of the need to define love before considering its effects for good and ill (237c5–d3, cf. *Rep* 1.354a13–c3) comes a setting of the problem that is essentially familiar to us: 'That love is some sort of desire is clear to everyone; and again we know that men desire the beautiful even if they are not in love. By what then shall we distinguish the man in love and the man who is not?' Eros here is specific, not generic; but the structure would seem otherwise to take us back to the *Symposium*: a genus of desire for the beautiful, within which a species of desire is to be marked off, presumably by its object. Yet that is not quite what follows here. Two principles of action in the soul are distinguished: an innate desire (*epithūmiā*) for pleasures, and an acquired judgement (*doxa*) which aims at the best (d6–9). These can agree, or be at variance (d9–10); when they are at variance, one or the other may prevail (e1–2). When judgement prevails in leading us rationally towards the best, its mastery is called self-control, or restraint (*sōphrosunē*); when desire prevails in dragging us irrationally towards pleasures, its rule is called excess (*hubris*, e2–238a2). Species of excess are then distinguished by the objects of specific ruling desires: gluttony comes about if a desire for food prevails at once over judgement of what is best and over other desires; similarly with a desire for drink; and so on (a2–b5). So emerges a definition of love:

The irrational desire which has gained control over judgement which urges a man towards the right, borne towards pleasure in beauty, and which is forcefully reinforced by the desires related to it in its pursuit of bodily beauty, overcoming them in its course, and takes its name from its very force (*rhōmē*)—this is called love (*erōs*) (b7–c4).

Here love is not itself a species of desire, but the state in which a certain species of desire prevails over reason, also prevailing over, or being reinforced by, other desires; it is a kind of excess, not of desire. What are the objects of the constituent desires?

If 237d4–5 imply (though they don't quite say) that all desires are desires for the beautiful (*ta kala*), that still leaves open two ways of distinguishing a kind of desire: by a kind of beauty, and by a kind of relation towards it. Here both are exploited: the kind of beauty is bodily beauty; the relation towards it is desiring to enjoy it (238c1–2). The phrase 'desire for beauty' is ambiguous: what it envisages as beautiful can be either the whole state of affairs I desire to obtain (my φ-ing, say), or some focal aspect of that state of affairs (if, say, my φ-ing is my possessing, or enjoying, some beauty). In some cases, both will be beautiful, in closely related ways: for example, with moral beauty (let us call it 'fineness'), doing a fine thing oneself is likely to be fine itself. But I may desire to possess a beautiful thing though it is not beautiful for me to possess it, or to enjoy a beautiful thing though it is not beautiful for me to enjoy it. What may be termed a 'desire for beauty' can take at least three forms in relation to making love (not the only, but no doubt the central, goal of this kind of lover, cf. 240d1–3):

(i) I want to make love to a beauty;
(ii) I want to make love beautifully;
(iii) I want to make love because it is beautiful to do so.[6]

---

[6] On the difference between (i) or (ii) and (iii), cf. Terence Irwin, *Plato's Moral Theory*, 327, on 'good drink' *versus* 'drink as a good'.

None of these entails any of the others; so which is intended within Socrates' definition of love? Most likely is (i);⁷ (iii) is ruled out by talk at 239c4–5 of 'the man who is under compulsion to pursue pleasure in preference to good' (given the Platonic coextensionality of the good and the beautiful). That shows that the fault of desire in pursuing pleasures instead of 'the best' (237d8–9) is not that of preferring the lesser to the greater good, but that of never prompting action on grounds of goodness at all (though of course the act may be good coincidentally, cf. d9–10). Most likely 'the best' is, in effect, *eudaimoniā* (best in the sense of most final, cf. *Symp* 205a2–3). The lover, lacking rule by reason, is motivated by innate drives (237d7–8), and not by an evaluation of an end to be achieved.

   Therefore, despite the initial suggestion of lines 237d3–5, we are not to be put in mind of the psychology of the *Symposium* (or of the *Lysis*), which focused all desires, including those for pleasure, upon a final good. Instead, we may be reminded of other occasions when Plato divides the soul into two parts: in *Republic* 10 these are the rational (604b4–5) and the irrational (604d9, 605b8); in the *Timaeus* the divine and the mortal (69c5 ff.). However, in both those places the lower part of the soul contains not only the appetites, but also the emotions (themselves two different parts in Plato's preferred tripartition): this is implicit in the *Republic* (where giving way to grief is indulging the irrational part, 606a2–7), clearer in the *Timaeus* (which mentions 'obstinate passion', 69d3, and proceeds to separate off a 'part of the soul which is the seat of courage, passion and ambition', 70a2–3). Here, the emotions are neglected. Opposed to reason is simply 'an inborn desire for pleasures' (237d7–8); and the only pleasures mentioned are those of food (238a6–b2), drink (b2–3), and sex (whether through sight, sound, touch, or whatever sense, 240d2–3, and so including attraction as well as satisfaction). The *Republic* associates at least sympathetic grief with pleasure (605d3–4), but it naturally assigns all the *Phaedrus* examples to appetite, and not to emotion (4.439d6–7). A closer parallel within the *Republic* is the initial opposition in Book 4 of reason to appetite alone:

Not unreasonably, said I, shall we claim that they are two and different from one another, naming that in the soul whereby it reckons and reasons the rational, and that with which it loves, hungers, thirsts, and feels the flutter and titillation of other desires, the irrational and appetitive—companion of various repletions and pleasures (439d4–8).⁸

---

⁷ So W. H. Thompson, *The Phaedrus of Plato* (London, 1868), 151.
⁸ This initial bipartition picks up a popular contrast between desires for pleasure and a wish for goodness that had already surfaced within earlier Plato, but could not be accommodated within the Socratic psychology of the *Lysis* and *Symposium*; cf. *Charm* 167e1–5, *Prot* 352d4–e2, *Gorg* 491d7–e1.

Significantly, spirit (*thūmos*) is then introduced as something falling outside both (439e3 ff.). It is as if Socrates' dissembling lover in the *Phaedrus* has taken over from the *Republic* what suits his immediate purpose, careless of what then gets left out. (In a way, neglect of the emotions suits his downgrading of love; but envy, which will loom large in the rest of his speech, becomes conceptually homeless.)

In one way this part of the *Phaedrus* is very close to a passage of the *Republic*, by which, indeed, it almost needs to be glossed. What are the desires akin to love that reinforce it in the direction of bodily beauty (238c1–2)? It helps to remember the tyrannical man of *Republic* 9:

There are among them feasts and carousals and revellings and courtesans and all the doings of those whose souls are entirely swayed by the indwelling tyrant Eros . . . And do not many and dread appetites shoot up beside this master passion every day and night in need of many things? . . . And so any revenues there may be are quickly expended (573d2–10).

It becomes clear that love's fellow-passengers are desires for the extravagances that are part of the erotic life. It may be a verbal difference that the 'Eros' of *Republic* 9 is *whatever* appetite is dominant (though the examples of 574b12–c5 are sexual). But the connection of thought is confirmed by two incidental parallels: Eros is associated with madness (*maniā*, 573a8, b4; 241a4); and the master appetite may itself be called a tyrant (573d4, 574e2; 238b2). The 'desires' of this section of the *Phaedrus* are indeed what in translation (the Greek word, *epithūmiā*, is the same) become the 'appetites' of the *Republic*.

For richer derivations, and departures, from the *Republic* we turn to Socrates' second speech.

3

A minor theme common to the first two speeches (of Lysias and of Socrates) is a contrast between sanity or self-control, and sickness or madness. Lysias's non-lover urged the following against lovers: 'They themselves agree that they are out of their mind, but cannot control themselves; so how, when they come to their senses, could they approve of the decisions they make when in this condition?' (231d2–6). Socrates' dissembling lover argues in the same way, contrasting 'sense and sanity' with 'love and madness' (241a3–4). Earlier, he

effectively expanded being 'sick' (of mind) into being 'ruled by desire and
enslaved to pleasure' (238e3–4). The conception of mental health as self-
control allows sanity also to be defined, with no blatant shift of sense, as
restraint ('sanity' and 'restraint' both translating a variably determinate
sōphrosunē): 'When judgement leads us by means of reason towards the
best and is in control, its control over us has the name of restraint' (237e2–
3).

never let go.
Diving

The same association between madness, lack of restraint, and sexuality
is emphatic in *Republic* 3 (402e3–403b2). In the *Symposium* Socrates
connects madness with erotic jealousy (213d1–6). In the *Republic*, and
elsewhere, madness is deemed a vice or defect (3.400b2), and linked with
excess (400b2, 403a2) and folly (2.382e2–3, *Tim* 86b3–4). Here Plato
exploits a feature of popular morality: K. J. Dover tells us that 'Aphrodite and Eros could . . . be feared and hated as a "sickness" (Euripides, fr.
400)' (*GPM*, 77), and again that 'Eros is a "sickness", a "madness"
(Euripides, fr. 161), a cruel god who robs us of our wits (Menander, fr.
79)' (ibid. 210). This must not be over-interpreted: Dover also observes
that 'the Greeks used all their words for insanity much more freely in
warning, reproach and vilification than we use our corresponding words'
(ibid. 129, cf. 127); hence it was easy for Plato to use 'illness' or 'madness'
as turns of the screw upon 'lack of restraint'. In these ways, Socrates' first
speech is at once popular and Platonic.

That makes more startling an apparent reversal of values at the start of
the palinode that is Socrates' second speech. Here, various types of
madness are credited with the greatest blessings for men (244a6–7): these
are prophecy, purification, poetry, and love. However, there is no real
paradox yet. What explains Plato's bold and innovatory extension of the
term 'madness' to these cases at the same time requires a partial revaluation: they are divinely inspired in a way that takes the agent outside
himself, and Plato ascribes to the gods benefits, not harms (cf. *Rep*
2.379b1–c7). More puzzling are two later features, which seem to generate material anomalies. On the one hand, Socrates' initial high praise of
the *activities*, when inspired, of prophesying, prescribing purifications,
and composing poetry does not seem to entail any corresponding ranking
of the various *lives*. In a later listing of nine different lives that may follow
on incarnation (248d2–e3), that of a prophet or official of the mysteries
comes only fifth, that of a poet or other practitioner of an imitative art
only sixth, even below those of a businessman, or a gymnastic trainer. On
the other hand, the lover who is reproached for being out of his wits by
the many (who do not realize that he is possessed by a god) is at the same

time the man who is best at passing, by recollection, from a plurality of perceptions to a unity brought together by a process of reasoning (249b6–d3), which seems to be an intuitive precursor of an academic and systematic method of collection (cf. 265d3–5). It is presumably connected with this that the 'man who will become a lover of wisdom or of beauty, or devoted to the Muses or to love' is a *single* character whose life is ranked first of the nine (248d4–5). Divine inspiration has become chameleon-like: it seems compatible both with a life of little value, and with a life of reason.

In fact, this is partly familiar. It is a recurrent discrimination in Plato to respect the song more than the singer. Gods use poets as their mouthpieces (*Ion* 534d3–4). Hence, what they say is valuable (even when it is contradictory, cf. *Laws* 4.719c7); but theirs is not to reason why (*Apol* 22c2–3, *Meno* 99d4–5). If R. Hackforth was right in reading the series of lives as 'one of decreasing worth to society' (op. cit. 83), the poet and prophet would rank higher.[9] Plato's criterion of ranking is different: it is not the utility of the activity, but the cognitive state of the agent (cf. 248d2). The thought must be that the poet who is best at escaping from his own mind is not the man with much of a mind of his own; poets put us vastly in their debt, but we owe them more gratitude than respect. Yet is that the only way of being divinely inspired? For the poet, being inspired is becoming out of one's wits, so that one's mind is no longer within one (*Ion* 534b5–6, d3). The lover and philosopher is the person who saw most before incarnation (248d2–4), of which he retains a memory sufficient to be activated by visible likenesses (250a5 ff.); it is his own memory that will be carried back towards the Form of Beauty (254b5–6). His inspiration is divine (so that he counts as being possessed by a god, 249d2, e1) both as the effect of a god's activity, and in that it carries him back to the Forms to which even a god owes his divinity (249c6); the inspiration is an involuntary exercise of his own cognitive powers. It is primarily his own reason that is affected by madness.[10]

---

[9] Of course he is sensitive to that; but there is nothing in the text to support his suggestion that the prophet and poet within the listing are the uninspired augur of 244c5–d5 and versifier of 245a5–8.

[10] In this paragraph I have adopted the views of Myles Burnyeat, 'The Passion of Reason in Plato's *Phaedrus*' (unpublished). To remove the appearance of contradiction, we need to distinguish, in English terms, two senses of 'reason': (i) that which desires and grasps truth (cf. *Rep* 9.581b5–6); (ii) a way of grasping truth, viz. rationally (cf. the epithet *logistikos*, first in the *Republic* at 4.439d5). New in the *Phaedrus* is an acknowledgement that reason can capture reality irrationally; as Plato might have put the point, 'that by which we learn' (581b5) is no longer to be viewed exclusively as 'that by which we reason' (439d5).

Can such inspiration amount to knowledge? It is tempting to suppose so (and supported by a natural reading of 249c4–e4); yet this cannot be right. Possession is a kind of madness (249d4–e4), and even the best madness falls within the genus of the irrational (265e3–4), and therefore (unless Plato is really ceasing to be Platonic) outside the state of knowledge. For a transition from inspiration to knowledge, the passive experience of being reminded by likenesses must give rise to an active exercise of memory, to the best of one's ability, which makes a deliberate use of reminders (cf. 249c5–7).[11] Only so will madness make straight the way for philosophy. No doubt the second will never wholly supersede the first: the method of collection must proceed by deliberate steps (265d3–5), but it cannot be either possible or desirable to close one's eyes to whatever reminders come one's way. If this is right, the philosopher, in the sense of the man who not only loves wisdom (cf. *Symp* 204a1–2) but possesses philosophical skill, was once, and remains, subject to inspiration (to which he owes his skill); but his exercise of skill is one thing, and his experience of inspiration another.[12]

Plato implies a similar transition within rhetoric from inspiration to science, or expertise (*technē*). Socrates ascribed the superiority of his first speech over that of Lysias to the spirit of the place or of its nymphs (238c9–10, 241e3–5), denying himself any knowledge of his own (235c6–d1). (Ironical or not, that implies that there is such an eloquence, effective but unschooled.) Later acknowledgements to the local divinities or the cicadas as mouthpieces of the Muses (262d3), and to the nymphs of Achelous and Pan (263d5–6), are less clear in their reference: Léon Robin first attached them to Socrates' first speech and not his second, though he later changed his mind and attached them to both.[13] His later view is confirmed by Socrates' disavowal, 'I don't think *I* share in any science of speaking' (262d5–6). It is true that he presented his second speech to Eros as 'the finest and best palinode of which I am capable' (257a3–4); but of course even the

---

[11] This is similar, but not identical, to the later distinction between recollection depending on external signs, and memory relying·on one's own internal resources (275a3–5).
[12] This seems the best way to reconcile 249c4–e4 with 265d3–266b1, taking the later passage to correct the natural reading of the earlier one. Alternatively, Plato could have distinguished two ways of being possessed by a god: involuntary and irrational, or deliberate and expert. That would have changed the terminology, not the substance.
[13] Cf. G. J. de Vries, *A Commentary on the Phaedrus of Plato* (Amsterdam, 1969), ad 262d1.

poet and prophet have an ability, though not a cognitive one, that other men lack. Socrates' modesty allows him to lay claim to a knack, but not to the science, of speaking: 'Of speaking, saith the Spartan, a genuine science, without a grasp of truth, neither exists nor will come into existence in the future' (260e5–7). Any genuine science of speaking requires knowledge, as of the nature of the soul (271a6–7), and of all the varieties of character (d1–3). Again, it need not be implied that inspiration is wholly supplanted by calculation;[14] but inspired rhetoric is not an exercise of the science of rhetoric. To apply Aristotle's distinction (*NE* 6.13.1144b26–7), practice may accord with science without manifesting it (*kata* without *meta*); even those who do possess a skill need not be guided by it whenever they act as it prescribes (and of course an interesting skill is one whose possession is never all or nothing).

At the end of the *Meno* Socrates distinguished two sources of practical guidance, knowledge, which involves understanding (*nous*, 99c8, e6), and true opinion, which in the manner (c2–5), or even in the form (d2–5, e6–7), of an inspired gift from the gods does not. Of the two it is only knowledge that is reliably transmissible (99a7–8, b7–9): a statesman who had the capacity to make another into a statesman would prove that he possessed understanding (100a1–2). The *Phaedrus* does not disagree: it is discourse conveying knowledge that can be written as it were in the soul of the learner (276a5–6), whence it may generate further discourse and knowledge in further souls (276e5–277a4). That, we shall see, is a goal of love, which thus needs philosophy for its success as much as philosophy needs love for its genesis. The best madness, that involving recollection, is indeed 'cause of our greatest goods' (266b1); but it achieves its function in preparing the way of reason. Plato, the arch-rationalist, is at last doing justice to unreason; but we shall not find him changing sides.

4

The new role that Plato accords to possession by a god in the *Phaedrus* fits an immediate feature of his treatment of the soul there: he brings divine and human souls closer together in ways that create a community between them. This makes it intelligible that divine inspiration, the retrieval of one's original self, and the recollection of reality should turn out to be different facets of a single process.

Socrates starts with a proof of the immortality of 'all soul' (245c5). In context (as Myles Burnyeat points out, op. cit.), he must mean by that soul both human and divine (cf. 245c3); and the proof that follows applies equally to both. We need not reflect here about its validity; even its conclusion is less important for us than the one fact that it depends on ascribing to souls of every kind the same 'essence and definition' (being a self-mover, 245e3). While most of the arguments to the same conclusion in the *Phaedo* and *Republic* rested on aspects of the life of the human soul (for example, its capacity for recollection, *Pdo* 72e3–78b3, and its survival of injustice, *Rep* 10.608d3–611a3), here a single argument grounds immortality, quite abstractly, upon an essence common to all souls, human and divine. The ensuing imagery of the soul as a chariot, though only a simile (cf. 246a6), both fits the essence of soul as self-moving, and allows divine and human souls to be depicted as moving *together*. While the proof asserts a common essence, the simile presents a community in operation; each complements the other.

A shared essence permits dissimilarities in nature. It is a sharp contrast that souls like ours are always liable to incarnation upon earth, but divine souls never. Yet it is disputed what differences in nature ground that contrast: do all souls share the same structure? do they share the same immateriality? On the answers to these questions rests the degree of assimilation of the human and the divine. The form of the soul is symbolized as follows:

Let it then resemble the combined power of a winged team of horses (*zeugos*) and their charioteer. Now in the case of gods, horses and charioteers are all both good and of good stock; whereas in the the case of the rest there is a mixture. In the first place our driver has charge of a pair (*sunōris*); secondly one of them he finds noble and good, while the other is of the opposite stock, and opposite in its nature (246a6–b3).

Here we seem to find two differences: one in constitution (the gods' horses are all good, ours mixed), the other in structure (we have two horses each, the gods an indefinite number). But are these certain, and are they permanent? It is possible to deny the structural difference altogether. Burnyeat takes both *zeugos* and *sunōris* to connote a pair, and stresses instead the word 'drives' (*hēniochei*, b2): while the gods' teams are easily dirigible (cf. 247b2), ours need management. He emphasizes a later unqualified restatement: 'At the beginning of this tale we divided each soul into three forms' (253c7–8). I think that he is wrong: an equally unqualified sentence at 253d1–2 ('Of the horses, one, we say, is good, the other not') is only true of human souls, and 253c7–8 may be likewise; even horses literally 'easy on the rein' (*euēnia*, 247b2) have to be driven; and the same pair of terms (*zeugos* and *sunōris*) suffices to make a contrast in the *Apology* (36d8). Nor should we want him to be right: a difference in the size of the teams would be a natural, if obvious, emblem of the disparity between the gods' capacities and ours. So a difference in composition is best accepted; is it equally permanent, or can the bad horse be schooled to share the obedience of the good one? Here Plato is not an optimist: avoiding incarnation, though possible for ever (248c4–5), never ceases to be an achievement (cf. the repeated 'always', c4–5, and 'scarcely', a4). For souls other than divine the price of escaping expulsion from the Platonic Eden is not self-transformation, but eternal vigilance.[15]

In our case, the distinction between driver and horses fits souls with conflicting parts. Though there is some unclarity in *Republic* 4 about the precise criterion of mental partition,[16] it obviously involves some kind of conflict of desire. But how are we to understand the complexity of divine souls? Hardly in that way. Maybe the complexity exists only at the level of imagery: as C. J. Rowe observes, 'A chariot, even a divine one, will be incomplete without horses.'[17] At the opposite extreme, Emil Groag inferred from the provision of a different food (nectar and ambrosia) for the horses from that (purely intellectual) of the driver that even the souls of the gods have a sensuous side; he ascribed to the gods a unity of will, not of soul.[18] Compatible with, but not dependent upon, that bold suggestion is another: that the horses symbolize the active life of the gods in governing the world (cf. 246b6–7). W. K. C. Guthrie is wrong to claim that the gods' eros 'is set in one direction only' (op. cit. iv. 425): their lives are complex, practical as well as theoretical, and perhaps

---

[15] As G. R. F. Ferrari wittily puts it, 'There is no tenure in Plato's paradise'; *Listening to the Cicadas* (Cambridge, 1987), 264, n. 16.

[16] Cf. Irwin, op. cit. 327.

[17] *Plato* (Brighton, 1984), 173.

[18] 'Zur Lehre vom Wesen der Seele in Platons *Phaidrus* und im zehnten Buch der *Republik*', *Wiener Studien* 37 (1915), 208; contrast W. K. C. Guthrie, *A History of Greek Philosophy*, iv. 424.

not free of the dilemmas of philosopher-kings (cf. *Rep* 7.540a7–b5).
To that extent, their souls must be complex also, if not as fields of a
conflict of desire.[19]

What is the make-up of non-divine, potentially human, souls that
they should be complex in the way of containing an evil element (and
so inescapably subject to conflicting desires)? Plato would seem to
have changed his position radically since the *Phaedo*, which located
conflicts of desire by ascribing appetites resisted by the soul to the
body, treating that (as I noted in Chapter 2) not just as a *sine qua non*,
but as a subject (83d6–7, 94b7–e4) of pleasures, passions, even
opinions, of a kind.[20] In *Republic* 4 we meet an explicit argument,
ostensibly from a principle of non-contradiction, for accommodating
conflicts of desire by a multiplicity of *loci* of desire (436a8 ff.); but
now the different *loci* are not soul and body, but three parts of the soul
itself. As we shall see, the description of the incarnate soul in the
Phaedrus is faithful in broad outline to the *Republic*'s tripartition; yet
one may be tempted to find in the *Phaedrus* a kind of reconciliation
between the *Phaedo* and the *Republic*. We meet a striking similarity in
the imagery of weight used to describe in the *Phaedo* how, even after
death, a bodily element can remain attached to weigh down the soul
(*embrithes . . . barunetai*, 81c8–10), and in the *Phaedrus* how the
bad horse weighs down the soul unless it is well schooled (*brithei . . .
barunōn*, 247b3–4). This parallel can suggest that the divided soul of
the *Phaedrus* is always liable to incarnation for the reason that it has
never fully escaped from some previous incarnation (cf. *Pdo* 81d9–
e2). Such a unifying interpretation goes back at least to R. D. Archer-
Hind,[21] and has been argued more recently by R. S. Bluck.[22] Its effect
is to find in the *Phaedrus* a story about reincarnation that presupposes
some account of an initial incarnation like that which we do find
elsewhere, in the *Timaeus*. There (69c2 ff.) it is by the decision of the
Demiurge that certain immortal souls are set in mortal bodies (as in a
chariot, c7), and thereby subjected to the accretions of spirit and
appetite (symbolized as horses in the *Phaedrus*); the mental conflict
results from the embodiment, and will last as long as it does. The

---

[19] Cf. Ferrari, op. cit. 126–32.
[20] The psycho-physical topography of *Phaedo* 83 may seem somewhat shifting. I
take it that these mental states of this non-Cartesian body may either bother the soul
from outside, or be accepted within it in a manner that contaminates it with corporeal
accretions (cf. 81b1–c6).
[21] 'On Some Difficulties in the Platonic Psychology', *Journal of Philology* 10 (1882).
[22] 'The *Phaedrus* and Reincarnation', *American Journal of Philology* 79 (1958).

present section of the *Phaedrus* could then be describing a later stage of half-embodiment which still carries with it, though no longer within a life on earth, the predicament of a divided soul; thence, as it narrates, further full incarnations are liable (though not bound, cf. 248c4–5) to follow. But this account faces serious objections.[23] There are two obvious misfits: the *Phaedrus* twice describes a first incarnation (248d1–2, 249a5), which can hardly, with no indication, merely mean the first subsequent incarnation, chosen instead of imposed; and it says that the soul 'lays hold of something solid, where it settles down, taking on an earthly body', *after* it has shed its feathers (246c2–4).

In any case, it was hardly a required presumption that, just because the language of weight was applied literally in the *Phaedo*, that must also be true of the *Phaedrus*. Rather than invoke the *Timaeus* (written later, on the orthodox view) as an essential prelude, we do better to look within *Republic* 10. That permits the *Timaeus* picture, of an originally simple ('single in form', 612a4) soul taking on mental accretions like the sea-god Glaucus encrusted with shells and seaweed (611c7–d7), so that the immortal is contaminated by the mortal, the purely mental by the partly physical. However, it also suggests an alternative picture, of an immortal soul always manifold ('many in form', 612c4), but consisting of elements put together in the finest manner (cf. 611b6). This alternative in turn might be explicated in two ways. The soul that is *not* put together in the finest manner and will not easily be immortal (b5–7) may be the corrupt soul of Books 8 and 9 rather than the tripartite soul of Book 4; the description there (443d1–e2) of the unity which can be achieved through temperance within the tripartite soul may have implied that there is no inherent deficiency in the interrelations of its parts (which need not imply that all those are perfect). Or else, the imperfectly related soul may be the tripartite soul of Book 4, 'marred by communion with the body' (611b10–c2) and so at least always liable to corruption, in contrast to a finer but also composite, and perhaps triple, soul before incarnation and outside the cycle of rebirth. An inherent complexity of a kind is confirmed by the signal fact that the proof of the immortality of the soul in Book 10 (608d3–611a3) rests on its indestructibility by injustice—a vice, precisely on the *Republic* definition (4.443d1–3), of the tripartite soul. That, from the point of view of the *Republic*, the purpose of the thought-experiment (as it is for us now) of denuding

---

[23] Many are well set out by Groag, op. cit. and D. D. McGibbon, 'The Fall of the Soul in Plato's *Phaedrus*', *Classical Quarterly* NS 14 (1964).

the soul of the body is to think away not the complexity but the typical disaccord of the incarnate soul seems further implied by a remark (too optimistic for the *Phaedrus*) that this will yield a paradigm of justice to contrast with injustice (611c4–5). It is true that Plato concludes by leaving the options open (612a3–5); in effect, he will explore one in the *Timaeus*, and a form of the other in the *Phaedrus*. Thus there is no need to amalgamate the *Phaedrus* with the *Timaeus* in order to provide it with a Platonic context.

Yet why, in contrast to the *Republic*, should Plato have chosen in the *Phaedrus* to present pre-incarnate souls as already in a state of internal strife? I have no confidence in any answer; but a simple thought (more consistent with my understanding of what is to come than more pregnant suggestions by Burnyeat, and Martha Nussbaum, *The Fragility of Goodness*, 222) is that if the prehistory of the incarnate soul is itself tripartite, the tasks and trials of the soul in heaven, and of the lover on earth, can mutually illuminate one another. If it is talk of heaven that is shedding light upon things on earth, the prehistory may be interpreted as a myth. (Notice how localized is a claim to be telling the truth, 247c4–6; cf. 265b6–8.) But one can also take the heavenly struggle quite seriously, as Groag does: 'The earthly struggle is only a preparation for the heavenly' (op. cit. 209). To convey the force of that one might borrow a sentence from Freud: 'The struggle which once raged in the deepest strata of the mind, and was not brought to an end by rapid sublimation and identification, is now continued in a higher region, like the Battle of the Huns in Kaulbach's painting.'[24]

5

Life in the heavens has various features that will be mirrored in love-life on earth: souls pursue in company a steep ascent towards an

---

[24] *The Pelican Freud Library* (Harmondsworth, 1973–86), xi. 379. I shall not try to decide here to what extent Plato intends Socrates' second speech to be presenting fact or fiction. Later admissions of an element of 'play' (262d2, 265c1, c8–9, 277e5–6, 278a7) leave open their own status as serious or playful (I take 277e5–278b4 more seriously than 265c8–d7), and also the relation of the serious to the playful (which need not be that of excluding one another). However, I shall be committed to taking Socrates' description of the predicament of the amorous soul on earth to be broadly assertory, and not, say, to constitute an erotic allegory of the task of pure philosophy; though its symbolism involves slight simplification (in ways that I shall note), it still captures recognizably Platonic psychology.

intellectual vision that directly nourishes reason, and indirectly orders and unites the whole soul. It is a contrast that heaven, but not earth, knows gods for whom the ascent is easy. But why should other souls lapse even into incarnation?

The broad lines of Plato's account are clear enough; and yet we are told no perfectly consistent story, because he seems not to have decided between two different ways of understanding the consequences of success or failure in the ascent. Socrates distinguishes three classes of non-divine souls:

1. Within the best souls the driver keeps his head in full sight of the Forms, though with difficulty, and disturbed by the horses (248a1–5).
2. The next best souls rise and sink as the horses impel them (presumably in contrary directions), seeing some realities, but not others (a5–6).
3. Souls of the last kind long to ascend but are unable to do so; instead, they jostle against each other, shedding much of their plumage. All fail to achieve any vision of reality, and feed upon appearance alone (a6–b5).

Which of these classes is subject to incarnation? The first escapes, and can even do so always (c4–5). The third must fall under this description of a soul: 'Through inability to follow it fails to see, and through some mischance is weighed down by being filled with forgetfulness and incompetence, and because of the weight loses its feathers and falls to the earth' (c5–7).[25] Harder to place is the second class: on the one hand, its members should be safe from incarnation as having seen something of reality (cf. c3–4); on the other, it should include souls that deserve to be incarnated as men precisely because they have achieved some knowledge (cf. 249b5–6, 249e4–250a1), and indeed, among them, those who, having perceived most, will become lovers and philosophers (248d2–4). Plato seems inconsistently to make both total cognitive failure a precondition of incarnation, and the degree of failure the determinant of incarnate role. He has partly lost control not just over his imagery, but over his aetiology. One thing at least is broadly clear: incarnation is the result of ignorance. This does invite two qualifications. Firstly, ignorance may not be the first cause: we

---

[25] Here, and hereafter in related contexts, I have replaced Rowe's 'wings' by 'feathers' (cf. Ferrari, op. cit. 265, n. 20): the wings themselves are not lost, though they may be broken (b3).

are not told why some souls see more of the Forms, and are less disrupted by the horses, than others; nor are we invited to ask. Secondly, ignorance is certainly not the last cause: there follows it, in whatever order, rivalry among the unsuccessful souls that further impedes them (248a8–b3), and indulgence in mere opinion (b5). The gods are better off in both ways: they derive their divinity from attention to the Forms (249c6), and they are free of envy (247a7). Yet it is noteworthy that, in Socrates' presentation, cognitive deficiency is the focus of explanation: hostile emulation is its effect, not its cause (248a6–b1). Though the account is incomplete, its message is that divinity depends on cognitive success, incarnation on cognitive failure.

It will be the task of heavenly love upon earth to reverse the decline into incarnation, to undo the catastrophe. This will involve a cognitive recovery that both reveals itself within, and is assisted by, a generous relationship to another. Mutual hostility was an effect of ignorance; mutual love will be a cause of knowledge.

6

Once a soul has entered into its incarnate life, the way backwards is the only way forwards; it must remember what it has lost in a manner that will inspire its retrieval. In outline, the task is nothing new in Plato: already in the *Phaedo*, recollection of the Forms that were originally the objects of the soul's devotion must motivate it to pursue the way of death that will release it from imprisonment in the body (cf. 67c5–e6, 80e2–81a9, 84a7–b4). But now that the soul to be liberated is tripartite, the task looks rather different. The soul apparently faces a dilemma: as the Forms are immaterial, it should suit the soul so far as possible to separate itself from the body and its sense-organs (cf. *Pdo* 79c2–8, 83a3–7), and depend upon reasoning alone (83a7–b4, 84a7–8); but since the soul is composite (containing, even before birth in a body, a part that, whether or not already recognizably appetite, naturally drew it down towards matter, *Phdr* 247b3–4), pure reasoning can only speak to a part of it. It is the soul as a whole that has to be redeemed, but the means of redemption were never accessible to the whole of it (cf. 248a2–3). Incarnation ensued when the lower parts of the soul had robbed reason of its vision; disincarnation should be achieved when reason can regain at once vision without and rule within. That evokes a puzzle of where to begin: how is either possible before the other? Plato offers a complicated narrative of a progression in understanding and self-control which conveys, with a striking vividness of style, how reason must achieve its goal by acting on behalf of the rest of the soul, and not in isolation from it.

The starting-point, and first crisis, is the perception of beauty. This is possible in two ways:

(i) The corrupt soul is not readily reminded of Beauty itself when it sees its namesake here; all it desires is sexual intercourse (250e1–251a1).

(ii) The richly and recently initiated soul is overcome by confusion at the sight of beauty (251a3–4); with no clear grasp of what it is doing (250a6–b1), which is seeing the object as an image of Beauty itself (d3–e1), it reveres the loved one as a god (251a6–7).

It is not necessary for the contrast to exaggerate either the animality of (i), or the intelligence of (ii). Like the lover of Socrates' first speech (cf. 237d3–5, 238b7–c1), the soul of (i) is set on beauty: beauty is its intentional object, of which it may, in its way, be a discriminating judge. (If the recollection of 249b6–c4 is a precondition of understanding language,[26] we must even allow that corrupt souls have a kind of submerged memory of the Forms; it is *quickly* that they cannot make the transition to Beauty itself, 250e2.) While the soul of (ii) is not initially described as remembering the Forms at all; if it was aware of doing that, and so of the distance between earth and heaven, it would not treat a boy as if he were a god. When the description is resumed, at 253e5 ff., it distinguishes an initial stage of longing (*pothos*) for Beauty lost from a later stage of recovering Beauty by conscious memory (compare 253e5–254a1 with 254b5–7). Cognitively, (ii) is not all gain on (i): the low-minded soul may have reliable opinions about beauties, while the high-minded one is as yet far from knowledge of Beauty; the first is clear-headed about this world, while the second is confused about this world and the other. Of course, first steps hold more promise than a dead end.

It is in a distinctively human way that we perceive both visible

---

[26] So David Bostock suggests, *Plato's Phaedo* (Oxford, 1986), 71; and attractively, since it is then clear why those who have never seen reality cannot be born as men (249b5–6).

beauties, and quasi-visible Beauty. Even the sensualist sees his objects as beautiful; he subsumes them under a concept. Plato is more explicit, in rhetorical vein, about the sighting of Beauty:

Beauty . . . shone out in company with those other things, and now that we have come to earth we have found it gleaming most clearly through the clearest of our senses. For of all the perceptions coming to us through the body, sight is the keenest: wisdom we do not see—the feelings of love it would cause in us would be terrible, if it allowed some such clear image of itself to reach our sight, and so too with the other objects of love; as it is, beauty alone has acquired this privilege, of being most evident and most loved (250c8–e1).

Can we capture this in our own terms? How is it that the invisible becomes visible? One looks, familiarly, to Wittgenstein on 'seeing-as': 'The flashing of an aspect on us seems half visual experience, half thought . . . Is it a case of both seeing and thinking? or an amalgam of the two, as I should almost like to say?'[27] This does apply, but not distinctively enough: what is it that the sensualist misses? Uniting Plato and our idiom, we may say that the lover sees the boy as an image of Beauty itself (initially with little awareness of that). But can we clarify what that is like without depending on the term 'image'? In a relevant context, Richard Wollheim complains of the unhelpfulness of the form of words 'I see *x* as the representation of . . .';[28] looking at pictures, he proposes, is better suited by talk of 'seeing-in'—not that he places weight on the phrases themselves (ibid. 209). Much of his subtle discussion, though quite applicable, is too far from the text of Plato, but not this: 'Seeing-in derives from a special perceptual capacity, which . . . allows us to have perceptual experiences of things that are not present to the senses: that is to say, both of things that are absent and also of things that are non-existent' (ibid. 217). His last phrase can put us in mind of de-mythologizing readings of Plato which may use similar language to Kantian effect. So C. Wenzig: 'The beautiful body as such is not this ideal which we see in it; rather, this ideal exists in us as an object of inner experience. It is we who think it into, or (to speak more accurately) see it into, this beautiful figure.'[29] Wenzig's addition to 'seeing-in' of 'seeing-into' fits some of Wollheim's cases (for instance, seeing Charles Laughton in

---

[27] *Philosophical Investigations* (Oxford, 1958), 197.

[28] *Art and its Objects* (Cambridge, 1980), 211.

[29] *Die Conception der Ideenlehre im Phaedrus bildet den einheitlichen Grundgedanken dieses Dialoges und liefert den Schlüssel zur Verständnis der Platonischen Ideenlehre überhaupt* (Breslau, 1883), 43.

Holbein's portrait of Henry VIII, op. cit. 206); and it fits his own Kantian construal of Forms as categories, which no longer takes participation seriously as a relation in which things stand to Forms independently of us. Apt to a more Platonic Plato (who actually believes at least the metaphysics of the *Phaedrus* 'myth', cf. 247c4–6) might be another variant: 'seeing-through'. The value of a pretty face to the Platonic lover is precisely that it is transparent (like, as it were, Venetian blinds open to the light) to the world of Forms beyond. Common to all these variations is an advantage, for our purposes, that 'seeing-as' lacked: while the lover can only see the boy as an image of a Form, he can be said to see the Form itself in or into or through the boy, even though it is the boy, and not the Form, that is present to his sight.

Earlier I cited Dover's pithy characterization of the wide sense of *kalos* in Greek: 'looks or sounds good (or is good to contemplate)' (*Plato: Symposium*, ad 201c2). That implies a relativity: looks good *to whom*? No embarrassing relativism need follow: Plato could say that the really beautiful looks good to the gods, that is to the best observers. But there is a problem for an idealizing theory of human love: what we can love most is what is most beautiful *to us*; how then can we have much love for Forms, or even for their participants, when it is only 'through dulled organs and with difficulty' that we can 'observe the nature of what is imaged in them' (250b3–5)? For his present purposes, Plato needs to connect his idealism with our actual capacities. That he has now achieved, and precisely in the case of that Form, Beauty, which constitutes the world of Forms as objects of love (in that other Forms are lovely through participating in Beauty). His claim becomes in our idiom that we can see Beauty in its manifestations in a way in which we cannot see the other Forms. This is not easy: if we can see any Form in sensibles, that must show (to lift from Wollheim, op. cit. 223) 'the relative dissociation of the cultivated experience from visual awareness of what supports it'; but if we 'leave the two visual experiences in such a way that one merely floats above the other' (ibid. 224), it becomes mere assertion that Beauty alone can be present to sight. For a better understanding we need to explore 'an ever more intimate *rapport* between the two experiences' (ibid.); but Plato does not try, and Wollheim disclaims knowing how to. In an abstract metaphor that would have to stand in for understanding, the picture might be that, although Beauty as a Form is 'pure, clear, unalloyed, not full of human flesh and hues and much other mortal trash' (*Symp* 211e1–2), yet its nature yields correspondences with visual aspects of things which connect it to *visibilia* as it were by lines of projection which the visual imagination can trace to their termination; thus seeing Beauty in a beautiful object is analogous to seeing a distant prospect in the surface of a picture. Though participation in other Forms is also a kind of similarity (250b3–5), it does not lend itself to the same imaginative operation. Of course the analogy breaks down where we most want help: a prospect is itself visible, while Beauty is not. Yet more abstractly, we might turn to the structural correspondences that survive within the causal chain that links the live performance of a piece of music to its broadcasting over the air; it is certainly an austere view that would hold that the beauty is realized throughout the chain, but one to appeal to the Pythagorean in Plato.[30]

How is the sighting of beauty to be located within the composite and incarnate soul? Eduard Zeller attempted, while aware of some obstacles, to attach perception, opinion, and knowledge to appetite, spirit, and reason, respectively.[31] That could have been a development out of the *Phaedo*, where sight and hearing, although the best of the senses (65b1–6), were still lumped together with them as a physical medium through which the soul may be distracted and deceived (65c5–9, 79c2–8, 83a4–5). However, the *Republic*'s criterion of partition, which is conflict in belief or desire (4.437b1–4, 10.602e8–9), does not directly apply to sense-perception; it is a judgement that things are as they appear that cannot be assigned to the same subject as a judgement that they are not (603a1–2). It might still be that, through causal association, opinion recruits perception to join its side; but later, in the *Timaeus* (45a6–b1, cf. *Laws* 12.961d8–10), the organs of sight and hearing are singled out as special servants

---

[30] Another reason for preferring the more abstract version is that it is also applicable to the other senses, which will turn out to be aesthetically inferior simply in being less keenly discriminating (cf. 250d3–4); it is true that Plato speaks here only of visual beauty, later remains silent about, for instance, beauty of voice, and implicitly denies (at 255e2 ff.) that tactile beauty is reminiscent of the ideal. On the other hand, implicit in context is a thought almost bizarrely concrete: it is specifically the beauty of boys that is transparent to Beauty itself (which is why they, and not women, let alone temples or landscapes, provoke the love that causes the soul's feathers to grow again). Walter Pater was alert to that, and trying to make sense of it in the only way he could, when he suggested that the Form of Beauty resembles a beautiful (by which he had in mind a male) body; *Plato and Platonism*, 170 (quoted in Chapter 2).

[31] *Plato and the Older Academy* (London, 1876), 416–17; contrast Groag, op. cit. 191.

to reason (all being located within the head). So it seems better to say that each sense-perception affects the soul as a whole (cf. *Tim* 67b2–5 on how sound causes a motion that starts in the head and ends in the liver), and yet may be primarily assigned to some part of the soul if tightly related, as cause or effect, to its operations. At least that fits what we find here in the *Phaedrus*. It is the driver (that is, reason) who 'catches sight of the light of his love' (253e5), precisely when (unlike as at 250e1–4) seeing a beauty is also, even if unawares, being reminded of Beauty (as at 251a1–3). And yet it is the whole soul that is affected: in a horticultural metaphor, 'With the incoming stream of nourishment the quills of the feathers swell and set to growing from their roots under the whole form of the soul; for formerly the whole of it was feathered' (251b5–7). The soul thus enjoys an experience whose like would have saved it from incarnation, arising from an activity *of* reason *for the sake of* the soul as a whole: 'The cause of their great eagerness to see the plain of truth where it lies is that the pasturage which is fitting for the best part of the soul comes from the meadow there, and that the nature of the plumage which lifts up the soul is nourished by this' (248b5–c2). In this world (cf. also 253e5–6) as in that, on a natural reading, the cognition is reason's, the benefit the whole soul's.[32]

It is the composite soul that is affected by the vision of beauty, and its response is complex. The two horses now, in representation of its incarnate state (which may differ, though neither structurally nor as involving conflict, from its previous state), quite clearly represent the spirited and appetitive parts of the soul as distinguished in the *Republic*, though in a somewhat distinctive form. It is perhaps for the sake of dramatic contrast that the horse of spirit is very, very good, that of appetite horrid. More serious explanations of the impeccability of spirit here seem faulty. D. D. McGibbon (op. cit. 61) finds no problem: 'Since the lower element is regarded by Plato as instrinsically evil, the process of corruption starts from it and before it has advanced to any significant degree the soul has fallen to earth.' He implies that Socrates is *only* describing souls incarnate for the first

---

[32] Ferrari raises a good question, 'why the philosophic character who is so stirred by physical human beauty does not go on to put it at the centre of his life' (op. cit. 149). The lovers of sights and sounds of *Republic* 5, who are blind to Beauty itself (476b4–8), follow just such a policy. However, no Form is an island: Forms share a pedestal (*Phdr* 254b6–7); they interweave (*Soph* 259e5–6). The true lover finds that the sighting of Beauty 'points him, in its immediacy, towards what is not immediately appreciable' (Ferrari, ibid.).

time, whose spirit cannot have been corrupted in a former life on earth. But that is less grounded than his main contention that Socrates is *also* describing such souls; and, besides, a man's spirit can be corrupted in the same life before he is out of the way of falling in love. Less ingeniously, Hackforth is unsurprised that in 'the subjugation of sheer lust' reason and spirit should be at one (op. cit. 107). He seems to be forgetting, despite a reminder at 232a1–6 (cited by Dover, *GPM*, 215), that one can boast of a successful seduction.

The good horse has two spirited features: he has a thirst for honour and renown (restraint and a sense of shame permitting); and he is governed by the word of command alone (253d6–e1). So, in the *Republic*, love of honour manifests domination by spirit (8.548c6–7); and spirit never takes sides with appetite against the prohibitions of reason (4.440b4–6)—an overstatement also (contrast 4.441a2–c2). The bad horse is prone to violence or excess (*hubris*), and hardly even yields to whip and goad (253e3–5). A connection between excess and appetite was central to the definition of love in Socrates' first speech (238a1–2). The unpersuadability of the bad horse is probably a corollary of appetite's not being directed at the good (cf. 239c4–5), so that it cannot register the evaluations of reason in the way that spirit can, being itself evaluative in its way (cf. *Rep* 8.553d4–6). However, in two ways the bad horse seems to have taken on the vices proper to spirit. It is called a 'companion of boastfulness' (253e3); that may just be impressionistic (cf. the assembled vices of *Gorg* 525a2–5), but goes better, once distinctions are made, with spirit's concern to keep face. More strikingly, irrational anger appears as a response of the bad horse (254c7), not of spirit (contrast *Rep* 4.441c2). So there is a degree of cross-classification: virtue against vice does not perfectly coincide with spirit against appetite. Fine points of substance are being sacrificed to bold strokes of presentation.

The first sight of the erotic object affects the whole soul (253e5–6), each part according to its nature. The good horse, constrained by a sense of shame, holds himself back from springing upon the beloved (254a1–3). Taken strictly, that implies a mental conflict within the one horse itself; no doubt it is not to be taken so. Unlike spirit in the *Republic*, the good horse is frequently said to feel shame (cf. 254c4, 256a6), never anger (except for a vexation shared with the driver, 254b1); contrast the state of Leontius (*Rep* 4.439e7–440a3), especially relevant if his motive was sexual perversion. But shame fits in well with love of honour: a sense of honour stands to the noble as shame stands to the base (*Symp* 178d1–2). The bad horse responds by springing,[33] and forcing the soul to approach and solicit the boy (254a3–7).[34] The driver at first forbids (a3–4, 7–8), and then consents (b2–3). There has been no explicit mention yet of any recollection of the Forms (which comes next, b5–7), though the dawning of the ideal is implicit in the ascription of the perception of the boy to the driver himself (253e5). No doubt we are to think of the driver as confused by a perceptual experience that he cannot himself understand (cf. 250a6–b1, 251d7–8); it is this confusion that the bad horse initially exploits.[35]

The driver only comes to his senses at the next stage: as the soul now approaches close to the boy (thanks, ironically, to the bad horse's insistence), and the sight of him really 'flashes' upon the driver (254b4–5), 'his memory is carried back to the nature of beauty, and again sees it standing together with self-control on a holy pedestal' (b5–7). He suddenly realizes that it is ideal beauty that he is seeing in the boy, so that the proper response to him cannot be sexual. He had a notion before of 'shocking and forbidden things' (b1);[36] but that went with a deference to 'the accepted standards of propriety and good taste' (252a4–5), which has to be replaced by a personal grasp of moral values at once cognitive and motivating, that is by his own apprehension of the moral Forms (notably, in context, that of Self-control, 254b7). He now sees seducing the boy not as something not done, but as a desecration. Before his new vision he falls back in fear and awe, which causes him to pull back the reins and force the two horses down

---

[33] More literally, 'prancing' (*skirtōn*, 254a4), here either phallic (cf. 'swelling', 256a2), or less specific (cf. *Rep* 9.571c6). Genital imagery can hardly surprise us here when it served in the *Symposium* to convey intellectual as well as sexual responses to beauty and ugliness (206d4–8).

[34] It is unclear whether its behaviour here is to be taken as different in manner from that provoked in a generally corrupt soul by a more prosaic perception of a sexual object as beautiful (250e1–251a1). Clearer is a difference in object-choice: whereas the corrupt soul was indifferent between women and boys, the bad horse takes its object, which can only be a boy, from the perceptions of the charioteer (253e5). If it is significant that 254a2–3 are more violent than 250e4–5, Plato may intend that the worst part of a good soul is more vicious in action than a bad soul as a whole. On the other hand, the sexual excitement of the bad horse must itself be a good as a symptom of the regrowth of its feathers. The paradox in Plato's account is precisely that if the bad horse too is to be saved (as part of the salvation of the whole soul), it must be at once stimulated and severely inhibited. The conflict that now ensues lies on the soul's path towards salvation; it does not take it out of its way.

[35] So Robin, *Platon: Phèdre*, p. ci.

[36] I find Rowe's 'improper' too prim for *paranomos*; cf. James Adam, *The Republic of Plato* (Cambridge, 1902), ad 9.571b5.

on to their haunches (b7–c1); thus (just as at the beginning, 253e5–254a1, but now to somewhat different effect) an involuntary response on his part is at once communicated to the rest of the soul. At a distance from the boy again, the good horse is left drenched with sweat from shame and horror; but the bad horse, once his pain is past, turns on his companions and rebukes them for cowardice and desertion (c3–d1). One would not expect him to get a hearing; but in the absence of the boy, and the loss of the ideal vision, he again gets his way (d1–2), and returns towards him with 'head down and tail outstretched' (d6–7, with *kerkos* certainly also phallic, and not even vulgar in this sense like the French 'queue' or German 'Schwanz'). The upshot is the same, only magnified: as the vision returns, the driver falls back even more sharply, and the bad horse suffers still more severely (d7–e5).[37]

Where does all this lead? We are told to the following:

When the same thing happens to the evil horse many times, and it ceases from its excesses, now humbled it allows the charioteer with his foresight to lead, and when it sees the boy in his beauty, it nearly dies with fright; and the result is that now the soul of the lover follows the beloved in reverence and awe (254e5–255a1).

W. H. Thompson reads this as surprising: 'The extinction of gross appetite by the actual presence of beauty coveted in absence, is a remarkable feature in the psychology of this passage' (*The Phaedrus of Plato*, ad 254e8). I take him to mean that even appetite now sees the boy as an object of dread, not sexual attraction; its fear corresponds to shame in the good horse (254a2, c4), and reverence in the driver (b8)—to spell out for the parts of the soul what e9 states of the soul as a whole. If so, appetite suffers not inhibition, but transformation. Bodily beauty has become for it not easy on the eye but 'a pain to the

---

[37] Ferrari (op. cit. 186–90) finds it contradictory of our expectations that it is the bad horse that attempts persuasion, whether of its colleagues (254b3, c7–d1, d4) or of the boy (a6–7, d5–6), while the charioteer simply applies force (a3–4, b8–c2, d7–e5). But the bad horse itself compels by force rather than persuasion (a4–5, b1, d1, d5–7), and it only respects force (contrast 253d7–e1 of the good horse with e4–5 of the bad); the seductive words to the boy are spoken by the whole soul, and it is ambiguous whether the bad horse intended them or just caused them. The charioteer and good horse do also play their role propositionally (254b1–3, d1–2), but there is more point in the bad horse's trying to persuade them than in their trying to persuade it (d2 records only a small concession on its part). To say of the charioteer that 'the goading and whipping he inflicts on the lascivious horse directly transfers the force of the goading he receives from the boy' (ibid. 187) is an inference from the repetition of the term 'goads' (254a1, 3) more Freudian, in both its style and its conclusion, than Platonic.

eyes'.[38] This is indeed remarkable; but is it right? It seems more natural to suppose, instead, that the object of appetite's alarm is not the sexual object, but the internal sanctions of the driver. What else can it be *frightened* of?[39] (Of course the boy might then become terrifying himself through association; but that is no longer so interesting.) If so, appetite has not changed its attitude; it is just that it is deterred from sexual pleasure by fear of the infliction of pain.

It would be good to confirm one or the other interpretation by parallels with the struggle in heaven. I noted earlier how the plumage of the whole soul is again nourished (248b5–c2), or begins to be restored (251b5–7), through the impact of reality. There is the same language of 'force' exerted by the horses, or the bad horse (248a5, 254d4), and of sweat caused by the conflict (248b2, 254c4).[40] Perhaps indicative now is that, as we saw, the progress in heaven of souls other than divine is never effortless.[41] And yet (one might try to argue), if appetite on earth could come not only to avoid certain pleasures out of fear of pain (compare the vulgar temperance of *Pdo* 68e3–69a4), but to be pained by what formerly pleased it (and, presumably, pleased by what formerly pained it), surely appetite in heaven could be transformed as well, so that the very risk of incarnation would be removed. However, that is not decisive: if in heaven even the good horse makes problems for the driver (cf. 248a4–6), so would also a redeemed bad horse. It is true that the bad horse is never described as anything but bad; and that its stock and nature is the opposite to that of the good horse (246b3) could indicate that its badness is incurable. Yet a crucial sentence (247b3–5) leaves open what counts as 'training' it well; so what we were told of heaven seems not to help.

Deterrence without reform is presumably unwelcome; so an inhibited appetite is unlikely to agree to the dominance of reason, which it must do if the soul is to achieve temperance as that is defined, somewhat artificially, in the *Republic* (4.432a7–9, 442c10–d3). Yet it remains more natural, looking at the *Phaedrus* on its own, to take what may be the less attractive view, that erotic appetite can be

---

[38] Dover cites this revealing phrase from Herodotus 5.18.4 (*GPM*, 211).

[39] Rowe's 'nearly dies with fright' (254e8) cannot be tamed into 'is filled with awe' or the like; it is far stronger than the description of the lover as experiencing, at his first sight of the boy, 'something of the fears he had before' (251a4).

[40] I take these parallels from Anne Lebeck, 'The Central Myth of Plato's *Phaedrus*', *Greek, Roman, and Byzantine Studies* 13 (1972), 278.

[41] Rowe's 'scarcely' is more literally 'with toil' (*mogis*, 248a4); cf. c4–5.

inhibited but not civilized.[42] There ought to be a third possibility, which is perhaps the most attractive of the three: of a transformed appetite that is no longer appetite at all, but a sublimated desire that now reinforces spirit or reason. That was clearly a goal in the *Republic* (6.485d6–e1), and if it is not mentioned here in the *Phaedrus* that may well only be because sublimation is virtually unrepresentable within the imagery of the soul as a chariot: a swollen driver with shrivelled horses would not ascend very easily. If we do bring the two books together we may envisage, rather as in Freud (though he vacillates about how to relate the two processes), an initial repression that forces the resurgent energies of appetite into sublimation. We would have to admit, given the obstinate imperfection of non-divine souls, even those free of incarnation, that the sublimation can never be complete. At least, this seems one compromise, not actually contradicting anything in the text, between what we do read in the *Phaedrus*, and what we might prefer to read.

7

Recollection starts, as we saw, as a state of fluctuation and confusion:

The man who observed much of what was visible to him before, on seeing a godlike face or some form of body which imitates beauty well, first shudders and experiences something of the fears he had before, and then reveres it as a god as he looks at it, and if he were not afraid of appearing thoroughly mad would sacrifice to his beloved as if to a statue of a god (251a2–7).

The case is one of unconscious memory: at the sight of one thing the soul feels an emotion appropriate to something similar, forgotten but previously experienced; that this is being recollected unawares will be confirmed if the memory ever becomes conscious.[43] The lover's response is superficially like that of Charmides' admirers: 'All looked at him as if he were a statue' (*Charm* 154c8). But it goes much deeper: the lover is unconsciously seeing in the boy not only Beauty itself, but also the god in whose train he (indeed, they) once saw Beauty (cf.

---

[42] That seems marginally supported rather later, when philosophical souls are described as 'having enslaved that part through which evil attempted to enter the soul' (256b2–3); however, while talk of slavery naturally suggests resentment, the *Republic*, at least, envisages artisans who are willing 'slaves' (cf. 9.590c9, d2).

[43] This is only half Proustian: Proust's narrator becomes alive to a similarity between two events, themselves equally trivial, which seems itself to exist outside time. It is not so easy to grant to that experience the intellectual significance that Proust claimed for it.

252c3 ff.). 'Godlike' takes on new force as the expression of a relation between individuals (that is, the boy and a god), rather as 'beautiful' expresses a relation (of participation) between a particular and a Form. The lover's attitude towards the boy betrays a confusion between this world and the other (is the boy 'a god' or merely 'a statue of a god'?); it is, precisely, a kind of idolatry.

The lover's behaviour takes on two aspects. On the one hand, he treats the boy as an object of experience: in his presence he receives the effusion of desire (*hīmeros*, 251c7) which eases the resprouting of his soul's feathers. On the other, he treats him as a subject: the boy has his own life to lead, and the lover tries to make it divine. In this respect, if not in the other, it matters not only that the boy should be beautiful (many may be that, cf. *Charm* 154b9–10, *Rep* 5.474d4–475a2), but that he should share with the lover a disposition towards a single way of life that he may inspire in the lover, and the lover may promote in him. Each such disposition is associated with having followed in heaven in the train of a particular god.[44] Plato is at last recognizing, as Socrates failed to do in the *Symposium*, that love must be sensitive to differences of character at once moral and cognitive. Socrates' description at first seems incoherent. The boy is viewed by the lover at once as himself a god, and as an image to be fashioned and adorned (252d6–7). The lover pursues the track of his own god within the person of the boy (252e7–253a2), and so draws from his memory of that god a character and way of life that he gratefully ascribes to the boy and not to the god (a2–6); and yet, as if nascently aware of his mistake, he also tries to *make* the boy similar to the god (252e4–5, 253a7–8, b5–c2). Very likely this matches the lover's own initial confusion (as already at 251a5–7). However, it will reconcile the lover's admiration with his activity that, for instance, the follower of Zeus chooses a boy who has the *capacity* to combine a love of philosophy with a talent for leadership ('naturally disposed towards philosophy and towards leadership', 252e3). In Aristotelian jargon, it is the boy's potentiality that inspires the lover to bring it, and his own, into actuality; and the potentiality that they share is the mark of the god in whose train they both followed. Without the mythology this exemplifies, in an unequal form, Aristotle's friendship of the good: these 'are thought to become better too by their activities and by improving each other; for from each other they take the stamp of the

---

[44] Of course it would be misplaced literalism to infer that, as there were twelve such gods (247a1–4), there are only twelve dispositions.

characteristics they approve of—whence the saying "fine deeds from fine men"' (*NE* 9.12.1172a11–14). The Bacchants provide a simile (253a6–7).[45] Nussbaum renders the experience elegantly as follows: 'They are both mutually active and mutually receptive: from the one the other, like a Bacchant, draws in the transforming liquid; and he pours liquid back, in his turn, into the beloved soul' (*The Fragility of Goodness*, 219). Yet it needs to be added, which alone for Plato explains all that can be achieved, that in origin the liquid is being drawn from the god (from Zeus in 253a6, cf. a3–4). The god is the final benefactor, lover and beloved his beneficiaries.

There follows in the text the description, discussed already, of the taming of appetite. Essential to that is that the lover's recollection of Beauty itself is brought into consciousness. With a new awareness of a difference between this world and another (to which it owes what is good in it), the lover will be able to place his response to the boy, and so escape his initial confusion. The result is an awakening, but not a disenchantment. The lover sees the boy now not as a god, yet as 'equal to a god' (*isotheos*, 255a1), while the boy realizes that the lover is 'possessed by a god' (*entheos*, b6). Each recognizes in the other the divine characteristics whose emergence each owes to the other; and it cannot impede further development to understand its ground.

That still leaves one major problem. It is the providential role of love to remind the lover, via beauties and Beauty itself, of the lost world of Forms. How then can he share that with a beloved who is not himself in love? We might suppose that the solution is simple: the love must be reciprocated. In effect, that will be Plato's solution also, and yet he clearly found himself in some embarrassment. In part, this may simply have been because he did not expect a boy to see beauty (at least of the required, Form-revealing, kind) in a young man. Further-more, Athenian opinion did not expect the younger partner in a pederastic relationship to return the passion of the elder. Briefly, they would have read into that a sexual passivity that would undermine pretensions to be fit for equal citizen status.[46] It better fitted the heroism of Harmodius and Aristogeiton to suppose, with Pausanias in the *Symposium*, that the elder felt love, but the younger friendship (182c5–6). Plato is willing to encourage both lover (*Phdr* 252a4–6)

45 On the punctuation of this, cf. W. J. Verdenius, 'Notes on Plato's *Phaedrus*', *Mnemosyne* 8 (1955), ad loc.
46 Cf. Dover, *GH*, 81–91; Michel Foucault, *L'Usage des plaisirs* (Paris, 1984), ch. 4.

and beloved (255a4–b1) to disregard the conventional proprieties; but he is still driven to construe a loving response on the boy's part in a charming but over-ingenious way that seems not fully interpretable. His purpose is to meet both objections by attributing the boy's love to the power of his own beauty and not to that of the other's virility. He returns to the metaphor of a effusion of desire, which before (251c5–d1) fitted the imagery of a regrowth of feathers to be watered in the lover's soul. It is now (255c1–d3) put to use to remarkable effect: desire overflows the eyes of the lover, and, like a sound echoing back towards its source, re-enters the eyes of the boy, who in turn finds his own feathers beginning to sprout again. So he too falls in love, but with what or whom he cannot tell (d3). In a way, he is a Narcissus in love with his own reflection (d6). Yet his emotion cannot stop there: it must become as true of him as of the lover that he sees his god (*their* god) in the other. His frame of mind is not sterile and self-regarding; he is not, to apply the first of Shakespeare's *Sonnets*, contracted to his own bright eyes, nor does he feed his life's flame with self-substantial fuel. And if the lover may be allowed to love *him* and not just the god in him, he may be allowed to love the lover. Like Ganymede loving Zeus (c1–2), who *is* a god, he loves the other as a god whom his own godlike beauty has attracted.[47] Harder to interpret are the metaphor of the overflow, and the simile of the echo. If visual beauty can remind the lover of Beauty itself, the moral beauty of the devoted lover (which so impresses the boy, 255b3–7) might be enough, though through 'dulled organs' (250b3–4), to put the boy in mind of the god.[48] But that is not what Plato has in mind: the boy's soul needs to be affected like the lover's in a way that stimulates it as a whole (horses as well as driver), provoking the same dangers and making possible the same triumph. It cannot be said that Plato succeeds in explaining how this can happen.[49]

So the boy too falls in love: 'His return of love (*anterōs*) is a reflection of love (*erōs*)' (255d8–e1). Yet he has his own reasons, additional to those which once affected the other, for failing to

---

[47] Lebeck's different reading of that allusion (op. cit. 278) is felicitous, but would rather fit the context of 253a2–5.

[48] Cf. Ferrari, op. cit. 178.

[49] Contrasted, and more credible, is Proust: 'It is the misfortune of the infatuated lover not to take into account that, while he sees a beautiful face in front of him, his mistress sees his face, which is not made more beautiful—on the contrary—when it is distorted by the pleasure which the sight of beauty brings there to birth'; *À la recherche du temps perdu* (Paris, 1954), iii. 181.

understand his own condition: the reflective path of the effusion of desire, and the conventional assumption (false in his case) that what he is feeling must be friendship, not love (e1–2). Hence he is as much at risk as the lover used to be when he indulges a desire, albeit weaker, 'to see, touch, kiss, and lie down with him' (e3–4). We might expect the lover to put him right, and may be surprised when this cannot be counted upon: the lover's unruly horse is again at his exercise (e5–256a1). The explanation seems simple: kissing and embracing undo the good work. This fits experience;[50] it also implies a plausible thought for Plato to have had, namely that the sense of touch, unlike that of sight, cannot put us in touch with another world.[51] This is a new predicament. Physical contact was already mentioned at 255b8, but in a different context and with different consequences: companionable and not erotic in origin, it took place, also through the boy's initiative, at a stage of deceptive security when, neither in love himself nor in any apprehension of falling in love, he was willing to flaunt in social gatherings the independence that he had achieved from conventional disapproval of even consorting with a lover (cf. a5–6); and visually rather than tactually erotic in effect, it was through his eyes (c6) that it caused him to receive back the effect upon his lover of a closer proximity to his beauty, above all naked in the gymnasium. The boy's confusion now, as he solicits his lover to take him in his arms not in a public tussle but in a private embrace, is intensified because he is unaware of his own sexual arousal (if that is the full way to read 256a2), and kisses the lover as an expression of gratitude for his goodwill (a2–3); so he is badly placed to take a hold upon himself (a4–5). Yet his own spirit and reason can play a part in overcoming their mutual temptation (a5–6); both lover and boy have already started to walk in the way of their god. Thus they may achieve unity of mind and self-control together through jointly enslaving the source of evil (b1–3). It is the boy's role to become in turn lover, tempter, and redeemer.

---

[50] On the dangers of kissing, cf. a Socratic anecdote in Xenophon (*Symposium* 3.8–14) cited by Dover (*GH*, 160).

[51] That fits the special role of sight in perceiving the Form of Beauty at 250c7–d4; also its special relationship to reason, stated elsewhere (*Tim* 45a6–b1, *Laws* 12.961d8–10). The *Hippias Major* finds it plausible to try out a definition of beauty as 'pleasure through hearing and through sight' (298a6–7), in contrast to the other senses (d8–e2); and the *Laws* will apply to the best kind of friend that phrase 'looking rather than loving' (8.837c4–5), in which 'looking' could certainly not be replaced by 'touching'. By contrast, it was characteristic of Socrates' first speech that it viewed all the lover's senses alike (240d1–3).

8

While the *Symposium* did not divide the mind into parts, it recognized three forms of vicarious immortality corresponding to the three levels of desire in the *Republic*: passing on one's philosophy, passing on one's name (through the fame of poetry, or legislation), and passing on one's blood (through sexual reproduction).[52] The *Phaedrus* now distinguishes three kinds of life which also correlate with the three parts of the soul.[53] Yet its present focus is not upon prolonging one's life here in ways that transcend one's own individuality (though that theme is coming, at 276e4–277a4), but upon preparing for one's individual fate after death (though that may be shared with another). Those who choose a philosophical life achieve inner peace here and now (256b1–2), and bring closer their return to the Platonic heaven (b4–5). I shall not pursue the details of the mythical eschatology (cf. 249a3–5). Instead, I shall consider two disputed questions: whether philosophers must not make love, and whether they must love boys. A modern moralist is likely to insist neither upon chastity nor upon pederasty; Plato was not a modern.

The orthodoxy, that the Platonic lover achieves (so far as is possible for a man) a kind of sexlessness, has been unsettled by Gregory Vlastos: 'That form of passionate experience invented by Plato . . . is a peculiar mix of sensuality, sentiment, and intellect—a companionship bonded by erotic attraction no less than by intellectual give-and-take. Body-to-body endearment is one of its normal features, though always subject to the constraint that terminal gratification will be denied.'[54] Nussbaum agrees precisely (op. cit. 217), with the extra thought that there is a kind of personal understanding that will otherwise be lacking: 'The lovers are . . . encouraged in any sensuous exploration of the other person that stops short of an act which they see as potentially selfish and/or violent' (ibid. 220). Both suppose that the foreplay of 255e2–256a5 is continued even *after* the victory of the higher elements of the mind (a8). I prefer Meredith:

[52] I take this from Iris Murdoch, *The Fire and the Sun* (Oxford, 1977), 34.
[53] Plato was clearly pleased with his trichotomy, for it reappears in the *Laws*, 8.837a6–d7.
[54] 'The Individual as Object of Love in Plato', *Platonic Studies*, 39–40. Ferrari cites a similar provision within a historical utopia (op. cit. 268–9, n. 47).

> I am not of those miserable males
> Who sniff at vice, and, daring not to snap,
> Do therefore hope for heaven
>
> (*Modern Love* 20.1–3).

It is hard to conceive how a perilous policy of deliberate mutual arousal without gratification could actually further a life of happiness and harmony (a8–9), of self-control and inner peace (b1–2). Even if it came off, it could only generate an obsessive sexual heroism; what motivation could these philosophical lovers have for making things so difficult for themselves? The bad horse must be reduced again to a state of fright (cf. 254e8), which is not one of titillation induced by petting. Plato is demanding; we need not suppose him so innocently unwise.[55]

More difficult to decide about, in my view, is the necessity of pederasty. A special dispensation from the ban on returning to heaven within ten thousand years is promised to the soul of 'the man who has lived the philosophical life without guile or who has united his love for a boy with philosophy' (249a1–2). Regrettably, 'or' is crucially ambiguous: it may introduce an alternative, or a gloss. Even if philosophy is compulsory, pederasty optional, 'the eschatological status of philosophical *paiderastiā* is still remarkable', as Dover remarks (*GH*, 165, n. 18). Can we even make intelligible a thought that mixing 'the philosophical sin' (to use an eighteenth-century French euphemism) with one's philosophy might go to prove a love of wisdom *without* ulterior motives?[56]

Less surprising glosses on honest philosophizing can be found elsewhere: fear of death proves that one loves the body, and not wisdom (*Pdo* 68b8–c1); one is an impostor with no share at all in true philosophy if one is not devoted to the truth, that is to 'the nature of each thing in itself' as opposed to 'the many particulars that are opined to be real' (*Rep* 6.490a1–b4). How might pederasty supply another gloss? This may depend on where one places the emphasis within the phrase 'uniting his love for a boy with philosophy'. If the stress is on

---

[55] And yet, while diverging from Vlastos and Nussbaum in practice, I am not so far from them in theory: we agree that the bad horse must respond to beauty in its own way, which demands stimulation as well as inhibition, if it is to regain its feathers; I think that it must cease to embark the lovers upon action, they that it must never take them into port.

[56] More teasing than thought-provoking was Socrates' description of himself in the *Gorgias* as 'a lover of two beloveds, . . . of Alcibiades the son of Cleinias and of philosophy' (481d3–4).

philosophical pederasty, the thought could be rather simply (to trans-
pose it into terms more familiar to most men nowadays) that it proves
quite a commitment to philosophy if one talks philosophy even with
one's girl. (Plato may simply be assuming that the reader, at least
within his circle, will love a boy, the question being *how*.) If, instead,
the stress is on *pederastic* philosophy, the thought cannot be so
commonplace; but there seem two ways of bringing out, to begin
with, the interpersonal demands of philosophy. We may compare the
philosopher-kings of the *Republic* who, while reluctant to rule as a
distraction from philosophy, nevertheless prove the sincerity of their
commitment to philosophy by respecting the call of the Good itself to
be a pattern for governing their state and educating their successors
(7.540a7–b7). They show that philosophy comes first by not treating
it as the servant of 'some senseless and childish opinion about happiness' (5.466b7–8) that would lead them to subordinate the impartial
demands of Goodness to their own interests, narrowly conceived.
The matter is notoriously difficult; but it must, somehow, be only a
superficial paradox that the genuine philosopher cannot be content to
do philosophy, in our sense, but must also *enact* it. We may compare,
in the *Phaedrus*, how soul that is perfect, moving on high with wings
unimpaired, still governs the whole world (246b7–c2). In another
way, interpersonal relationships may be not a corollary, but an aspect,
of philosophy. As Karl Schirlitz puts it in a good discussion, there
may be no real separation possible between *Lernen* (learning) and
Lehren (teaching).[57] That is one reason, he suggests, why it was not
frivolous of Plato to present his thinking in dialogue-form. In the
possibly Platonic *Seventh Letter* we explicitly read of philosophy,
'Only after long partnership in a common life devoted to this very
thing does truth flash upon the soul, like a flame kindled by a leaping
spark' (341c6–d1). If so, a commitment to another person may fall
inside a commitment to philosophy: philosophizing with and for
another may be the only way of philosophizing oneself.

But why should the relationship be erotic? The *Phaedrus* makes the
answer easy: it has described how personal physical beauty alerts, and
(we may suppose) keeps alert, the whole soul to the world of Forms. A
pure course in philosophy, even if itself successful (which Plato would
never conceive), could not convert the soul as a whole; and it is the
tripartite soul that has to regain its way to heaven. 'Why particularly

[57] *Beiträge zur Erklärung der Rede des Sokrates in Platons Symposion* (Neustettin,
1890), 30–2.

pederasty?', we may still ask. Plato may not even have been conscious
of provoking that question. He was, in that respect, conventional
enough. So Dover (*GH*, 164): 'It is . . . easy to see why an eros which
perpetually restrained itself from bodily gratification should be
homosexual: it was after all the prescribed role of women to be
inseminated, whereas popular sentiment romanticized and applauded
the chastity of an eromenos and the devotedly unselfish erastes.'
Contingently (not that Plato approved), boys were educated, and
girls not. Further, whatever speculations may suggest themselves to
us about Plato's personal penchants (Vlastos romances, op. cit. 25–6),
he clearly assumed that an instinct towards sexual reproduction was
always liable to be dominant in relation to the opposite sex.[58]

So much for the philosophic life. There follows a second way of life,
of which Plato writes with unexpected sympathy. In essence, it is
familiar to us as the timocratic life of *Republic* 9: it is devoted to
honour (256c1, 549a4); it is less cultured (256b7, 548e4–5); it is not
pure in respect of virtue since it lacks the best of guardians (549b3–4),
and so can be caught off its guard without the consent of the whole
mind (256c2, 6–7); we may expect of it a taste for militarism (549a5–
6), and so connect it to allegiance not to Zeus but to Ares (cf. 252c4–
7). Lovers who pursue this life do make love, recurrently but occasionally, since they partly disapprove (256c5–7). That is less remarkable than what follows: 'So these too spend their lives as friends,
though not to the same degree as the other pair, both during their love
and when they have passed beyond it, believing that they have given
and received the greatest pledges, which it would be wrong to break
by ever becoming enemies' (c7–d3). That astounded J. A. Stewart,[59]
in a way rightly. It shows that, oddly enough, Nussbaum's supposition that Plato deprecated full intercourse 'as potentially selfish and/or
violent' (op. cit. 220, already cited) overstates his severity: he here
acknowledges that going the whole hog (if that is what the phrase 'the
greatest pledges' alludes to) can cement a friendship, and thereby
implicitly concedes that even sterile love-making can have a partial
justification. However, it partly disarms his concession, without
cancelling it, that it is not he but the lovers themselves who are
attaching such a positive significance to making love: what so helps to
bind them may rest, from a philosopher's point of view, on a shared

---

[58] A deeper reason why Platonic love must be homoerotic in nature will emerge in
Appendix 3.
[59] *The Myths of Plato* (Fontwell, 1960), 297.

mistake.⁶⁰ More remarkably still, these friends who are not philosophers die featherless but having begun to regrow their feathers (d4–
5); they are rewarded by happy *Wanderjahre* together not below
earth but somewhere in the heavens (cf. 249a7–b1), and will 'acquire
matching plumage, when they acquire it, because of their love'
(256d8–e2). As a means towards happiness, making love may seem to
have become an ersatz for philosophy. However, it is no doubt
important that the love-making is not, in Aristotle's terminology,
chosen by either party. (In viewing it as so significant they may be
making the extra mistake of overvaluing action without choice.) The
foundation of their friendship must be something other than sex,
which survives their becoming only good friends (d1) as they grow
older; we are not told what it is, but it must accord with their better
judgement, and provide a preliminary to philosophy. Plato's silence is
unhelpful; but only so can we understand how the honour-loving man
of the *Phaedrus*, unlike that of the *Republic*, is on the way up, not
down.⁶¹

Finally, and most cursorily, there is the acquaintance (we are not
invited to term it a friendship) of the non-lover which 'engenders in
the soul that is the object of its attachment a meanness that is praised
by the majority as virtue, and so will cause it to wallow mindlessly
around and under the earth for nine thousand years' (256e4–257a2).
No doubt we are not to read this as a rejection of non-erotic friendship: the context is still provided by Lysias's case for sex without love,
and it is that combination which is being condemned.⁶² From Plato's
point of view, although this may be superficially prudent (as Lysias
argued), it must be as profoundly dangerous as love that is set on sex:
by confirming a perception of beauty which is not one of Beauty itself,
both put off still further the day of recollection (cf. 250e1–4); by
letting the bad horse run out of control, both lead souls (to apply some
wording of Freud's) to repeat over and over again the mechanism by

⁶⁰ I owe this point to Edward Hussey. It reassures me in disagreeing with Dover,
who takes the pledges to be not 'their copulation but the rest of their relationship' (*GH*,
163, n. 16): giving and receiving pledges is a precise notion that exactly fits making
love; we should not apply the notion otherwise here unless we have to—which, given
Hussey's point, we do not.
⁶¹ In the *Laws*, Plato conceives this love not in relation to spirit, but as an unhappy
mixture of the other two loves (8.837b4–7); accordingly, he detects in it a more acute
mental conflict (compare 837b7 with 256c6–7 here), and would like to prohibit it
(837d6–7).
⁶² This is confirmed by the parallel in the *Laws*, 8.837b8–c3.

which they became incarnate. The proper goal of human life is still to regain the use of one's wings by means of a partial, and for the sake of a fuller, cognitive recovery.

Thus love as madness is justified not as itself constituting wisdom, but as a prelude to philosophy (and most likely, as I speculated earlier, a continuing accompaniment to it). Socrates has construed his task as a justification of love of a kind, not as a definition of love; the result is less than systematic and exhaustive. The programmatic demands that prefaced his first speech (237b7–d3) have been neglected in his second (*pace* 265d5–7, curiously). Much later, Socrates will sketch the problem and the solution. 'Love', like 'just' and 'good', unlike 'iron' and 'silver', is a disputed term (263a2–d1), and so lends itself to rhetorical exploitation; by that Plato has in mind not sound without sense, but the assimilation of one thing to another (cf. 261c4–262a7) for the purposes of praise or blame, and advice for or against. To sort things out (whether in order to practise or to resist such exploitation), we need to carry through collections and divisions: all love is subsumed under madness and (still more generically, I take it) irrationality, whether it comes within a 'left-hand' species that is to be blamed, or a divine 'right-hand' species to be praised (265e3–266b1). We may regret that the solution is not spelled out in any detail; even whether there is something common to all cases of love that makes them that is left open.[63] One would like to know whether the imperfect lovers of 256b7–e2, who are friends to a lesser degree than those who achieve chastity (c7), also count as less in love, or in love in a partly different sense; also whether their carnal love falls within left-hand love, or is crucially different (possibly even expressing, in a distorted form, the erotic point of view from which it can never be an object of choice). Such clarification could have made Socrates' second speech more acceptable to the gods (cf. 273e6–7) without making it less persuasive to Phaedrus. As it is, his first speech remains less edifying but more rigorous (cf. 263d1–4).[64]

---

[63] The term 'homonymous' twice occurs here (266a1, 7); but its technical use to exclude any common definition is not Platonic but Aristotelian (cf. *Cat* 1.1a1–6).

[64] However, I accept Rowe's explanation of what Socrates is up to: offering Phaedrus a 'variegated' speech (cf. 277c2–3) intended not to communicate the speaker's knowledge but to appeal to a nature more enthusiastic than analytical; 'The Argument and Structure of Plato's *Phaedrus*', *Proceedings of the Cambridge Philological Society* NS 32 (1986), 112–13.

9

Especially in the old days, when each Platonic dialogue was expected to display a single unifying theme (contrast Guthrie, *A History of Greek Philosophy*, iv. 130–1), there was much debate about the topic of the *Phaedrus*: love, and rhetoric, seemed obvious, yet incompatible, candidates. (Plumping for rhetoric had the advantage of playing down the pederasty.) Free of any a priori conception of the dialogic unities, we may look around in a more relaxed frame of mind for whatever connections may suggest themselves. Most simply, of course, the three speeches (Lysias's one, and Socrates' two) are specimens of rhetoric, good and bad, and are later cited as such (262c5–e6, 263d1–266b1). Less superficially, on an adequate conception of love, such as was achieved only in the third speech, it turns out that rhetoric is its tool. Rhetoric is to be understood quite generally, as an art of influencing souls by means of words, even in private (261a7–9). Examples of the art should aim at once to be persuasive (259e7 ff.), and to please the gods (273e5–274a2). To realize that double goal most fully they must at the same time be exercises of the art of dialectic, achieving through individual communication an immortality quite different from the death in life of written words stiffened for ever into one unresponsive fixity: 'If you ever ask them about any of the things they say out of a desire to learn, they point to just one thing, the same each time' (275d8–9). To a truer immortality the means are personal and transient:

It is far finer if one is in earnest . . . when a man makes use of the science of dialectic, and taking a fitting soul plants and sows in it words accompanied by knowledge, which are able to help themselves and the man who planted them, and are not without fruit but contain a seed, from which others grow in other soils, capable of rendering it for ever immortal, and making the one who has it as happy as it is possible for a man to be (276e4–277a4).

Such words are 'genuinely written in the soul' (278a3) not in the sense of being inscribed, quasi-materially, in a mental medium, but in that the speaker communicates an understanding of them that manifests itself not in repetition, but in defence and development; in contrast to the written matter which 'is incapable of defending or helping itself' (275e5), the spoken word can implant 'offspring and brothers . . . in other souls' (278a7–b1). Of course it is not that hearing has magical properties denied to reading: rather, training in discussion, which

demands participation, not overhearing, alone develops and transmits that discursive capacity to deduce derivations and adduce con-
firmations which in Plato's view constitutes understanding. A logical
grasp of the things that most matter to men (the just, the beautiful,
and the good, 278a3–4) bestows such happiness as men are capable of;
if it is passed down an unending chain of transmission, it yields a kind
of immortality (not of the individual human being, but of a stream of
human life). Thus a rhetoric that is at the same time dialectical (and so
transmits to another through persuasion a memory that is also an
understanding) needs to be exercised within personal relationships
(within which alone genuine understanding can be either achieved or
communicated). And a love that sets as an object of mutual imitation a
god who owes his individuality and divinity to a distinctive grasp of
the Forms (cf. 249c6) needs to develop into a philosophy of which
dialectical rhetoric will be at once the cause and the manifestation.
Thus the best love will achieve its goal through the best rhetoric.

The lover thereby takes a god as his model in two ways, contemplative and practical: he retrieves for himself the same kind of
grasp of the Forms; and he shares that grasp generously with another.
It was characteristic of the gods to welcome anyone willing and able to
follow in their train (247a4–7); by contrast, hostile emulation
between their followers in cognizing Forms was a cause of the fall
from heaven (248a8–9). Dialectic demands the divine attitude: questions and answers must be exchanged with a lack of envy, a willingness to share discoveries (cf. *7th Letter* 344b6). Such generosity is not
optional for the investigator: partly obscurely, it must be required
both by the content of the Forms themselves, so that no one could
grasp *them* in a mean spirit, and by our manner of grasping them, so
that *we* in particular could not so grasp them. (Possibly even the gods
of the *Phaedrus* need followers with whom to share a dialectical
understanding of Forms.) But this generosity in cognition falls
within—and, we may suppose, via grasp of the moral Forms generates—a wider generosity, that which in the *Timaeus* motivates creation itself, a lack of envy on the part of the Demiurge that takes the
form of a willingness that everything should resemble him as much as
possible (29e2–3). In a human lover this takes the form of an eagerness that another should share the divine inheritance in all its aspects:
'Imitating the god themselves and persuading and disciplining their
beloved they draw him into the way of life and pattern of the god, to
the extent that each is able, without showing envy or mean ill-will

towards their beloved' (253b5–c2, with 'envy' for Rowe's 'jealousy', cf. a6–b1). This contrasts the Platonic lover sharply with the envious lover of Lysias, and of Socrates' first speech. There is even a kind of selflessness (though a less welcome one) in followers of Ares who, thinking themselves wronged by their beloved, 'are ready to sacrifice both themselves and their beloved' (252c7); this is a perverted kind of mutuality, in which the agent freely inflicts the suffering that he wishes to share, while retaining the freedom as his own prerogative, which is an element of possessiveness. (As a god Ares is no doubt a problem.)

10

It is natural, perhaps, that the very high-mindedness of Plato's conception of love should have provoked strictures that might at once seem priggish in a different context. It is not easy to identify just how demanding a critic can be without lapsing into unreality. I think that Ferdinand Horn becomes slightly absurd when he complains that the lover loves the boy not for his own sake, but to win him over (253c7), and to find pleasure and relief in his company (251e4–5, 252b1) (*Platonstudien*, 211); to apply an exclamation from a similar context of moral one-upmanship in Henry de Montherlant's *Les Garçons*, 'How quick, the higher bid!'[65] L. A. Kosman more sensibly remarks, 'We should feel some apprehension if we thought our lovers didn't get satisfaction from their love of us' ('Platonic Love', 64). But reflection upon some other criticisms may help us to understand Plato better.

Vlastos finds in Plato's treatment of love a presupposition of egoism which he evidently takes to be self-condemning: 'If A loves B, he does so because of some benefit *he* needs from B and for the sake of just that benefit . . . No reason is offered why we could love anyone except for what we could get out of him' (op. cit. 8). (He bases this initially on the *Lysis*, but does not intend to take it back.) In part, this just raises the general issue of psychological egoism, but there is a sting in the clause 'what we could get out of him'; is that deserved? Applied to the mature doctrine of the *Symposium* and *Phaedrus*, not easily. Here the lover is described as set on a kind of vicarious immortality

---

[65] *Romans II* (Paris, 1982), 616.

whereby aspects of his life are duplicated and developed within another's life.[66] But how could that be compatible with an exploitative attitude towards one's inheritors? If bequeathing a way of life is to satisfy, even to some extent, an innate desire for survival, I must value its realization in another rather as I value it in myself. If I view him as a means and not an end, then his happy life cannot count in itself as a success for me. The further we extend the desire for the good to belong to oneself always (*Symp* 206a11–12), the less we can oppose it to a desire that others should possess the good, and for their own sakes. Some may feel that Plato's transfigured egoism is a characteristically philosophical invention (I tried at least to make sense of it in Chapter 2); it is not a deserving target for familiar moralizing.

Another of Vlastos's criticisms perhaps takes us deeper: 'Plato's theory . . . does not provide for love of whole persons, but only for love of that abstract version of persons which consists of the complex of their best qualities' (op. cit. 31). In fact, this raises a quite general dilemma (as Kosman displays, op. cit. 56–7). If I love you for qualities that differentiate you from others, is it that complex of qualities (which you might have lacked or others have possessed) that I really love? If I don't love you for any differentiating qualities, is it more than accidentally and superficially true that I love *you*? In this form, the problem may not particularly undermine Plato. Nussbaum well notes of the *Phaedrus*, in a sentence that says all that needs to be said, 'The focus on character takes away much of love's replaceability; the focus on history removes the rest' (op. cit. 218). It is a mistake to try to solve the problem for love at first sight; once love has got going, the beloved will be singled out by a unique role within a historical relationship. (It ought not to worry the lover that he might have had a relationship, perhaps even preferably, with someone else; that element of contingency has simply to be accepted.) To infer that what I really love is not a person, but a complex of repeatable qualities and irrepeatable relations, seems a category-mistake: we must not confuse the object of an emotion with its grounds (whether these are its reasons, citable by the subject, or its causes, perhaps hidden from him).

---

[66] The *Phaedrus* is more explicit than the *Symposium* in envisaging a chain of transmission down a sequence of lives that might constitute not just a doubled life, but immortality (276e4–277a4).

However, Vlastos is on to something distinctive when he talks of
the loved one's *best* qualities: Platonic love is peculiarly evaluative.
The lover need not suppose that everyone ought to be like his
beloved: he should be capable of the detachment to recognize, in
Plato's terms, that different lovers follow different gods. Yet it does
seem that what one loves in someone is a way of being *good*, and not
just attractive or winning to oneself. Here there is doubtless a presumption of objectivity alien to us (at least when love is the topic). Yet
it is important to notice that Plato is envisaging evaluations common
to lover and loved one. This is even true, to rather peculiar effect, of
the lover's physical evaluation of the other ('How beautiful you are!'):
that is why the beloved can fall in love through seeing his own
reflection in his lover's eyes (*Phdr* 255d4–6). Very likely Plato expects
that agreement only because he is not thinking of differences in taste
(aware though he can be of these in a different context, cf. *Rep*
5.474d4–e5). In any case, those are not the evaluations that do the
selecting: the boy is chosen for the capacities and aspirations that
constitute his character, actual or potential. Now a character is partly
constituted by the evaluations that it sustains; thus what the lover
values includes the boy's own values, present or incipient. Of course
Plato does not intend the evaluative subservience by which an infatuated lover may value *whatever* his beloved values (though that was
known to him, cf. in Lysias's speech 233a5–b1). But neither does he
assume that the lover will come to the relationship with his values
already fixed: the *Phaedrus* envisages lovers who can imagine that
their ideal is taking its form from the qualities of the beloved rather
than from their memory of the god (252e7–253a6). Here, though
there remains a difference in role, there is a need of mutual self-
discovery: each comes to recognize his god in and through the other.
Such initial indeterminacy on both sides is assumed in the *Symposium*
ascent: there the beloved is guided by a lover himself simultaneously
guided by someone else (210a6–7, c7, e2–3, 211c1). Such a psychagogue is not mentioned in the *Phaedrus*; but there may be an allusion
(cf. 'learning from wherever they can', 252e6), and that, after all, is
Socrates' actual role towards Phaedrus (though they play with the
fancy that Phaedrus is the loved one, 243e4–8). There is the implication, intended or not, that, if the beloved later falls in love himself
with another (as he must if the erotic succession is to be carried
down), this will be with full self-knowledge from the first, so that *their*

roles will be more sharply unequal. Yet in that case the evaluations actually present in the lover at the start of their relationship will again be already potentially present in the loved one.

Is it still an objection that the qualities admired by the lover that ground his love are not *all* the other's qualities? It is hard to see why it should be, unless, perhaps, we identify persons with the total set of their qualities (all of which, bizarrely, will count as essential to their identity), so that to love a person fully is to love all his qualities. But it would seem just a fallacy to infer that if I love someone only for his 'better self', it is that self, not the 'whole person' (in Vlastos's phrase), whom I love: why should we identify *whom I love* with *what I love him for*? It is not even clear that we could make sense of a love of persons as totalities. In any case, such a love could hardly take as its object the divided souls of the *Republic* and *Phaedrus*. It is in the nature of such souls to refuse to identify with all that is true of themselves; so love has to take sides. To respect the integrity of the other his partner must apply to him a critical evaluation that may be the mirror or the catalyst of his own self-evaluation. The supportive lover who affectionately seconds the other even through his internal dissensions can say with Michelangelo, 'If I only love in you, my dear lord, what you love most in yourself, do not be offended; for the one spirit falls in love with the other' (*Rime*, Girardi 60.9–11). It is important that the better self that I detect in the other is that which it is in his nature to prefer: my initial task is one of appreciative *recognition* (cf. Kosman, op. cit. 64). If we bear in mind that, for Plato, the sort of person that I ought to become is also the sort of person that I used once to be (which exemplifies 'the archaeology of love taken up in its teleology', Kosman, ibid. 65), history as well as idealism will encourage the lovers to think of themselves as each recalling the other to his 'true self', as restoring to him what in the *Lysis* was termed 'one's own' (*oikeios*, 221e3). It is then an undiscriminating love that will seem to be missing its target.[67]

In assessing a practical theory, however, it is important to distinguish its intended effect from what might actually come of trying to live it. Taken on its own terms, Plato's conception of a higher love

---

[67] Cf. Kosman, 'Platonic Love', *passim*, and Denis de Rougemont, *The Myths of Love* (London, 1964), 206–7; also, more concisely, the poet Angelus Silesius, 'Mensch, werde wesentlich!' or 'Man, achieve your essence', in his epigram 'Zufall und Wesen', and Nietzsche, '*What does your conscience say?*—"You shall become the person you are"', *The Gay Science* (New York, 1974), 3.270.

may defy revaluation; but if we think of it as a glorious illusion, what is the reality of the love that it reconstrues and thereby justifies? Perhaps one not altogether unexceptionable. As an interpretation, it is just a mistake when Terence Irwin reads off the metaphor of the lover as sculptor and the beloved as statue (252d7) that the beloved is 'simply the passive material which the lover moulds to his own design' (*Plato's Moral Theory*, 269): that neglects all that we read about the boy as himself a follower of the same god. But set aside the prehistory, and what prevents the criticism from becoming a fair one?[68] What confirms that the better self, as conceived by the lover, is the true self? The only test remaining would seem to be the future, and that can be made to measure. Nietzsche is salutary: '*Ingenious and limited*.—He does not know how to love anyone but himself; and when he wants to love others he always has first to transform them into himself. But in that he is ingenious.'[69] Or else, more attractively but confusedly, each partner may try to model himself on the other:

'*Love makes the same*'.—Love wants to spare the person to whom it dedicates itself every feeling of *being other*, and consequently it is full of dissimulation and pretence of similarity, it is constantly deceiving and feigning a sameness which in reality does not exist . . . There is no more confused and impenetrable spectacle than that which arises when both parties are passionately in love with one another and both consequently abandon themselves and want to be the same as one another: in the end neither knows what he is supposed to be imitating, what dissimulating, what pretending to be (*Daybreak*, 5.532).

The dangers here are different, and imply the possibility of success, whereby each models himself on the same preconception of the other. But it is more likely that similarity will only be achieved if one of the parties is domineering, and indifferent to the other's individuality. Plato hopes for a sensitive dominance; but the dominance risks being real (firmly grounded on a difference in age), the sensitivity imaginary (if its criterion is faithfulness to a mythical prehistory). With the best of intentions, the lover is liable to be colonizing the other's mind (love as imperialism?).[70]

[68] The same temptation to become a 'lord of souls', with the same sculptural imagery, is offered by a Satanic Eros in Baudelaire, *Le Spleen de Paris* 21; *Œuvres complètes* (Paris, 1975–7), i. 308. What Plato intends by the imagery here (at 251a6 and 252d7) is more fairly captured by Ferrari (op. cit. 171–5).
[69] *Daybreak* (Cambridge, 1982), 4.412; cf. *Human, All Too Human* (Cambridge, 1986), 2.1.37.
[70] Cf. Baudelaire: 'Love wishes to exit from itself, to confound itself with its victim, like the victor with the vanquished, and yet to preserve the privileges of a conqueror' (*Journaux intimes*, 'Fusées' § 1); *Œuvres complètes*, i. 650.

But suppose that the unlikely is achieved, and the lovers actually become similar, even indistinguishable in important respects, through freely modelling themselves on the same ideal. Would that give rise to a forgetfulness of self whereby it became indifferent to both which of them was the subject of some characteristic experience? We may compare the situation (somewhat idealized) of identical twins who find themselves already related rather as Plato's lovers aim to become. In their case do the barriers between lives collapse? It may be that these stand out all the more clearly where there are no accidental differences. Perhaps the deepest doubt about the prospects for the Platonic project is raised in a sentence of Michel Tournier: 'The motley cloak of personality which halts the unique gaze is colourless and transparent to the geminate gaze, and allows it to see abstract, bare, disconcerting, vertiginous, skeletal, terrifying: Otherness.'[71]

[71] *Les Météores* (Paris, 1975), 248.

4
PERFECT FRIENDSHIP IN ARISTOTLE

I

A central question for any philosophical theory of friendship is what it is to love an individual for himself. The question rapidly yields a dilemma. If we start by trying to identify the essence of an individual, that is what differentiates him from all other individuals essentially and not accidentally (and would still have differentiated him from them whatever might have happened to him), we are likely to look to his begetting, and propose as essential either his origination from a particular sperm and egg, or his conception at a certain time and place. That will indeed supply an essentially individuating description, but what would it be to love a person as falling under such a description? How is the identifying description related to any appropriate mode of loving? Within the phrase 'loving someone for himself' the words 'for himself' grammatically qualify 'loving'; if the notion expressed is to have any practical significance, the qualification must signify, or imply, one mode of loving among others (so that looking, say, on some instance of sentimental or exploitative affection, we can assert that its object is *not* being loved for himself). But what would it be to display in action a respect for the details of a friend's biological prehistory (most likely unknown to both)? Alternatively, if we start by distinguishing different ways in which an individual might be lovable, or different reasons for which one might love him, that is more likely to imply corresponding modes of loving him, but also liable to ground the love on qualities that he might have lacked, and others may also possess. Loving him for those qualities, though intelligible, will then seem to contrast with loving him for himself: its focus is not his essence, but accidents that may not even differentiate him from others as things are.[1]

[1] Richard Kraut likens loving another for himself to choosing an act for itself (e.g. *NE* 2.4.1105a32); 'Aristotle on Choosing Virtue for Itself', *Archiv für Geschichte der Philosophie* 58 (1976), 236–8. The latter must differ slightly in that the act one chooses, unlike the act one does, is a possibility (however specific), and not a particular. It also

This dilemma may be deep, or dispensable. An easy solution is to retain the notion of loving an individual while rejecting that of loving him 'for himself' as familiar but unintelligible. Another is to accept the qualification 'for himself' as multiply ambiguous, serving in one context to exclude self-interest, in another deference for rank, and so on. Aristotle takes a different line, which we shall better respect if we take him to intend it as the solution of a problem, and not as a piece of moralizing. He schematically divides the grounds of 'friendship' (*philiā*) into three: utility, pleasure, and goodness. Utility and pleasure, he then claims, ground loving another not for himself, but as he happens to relate to oneself:

Those who love because of utility love because of what is good for themselves, and those who love because of pleasure do so because of what is pleasant to themselves, and not in so far as the person loved is the man he is, but in so far as he is useful or pleasant. And thus these friendships are only incidental; for it is not as being the man he is that the loved person is loved, but as providing some good or pleasure (*NE* 8.3.1156a14–19).[2]

It is goodness alone, in both friends, that can ground loving the other not coincidentally but for himself:

Perfect friendship is the friendship of men who are good, and alike in virtue; for these wish well alike to each other *qua* good, and they are good in themselves. Now those who wish well to their friends for their sake are most truly friends; for they are so disposed by reason of the friends themselves, and not incidentally (1156b7–11).[3]

However, it is unclear quite what is going on. There is a shift from the familiar 'loving someone for his sake' to a newly inflected 'loving someone for *his* sake', that is for the sake of the person who he

seems less problematic, in that it is harder to think away intrinsically desirable features of an act, at least as an object of choice (and so a type, not a token), while respecting its identity. Even being enjoyable, which we might classify as intrinsic yet inessential, is according to Aristotle necessitated by other features which it may be impossible to think away (cf. 10.4.1174b31–1175a3).

[2] On the text of a16, cf. M. van Straaten and G. J. de Vries, 'Notes on the 8th and 9th Books of Aristotle's *Nicomachean Ethics*', *Mnemosyne* 13 (1960), 198–9; as I have translated it, it simply anticipates a17–18.

[3] Following Jonathan Barnes, I retain W. D. Ross's 'perfect' here in translation of *teleios*; Terence Irwin consistently prefers 'complete'. Neither English word (nor perhaps the Greek one) suits Aristotle ideally: against 'perfect', some instances must be better than others (if more than the perfect are to be capable of 'perfect friendship'), and some varieties may be better than others (notably if equality is preferable to inequality, cf. *NE* 8.7, *EE* 7.3); against both, we shall see that this kind of friendship can be realized imperfectly and incompletely, because only partially or fragmentarily.

is (compare 8.2.1155b31, which states a commonplace, with 8.3.1156b9–10, which in context mean something quite new); that is accompanied by an unargued assumption that *how* one is is part of *who* one is, that one's character is part of one's identity. But that seems strange: we need to distinguish self-interest from disinterestedness within personal relations, and we may associate the former with a kind of relational evaluation (of another person as being useful or pleasant to oneself); but why should we connect disinterestedness with a kind of intrinsic evaluation (of him as being of good character)? It is a recurrent complaint against the lesser friendships that they involve ranking attributes above persons (e.g. 9.1.1164a10–11, 9.3.1165b1–3); yet it seems that all friends do that. There is force in a complaint against Aristotle by Gregory Vlastos:

His intuition takes him as far as seeing that (a) *disinterested affection for the person we love*—the active desire to promote that person's good 'for that person's sake, not for ours'—must be built into love at its best, but not as far as sorting this out from (b) *appreciation of the excellencies instantiated by that person*; (b), of course, need not be disinterested and could be egoistic ('The Individual as Object of Love in Plato', 33, n. 100).

The question arises why Aristotle presents (b), within the context of friendship, as an aspect or precondition of (a): is he just confused, out of carelessness or prejudice, or does he provide the materials for articulating a bridge between the two notions?

Crucial to this problem, I believe, as to Aristotle's whole account of friendship, is an ethical conception of the self, and the life (mental and physical) that constitutes it in action, as being rooted in but not exhausted by the identity of the living physical substance that is a man. There is an implicit distinction between two notions of the 'self': a subject of choice and desire (a person and a substance), and a persona constructed by forming desires and making choices (compare the phrase 'my better self'). A practical persona is realized in sequences of, especially, desires, choices, actions, and results; these are what are most relevant to a man's success in the life he leads, to his *eudaimoniā* or 'activity of soul in accordance with virtue' (*NE* 1.7.1098a16–17).[4] Now while, normally, no organ is shared by two

---

[4] This is only roughly equivalent to 'happiness'; cf. J. L. Ackrill, 'Aristotle on *Eudaimonia*', in A. O. Rorty (ed.) *Essays on Aristotle's Ethics* (University of California, 1980), §5. Like Irwin, I have retained the traditional 'virtue' in translation of *aretē*, where Barnes has 'excellence'; one is not, indeed, to think exclusively of 'moral' virtue in our sense (whatever that is).

organisms, parts of lives can be shared: one and the same act may count as contributing, as a constituent and not a cause, to the *eudaimoniā* of two persons. It is this possibility that grounds Aristotle's ideal of friendship. In that it dissolves the obstinate dichotomy between egoism and altruism, it may attract us; however, its application is seriously restricted by other features of Aristotle's ethical theory, which have the effect that only the good can be perfectly so related. Hence, in brief, a special connection for Aristotle between being friends and being good.

2

'Virtuous acts', we are told, 'are fine and done for the sake of the fine' (*NE* 4.1.1120a23–4).[5] More precisely, the good man acts to get possession of the fine (9.8.1168b27, 1169a21–2); this he can only achieve in acting if he identifies (from his own point of view), and can be identified (from an impersonal point of view), with his act. It must hold of acts, as we read of their results (9.7.1168a5–10), that their fineness is also the agent's only if they *are* the agent, in a way, only if (as we might express it) the agent *realizes* himself in them. Of the motive of fineness, at least, Aristotle might say with F. H. Bradley, 'Nothing is desired except that which is identified with ourselves, and we can aim at nothing, except so far as we aim at ourselves in it.'[6] Does this extend to other motives? It is only to the fine that Aristotle explicitly extends a wide claim that 'the end of every activity is conformity to the corresponding state' (3.7.1115b20–1); and while more, no doubt, aim for the fine than achieve it, the fine is not a goal of choice for the vicious, for instance neither for cowards (3.8.1116b22), nor for

----

5 Like Irwin, I use 'fine' here to translate *kalos* (which Ross and Barnes render, appropriately enough in these contexts, as 'noble'). The fine ranks as an object of pursuit beside the expedient and the pleasant, in contrast to the base, the harmful, and the painful as objects of aversion (2.3.1104b30–2). The fine is good absolutely, while the expedient is good for oneself (*Rhet* 2.13.1389b37–1390a1), and the pleasant often an apparent good (e.g. *EE* 2.10.1227a39). *Kalos* connects with commendation: close relations are 'honourable' (*entīmos*; compare *NE* 4.3.1125a26 with a29), and 'praiseworthy' (*epainetos*; cf. *EE* 8.3.1248b19–20). However, it would be anachronistic to look here for a speech-act analysis of the fine (though a prescriptivist might well relate its implicit supervenience upon other qualities to the logic of praise, citing *NE* 1.12.1101b12–14); the concept in Aristotle remains basic, and elusive.

6 *Ethical Studies* (Oxford, 1927), 68; cf. D. J. Allan, 'Individual and State in the *Ethics* and *Politics*', in Fondation Hardt, *Entretiens 9, La 'Politique' d'Aristote* (Geneva, 1964), 60.

spendthrifts (4.1.1121b1), nor for all those who are sacrificing the fine to their own advantage (8.13.1162b35–6). However, presumably they too identify with their acts under some desirability-characterization, in the light of which *we* apply terms indicative of vice (in contrast to acrasia or negligence) at once to act and agent. These are still identified both by agent and by moralist, but under contrasted descriptions.

More precisely, we may say that acts can help realize a self that is a moral persona of the agent. They do this when they are *chosen* (or even, in a specially restrictive sense, when they are *acts*, cf. 6.2.1139a31). It is true that not all voluntary acts are chosen (3.2.1112a14–15): others are done spontaneously in accordance with wish (*EE* 2.8.1224a1, 3–4), or with irrational desire, whether anger or appetite (*NE* 3.1.1111a24–b3).[7] Yet it is 'the things men have done from reason' (and so from choice, 6.2.1139a32–3) that 'are thought most properly their own acts and voluntary acts' (9.8.1168b35–1169a1): the chosen is the paradigm of the voluntary. To identify fully with an act, then, is to choose it; the self is primarily realized in its choices. So Aristotle is willing to declare of choice, 'Such an origin of action is a man' (6.2.1139b5).[8]

When Aristotle is spelling out a restricted notion of the self, he tends to use the pronoun 'each' (*hekastos*, most easily translated as 'each man') with a special emphasis. The equivalent of the friendly 'for his sake' (e.g. 8.2.1155b31) within self-love is 'for his own sake' (compare 9.4.1166a4 with a16), which is glossed as 'for the sake of his thinking element, which is thought to be each man' (a16–17, cf. a22–3); it becomes unambiguous later that this 'most authoritative element in himself' includes his practical reason (9.8.1168b30–1). As reason acts through choice, this confirms choice's centrality. The practical mind (*nous*) of 9.8 (1168b35, 1169a18) surfaces again in 10.7 (where the terms 'rule' and 'guide' clearly indicate practical reason, 1177a13–15), but is soon supplanted by theoretical reason (a17–18): it is of *this* that Aristotle then remarks that it 'would seem, too, to be each man (*hekastos*), since it is his authoritative and better part' (1178a2–3). Thus it depends on the context how far Aristotle pushes his tendency to single out some element within a man honorifically as his 'self'.

<hr>

[7] On the distinction between 'choice', 'wish', and 'appetite', cf. *NE* 3.2–4.

[8] Cf. *EE* 2.1.1219b39–40, as emended by Michael Woods, *Aristotle's Eudemian Ethics: Books 1, 2, and 8* (Oxford, 1982), 203.

From the self realized in choices derives a less restricted notion. Choice is only one species of desire, and a man's other desires may, or may not, form a unity with his choices. (This unity is already implicit in the virtue in respect of choice which constitutes virtue of character; that amounts to more than that capacity to choose well which even the acratic possess, cf. 7.10.1152a17.) When a man's desires are in agreement, he may be called 'one and indivisible' (*EE* 7.6.1241b14–15); the two parts within himself (the rational and the irrational, cf. *NE* 1.13.1102a28) are 'impossible to draw asunder' (*EE* 7.6.1241b30). Of course, in an ordinary and important sense, even an acratic man is one man: his 'whole soul' acts voluntarily even if its rational part is coerced by its irrational one (2.8.1224b21–9); he is 'still one so long as he is alive' (7.6.1241b37). Otherwise, his situation would not be what it is, and how Bradley describes it: 'The self feels itself divided against itself; and, unless they both fall within one subject, how is this possible?' (op. cit. 323). His predicament is precisely that he is one but not at one, one mind but not a single will. In terms of the 'self', we could talk either inclusively (like Bradley) of a divided self, or exclusively of a beleaguered self.

It is in the light of a notion of the self as a persona realized in choices and desires, or as an instantiation of a character, that Aristotle chooses to understand the commonplace that a man should love his friends 'for their sakes' (e.g. *NE* 8.3.1156b10). He associates that phrase with 'in themselves' (1156b9), and 'because of themselves' (b10, cf. 8.4.1157a18, b3), which in turn he connects with a man's character (1156b12, 1157b3). Similarly, enjoying a man *qua* himself goes with enjoying him for his character (*EE* 7.2.1237b2–4). In a way, that was just the problem. What has become clear by now is that Aristotle is being idiosyncratic, not careless: he is not confounding common concepts, but reinterpreting them. So far, this is just an alternative diagnosis; to grasp what motivates the idiosyncrasy, we need to pursue how Aristotle's view of character as what friendship is ideally *about* lends itself to an intelligible reconstrual of the structure of friendship.

Before we set off on that pursuit, however, we may derive some preliminary illumination from Jean Buridan's commentary. To the proposal that a moral persona is the focus of friendship he foresees an objection: does the real object then become 'not the loved person, but his virtues, which neither are animate nor love in return'?[9] In a way

---

[9] *Quaestiones in decem libros Ethicorum Aristotelis ad Nicomachum*, 8.4.

that I have already discussed with reference to Plato's *Phaedrus*, the objection confuses the object of love with its ground; but that confusion is rather invited than avoided by Aristotle's restrictive identification of 'each man' with a moral persona. Buridan's reply, without sorting that out, enriches Aristotle's appeal to what friends are 'because of themselves' and not incidentally (*NE* 8.4.1156b10–11, 1157b4):

> The virtues are spoken of in this way: they are said to be present in the possessor because of himself, to the extent that it is in man's power to become virtuous, or that virtue cannot be taken away from him against his will. But it is not in the same way because of himself that a man may be useful or pleasant to another: for it is not in his power to be young and pretty, nor to be rich or able to serve the other's business; nor, indeed, is the life of the other in his power, though if it is lost he will no longer be useful or pleasant to him (loc. cit.).

Here a simple distinction between intrinsic and relational properties prepares the way for a more reflective one between properties that are, or are not, within a man's power to acquire and to keep. Buridan assigns a special status to qualities that a man gains and retains by his own will, not by luck. (Even the man who repents too late of a bad character is what he is by his own will, if not his later wishes; cf. *NE* 3.5.1114a13–21.) Of course, we may wonder whether Aristotle might not have given more thought to the ways in which luck affects even character; but that is a point against him (if also one derivable from him, cf. 10.9.1179b21–31). It remains helpful to bring together, as Buridan does on Aristotle's behalf, a man's supposed responsibility for the character that he has, and Aristotle's focus upon a self that is his instantiation of that character. We can thus understand more fully why liking a man *qua* musical or medical is not to be counted as a way of liking him *qua* himself (*EE* 7.2.1237b1–5), and involves preferring a man's possessions to the man himself (b31–2). Although being medical or musical are capacities that one acquires oneself, and does not lose through a mishap like, say, being stranded on a desert island (two features which do differentiate them from Buridan's examples of being young or rich), yet the value of those capacities is purely instrumental and relational: a musician is pleasant, a doctor useful, to another (or, if he entertains or cures himself, to himself *qua* other). By contrast, a good character has an intrinsic value (though it is also pleasant and useful) that it does not owe to any accidental relation to someone else. This point already helps to explain why, if we *are* to attach a man's 'self' especially to certain of his qualities, being good is a better candidate than being pleasant or useful.

3

When a man's desires do form a unity, they provide an intrapersonal model for interpersonal friendship (cf. *NE* 9.4.1166a29–31, *EE* 7.6.1240b3–4). Indeed, so long as we think of the parts of the soul as apart, we may even take their relationship as a paradigm of friendship (1166a34–5, 1240b28–31).[10] The ideal is that one's friend should be 'another self' (*allos* or *heteros autos*, *NE* 9.4.1166a32, 9.9.1170b6, *EE* 7.12.1245a30); in a phrase apparently familiar, friends should have, or be, 'a single soul' (*NE* 9.8.1168b7, *EE* 7.6.1240b3). To gloss 'another', 'A friend wishes to be as it were a separate self' (7.12.1245a34–5). To add a little content by a commonplace, 'The like is friend to the like' (*NE* 9.3.1165b17, *EE* 7.1.1235a6); in short, 'Likeness is friendship' (*NE* 8.8.1159b3). What sort of unity is Aristotle envisaging?

Two kinds of unity are not intended. One is the extreme fusion envisaged by the Aristophanes of Plato's *Symposium*, that of the lovers 'who desire to grow together in the excess of their affection, and from being two to become one, in which case one or both would certainly perish' (*Pol* 2.4.1262b12–14). Aristotle's complaint is not clearly just: how can both perish if someone survives, and how can one be said to perish if there could be no way of deciding which one? It is at least clear that he does not himself look for the obliteration of those distinguishing differences which, whether within the soul or between souls, are presupposed by the language of friendship. For instance, a man may prefer causing a friend to act well to acting well himself (*NE* 9.8.1169a33–4), which requires an interaction that still displays a difference in role. Another kind of unity that needs to be set aside is that variously achieved in the relations between master and slave, and parent and infant, where one can be called 'part' of the other

---

[10] That is what Aristotle says; but to what extent an individual can internalize the features ascribed to friendship not by common opinion (cf. 1166a3–8, 1240b4–11), but by Aristotle's theory (as I shall be expounding it), would need examination.

(e.g. *NE* 5.6.1134b11, *Pol* 1.6.1255b11). But how is that so different from a free adult's being 'another self', whether to his parents, or to his friends? One way of glossing the phrase 'a single soul' might be by way of a sentence in Augustine's *Confessions*: 'Well did he say of his friend, "half of my soul"; for I felt that his soul and mine had been one soul in two bodies' (4.6). Stephen Clark quotes this, but adds a warning: 'This life is not simply one's own, for that would be to treat one's friends as mere appendages. Kings get many eyes, ears, and hands by making colleagues of their friends (*Pol* 3.16.1287b29–31), but one who is treated as a tool, for utility or pleasure, is not being treated as a free man, one who is for himself.'[11] This is well said: another person who was somehow part of oneself would be a natural object of exploitation. Even if one viewed him as more than a 'mere appendage', and had some concern for his welfare as part of one's own, there would be nothing to exclude a 'trading off' whereby one might repeatedly balance his loss by one's own gain elsewhere and profit against his will at his expense. For Aristotle, the demands of friendship extend as widely as those of justice (*EE* 7.10.1242a19–22), and a man can exercise no injustice in an unqualified sense towards a chattel or child that are 'as it were part of himself' (*NE* 5.6.1134b9–11). Such behaviour might seem perfectly reasonable from certain points of view (if it maximizes welfare), and quite different from the mutually harmful treatment of friends that Aristotle expects of the vicious (9.8.1169a13–15) and the pleasure-seeking (*EE* 7.2.1236b16); but it is not to treat the other as a friend. A crucial point is that 'another self' is be set beside 'I myself', not (say) 'my present self' (on whom it may simply be right to impose hardship for the sake of future benefit). I am to care for my friend in the kind of way in which I care about my whole welfare, not just part of it.

Yet, if we construe 'welfare' independently of morality, this may not take us far enough, for we may want to exclude any thoughts like these:

May we not at least treat our neighbour as we treat ourselves? . . . Supposing we acted in the sense of self-sacrifice, what would forbid us to sacrifice our neighbour as well?—just as the state and as princes have done hitherto, when they sacrificed one citizen to another 'for the sake of the general interest', as they put it.[12]

---

[11] *Aristotle's Man* (Oxford, 1975), 109.
[12] Nietzsche, *Daybreak*, 2.146.

The interests that I may be willing to sacrifice for some cause may be all my interests, and not just some of them for the sake of others; so why should not loving another as myself involve an equal willingness to sacrifice his interests for the sake of interests not his own? If we want to resist this, we need to distinguish two kinds of 'other-sacrifice', as one might call it, in order to permit only the second and more friendlike:

1. I sacrifice your interests against your will, or without your knowledge, for some good cause; then the moral advantage (such as it is) is all mine, the material disadvantage all yours.[13]
2. Instead of sacrificing my own interests I stand back, and let you willingly sacrifice your interests; then we share the moral advantage, you through material sacrifice, I through moral sacrifice.

It is (2) alone which Aristotle envisages between friends: 'He may even give up actions to his friend; it may be finer to become the cause of his friend's acting than to act himself' (*NE* 9.8.1169a32–4).

Of course the upshot is a paradox: my moral sacrifice is at the same time, if moral generosity is indeed a virtue like material generosity, a moral gain. Is the paradox endurable? I think not. A close relation of it has been noticed by Anselm Müller. Suppose that *A* is an altruist who can escape suffering wrong from *B* only by wronging *B* himself. (Perhaps *B* will slander him and be believed unless he gets in quickly by slandering *B* first.) What should he do? Müller diagnoses a quandary:

On the one hand, he ought to opt for the (moral) disadvantage of doing wrong himself; on the other hand, though, this 'generous' conduct is in turn a moral advantage which he ought to relinquish to the other person. One could thus (by using a recursive definition) construct an unending list of incompatible advantages. But unfortunately a theory dies of one single irremediable contradiction.[14]

If we replace, within the first sentence just quoted, the phrase 'doing wrong himself' by 'not doing good himself', the paradox becomes precisely that into which Aristotle has stumbled. Müller's way out is to reject 'the concept of moral advantage': 'The contradiction which has just been made evident only confirms the suspicion that my (morally) good conduct has nothing to do with that which is good for

---

[13] I might, for instance, imitate Walter Raleigh's courtesy to a monarch using your cloak.

[14] 'Radical Subjectivity: Morality versus Utilitarianism', *Ratio* 19 (1977), 128.

me in the sense of "advantageous".[15] But that concept is most explicitly expressed by Aristotle in the very passage under discussion: the good man spurns material goods in order to *get possession of* the fine (9.8.1169a20–2, cf. 1168b27). This is not an optional misstatement: the whole argument of the passage is that notional 'self-sacrifice', which would seem to be a refutation by example of the doctrine that each man's *eudaimoniā* is his own exclusive goal, in fact displays a higher possessiveness.[16] The good man who takes less than his share of material goods is taking more than his share either of reputation or of the intrinsically fine (5.9.1136b21–2). Wealth and fineness can be compared as objects of acquisition: the latter is the greater (9.8.1169a26–9). It is true that fineness is also contrasted with 'the goods that are objects of competition' (a21); but that expresses not an awareness of the fatal paradox, but a dim view of most people (cf. 1168b17–19).[17]

Though radically faulty, Aristotle's conception, by articulating the second kind of 'other-sacrifice', at least provides an answer to Nietzsche's question about sacrificing one's neighbour like oneself: even if I allow, or enable, my friend to sacrifice himself (perhaps for my sake), there is no exploitation so long as, by offering him an opportunity of acting finely, I am not putting him to use in a way from which he derives no sufficient benefit. A wish to share with one's friends benefits of all kinds, moral and material, is implicit in a later remark: 'As a man is to himself, so he is to his friend' (9.12.1171b33–4). A pre-eminent part of my own good, in Aristotle's evaluation, is possession of the fine; if I trick or conscript another into subserving some overriding cause, I monopolize the fineness myself. He is to me more nearly 'another self' if I wish him to enjoy every kind of good that I value for myself.[18] However, a kind of moral partiality on one's own

---

[15] Ibid. 129. Cf. Nietzsche, *Twilight of the Idols* (Harmondsworth, 1968), 'Maxims and Arrows' 19: 'With virtue one renounces "advantage".' However, Nietzsche appears to allow moral advantage within a higher morality in *Human, All Too Human*, 1.2.95.

[16] Ascription of the doctrine to Aristotle is admittedly controversial; it is defended in Ackrill's 'Aristotle on *Eudaimonia*', and my 'Aristotle's Ethical Holism', *Mind* 89 (1980).

[17] Notice that, in weighing moral against material goods, Aristotle assumes that they are goods irreducibly different in kind, but not that they escape generalizable quantitative comparisons. Here (and I believe elsewhere) he can be cited on the side of the multiplicity of values, but not of their incommensurability.

[18] Cf. Roger Scruton, *Sexual Desire* (London, 1986), 230, final paragraph. In general, Scruton shows a natural sympathy with Aristotle which compensates for his hostility to Plato (and Freud).

behalf is even commended: 'In all the actions, therefore, that men are praised for, the good man is seen to assign to himself the greater share in what is fine' (9.8.1169a34–b1, cf. 8.7.1159a8–12). (Thus 9.12.1171b33–4 are really an overstatement.) What Aristotle does seem to expect of me is that I should have for 'another self' the same kind (if not degree) of concern that I have for myself; and hence that I should hate to sacrifice him for the sake of my own fineness in a way that does nothing for his. Such a sacrifice of another might yet, on occasion, be the fine thing to do (consider Agamemnon and Iphigenia); but it would not be to treat him as a friend.

4

So far, talk of a friend as 'another self' has not amounted in substance to anything at all startling; yet Aristotle's conception does contain surprises, which it is time to attend to. Let me begin with an utterly un-Aristotelian quotation. Proust is not betraying a deviant idiosyncrasy when he declares, in the tone of an anathema, 'Despite the illusion of which we would wish to be the dupes and with which, out of love, friendship, politeness, human respect, or duty, we dupe one another, we exist alone. Man is the creature who cannot exit from himself, who only knows his fellows in himself, and, in saying the contrary, lies' (*A la recherche du temps perdu*, iii. 450). He is taking over a melancholy, yet flattering, idea from the legacy of romanticism: every human being is unique, and condemned to misunderstand, and be misunderstood by, every other.[19] Aristotle had no such isolationist picture of man even to react against when he remarks, 'No one would choose all good things on condition of being alone, since man is a civic creature and one whose nature is to live with others' (*NE* 9.8.1169b17–19). However, he had at hand an older contrast, with the nature of God: 'For us well-being has reference to something other than ourselves, but in his case he is himself his own well-being' (*EE* 7.12.1245b18–19). The thought applies especially within friendship, but generally to the whole range of social activity. To impose a dichotomy, this may take, among desirable forms, that of (a) *beneficence* (cf. *NE* 9.7, especially 1168a3–9), or (b) *co-operation*. It holds of human beings that 'by oneself it is not easy to be continuously

---

[19] Cf. Nietzsche, *Daybreak*, 5.491.

active, but with others and towards others it is easier' (9.9.1170a5–6). Here 'with' primarily signals (b), while 'towards' signals (a). Through (a) a man's *faring well* (which is passive), through (b) a man's *acting well* (which is active)—both falling under an ambiguous 'doing well' (*eu prattein*)—become the product or result of another man's actions.[20] Both kinds of benefit, and not only the acts that are movements of his own body, can be identified with the agent *qua* active: consider, in the case of (a), 'The handiwork *is*, in a sense, the producer in activity' (9.7.1168a7), and, in the case of (b), the characterization of a friend's acts as 'one's own' (*oikeiās*, 9.9.1170a3). Both may serve as objects of the choice that most intimately is a man (6.2.1139b5), that is a human self or persona primarily realized in choices. We are not to suppose that what such a self really is, or is realized in, stops dead with a man's choices and falls short of what he chooses ('primarily' does not entail 'only'). Just as Aristotle lacks the sceptical, moral, or metaphysical grounds that have tended since Descartes to push back the identity of the practical self behind its actions to its acts of will, so he allows that self's identity or realization to overflow in the opposite direction, so as to extend into the life, active and passive, of another.[21]

The drawback with beneficence is that it is more blessed to give than to receive: 'To the benefactor that is fine which depends on his action, . . . whereas to the patient there is nothing fine in the agent, but at most something advantageous, and this is less pleasant and lovable' (*NE* 9.7.1168a10–12). The fineness is at once (to us paradoxically) the monopoly of the benefactor, and locatable in the beneficiary; the benefit, being the benefactor in action, has itself within that perspective a moral quality. While the benefactor is thus linked forwards to the benefit, the beneficiary is linked backwards to the benefactor's choice or disposition; but while the benefit shows up as fine from the point of view of the benefactor, the disposition merely shows up as useful from the point of view of the beneficiary. The

---

[20] For Aristotle, to fare well is to become in a good or better position to act well (cf. 1.8.1099a31–b7).

[21] For an early indication, take 1.7.1097b8–11. The moral ground I have in mind is the recoil from the notion of moral luck, here expressed in assessing an agent's moral success solely in terms of the content of his intentions; Aristotle's *eudaimoniā* is not so insulated from external and interpersonal contingency. Robert Gay has pointed out to me that Aristotle's view of the benefit to a friend as belonging within the lives of both friends reiterates the structure of his general view of change as present in the patient but actualizing the capacities at once of patient and of agent (cf. *Phys* 3.3).

picture is complex, and yields a superficial inconsistency: on the one hand, 'the better should be more loved than he loves' (8.7.1158b25); on the other, benefactor loves beneficiary more than beneficiary loves benefactor (9.7.1167b17–18). That is explicitly resolved: in loving the beneficiary *qua* beneficiary, the benefactor is loving himself in action (1167b34–1168a9). An objector might extract a contrast between loving someone *qua* oneself in action, and loving him *qua* himself, but that would be merely verbal: where the benefit goes deep (as in moral education), the beneficiary owes himself (that is, his choosing self) to the benefactor. More troublesome, again, is the notion of moral advantage: if the benefactor gains the fine while the beneficiary merely gains the advantageous, the benefactor owes more to the beneficiary than the latter owes to him, which should mean that the beneficiary gains yet more of the fine, and so on through 'an unending series of incompatible advantages' (Müller). The regress of contradictions can be evaded so long as it is no merit in the beneficiary to be capable of being benefited. In that case, while merit and goodness are equivalent in moral benefactor *qua* benefactor, they come apart in moral beneficiary *qua* beneficiary, since the latter, through owing his goodness wholly to the former, achieves goodness without merit; hence more gratitude is owed to benefactor than to beneficiary, even though the moral benefit to the benefactor is greater (as it ought to be, cf. 8.14.1163a26–7) than that to the beneficiary. However, where it is a merit in the beneficiary to be benefitable (as usually in the case of moral benefit, given the doctrine of the natural virtues that make a man morally educable, 6.13.1144b4–6), it will become irresolvably contradictory which party owes more to the other.

In co-operation, each party helps the other not merely to be capable of action, but *in* action. More interestingly than in the case of beneficence, there is a range of possible ways in which their activities may be correlated. The simplest case involves precise similarity: one may think of David Wiggins's somewhat bookish examples of 'digging a ditch with a man whom one likes, or helping the same man to talk or drink the sun down the sky'.[22] Yet there is also similarity-cum-complementarity: a pair of piano-duettists are describable jointly as performing some piano duet, separately as playing different parts. There may even be great inequality, as in the role that Alfred Brendel

---

[22] 'Truth, Invention and the Meaning of Life', in *Needs, Values, Truth* (Oxford, 1987), 101.

ascribes to the silent section of the audience at a piano recital: 'In the concert hall, each motionless listener is part of the performance. The concentration of the player charges the electric tension in the auditorium and returns to him magnified; thus the audience makes its contribution, helping the pianist.'[23] In all these cases, the activity of each party can be viewed as the exercise at once of a capacity of his own, and of a capacity (whether similar or complementary) of the other's; hence the activity of each is not only himself, but also the other, in action.

Less satisfactory, so far, is another kind of case. Suppose that two people, A and B, could *each* become a ditch-digger or a concert-pianist, but not *both*; so they decide between themselves that, say, A will dig ditches, while B plays the piano.[24] To rephrase their decision more suggestively, A becomes *the* ditch-digger, B *the* piano-player (where the 'the's make implicit reference to the pair of them in describing the occupation of each). Here each pursues a career of which the other is also capable, in accordance with a mutual decision. If this case is less happy, it is because A's ditch-digging and B's piano-playing are exercises of a capacity which the other happens to share, but not of his possession of that capacity. B can tell A 'I owe this piano-playing to you'; but A is not realized in B's playing as he is in his own digging.[25] Yet the example is illuminating: it indicates that what has so far shown up as crucial is the relation between capacity and activity. In the more satisfactory cases, the activity of one man is in part an actualization of the capacity of another.

This last case has a further defect: it exemplifies not co-operating in an activity, but ministering to one. Suppose that I am philosophizing with a colleague over coffee: even if the coffee stimulates my progress, the steward and my interlocutor contribute in quite different ways; for the steward sharpens my capacity (so acting upon me *qua* passive), while my interlocutor joins in its exercise (so acting with me *qua* active). If other colleagues refrain from interrupting us, they promote the exercise of our capacities, but without being party to it; they may

---

[23] *Musical Thoughts and Afterthoughts* (London, 1976), 138–9.

[24] I owe the substance of this example to a helpful paper which I heard Irwin give in Oxford in November 1982; an actual story with the same structure is told about Dürer and a fellow apprentice.

[25] It might be different if A could solve his own dilemma by splitting into A* and A**, so becoming *himself* at once manual labourer and musician (cf. Derek Parfit, *Reasons and Persons*, 264).

be ranked with the steward as supplying the right background conditions. In the previous example, A makes possible B's piano-playing, while B makes possible A's ditch-digging; but neither participates in the other's activity. If two people are to come together in an activity, it is necessary that the contribution of each should be the result, and not just a consequence, of the contribution of the other. Indeed, such simultaneous mutual dependence is possible between results, but not consequences. In co-operation, but not beneficence, the well-doing (*eupráxia*) of each is so intimately and immediately connected with the well-doing of the other as to count as both agents in action.

Aristotle himself gives us some general characterizations, and some examples; he hardly uses the one to illuminate the other. 'Living together' (*suzēn*, which means a life, not a home, in common) is glossed in various ways: 'the sharing of words and deeds' (*NE* 4.6.1126b11–12), 'the sharing of words and thought' (9.9.1170b11–12), 'perception and knowledge in common' (*EE* 7.12.1244b15–16). The variations are not inconsistencies, and the total generality is intentional: 'Whatever existence means for each class of men, whatever it is for whose sake they value life, in that they wish to occupy themselves with their friends' (*NE* 9.12.1172a1–3, cf. a6–8 as emended by Bekker, *EE* 7.12.1245b7–8). Shared pleasures may range from the vulgar to the more divine (*EE* 7.12.1245a37–9, cf. a19–22). Yet mere eating and drinking together, such as we find among animals without speech, take on no new value: 'For what is the difference between doing these things near to others or apart from them, if you take away speech?' (a13–14). Of more point than feeding together is feasting together (b5). Less than ideal too are teaching and learning: 'For if one learns, he is not as he should be, and if he teaches, his friend is not; and likeness is friendship' (a17–18). That seems rather severe: if learning is an activity, the inequality does not exclude co-operation. More illuminating, however, is a description of mutual improvement:

The friendship of good men is good, being augmented by their companionship; and they are thought to become better too by their activities and by improving each other; for from each other they take the stamp of the characteristics they approve of—whence the saying 'fine deeds from fine men' (*NE* 9.12.1172a10–14, cf. 9.9.1170a11–13, 10.9.1180a31–2).

Here the metaphor of stamping an impression upon wax is used to convey the close causal connection between the virtue of each and the activity of the other (both in development). It must be because of this that a man may contemplate 'good actions and actions that are his own' in the form of 'the actions of a good man who is his friend' (9.9.1170a2–4, cf. 3.3.1112b27–8). There can be many variations, so long as the right kind of causal structure is maintained. In some cases action may be shared simply through a preliminary sharing in thought: if, in a friendship involving inequality, one party possesses practical wisdom, which is 'prescriptive', while the other possesses understanding (*sunesis*), which is 'only critical' and serves for 'judging what someone else says about matters with which practical wisdom is concerned' (6.10.1143a8–10, 14–15), they may directly share in choice, indirectly in action. In other cases the action itself may be co-operative, either in such a way that the acts of both have to be taken together for the purposes of assessment (as when it is only in conjunction that they count as repaying a debt, or achieving some other 'threshold'-effect), or just in that the activity of each is an intended result of the activity of the other (as when two soldiers make a stand in battle, each keeping the other to the mark). Emphasis on the ethical aspect of the action (that is its relation to choice and character, but not necessarily what we might isolate as its 'moral' import) may seem restrictive, but in fact extends the possibilities: in the example of ditch-digging and piano-playing, *B*'s playing is no actualization of *A*'s ability to play, but it does put into action *A*'s and *B*'s shared decision that *B* should be the pianist; interpreted in relation not to technical capacities but to states of character, *B*'s activity can, after all, be viewed as a realization in action of a state of *A*'s.

Thus there are two distinctions to be made between ways in which activity may constitute a deliberate part of the life not only of the direct agent (the owner, say, of the relevant hands and feet), but of a collaborator: they may share only in the decisions, or also in their execution; and the activity may manifest their capacities (similar or complementary), or just their states of character. I have already said that emphasis on character (which may strike us, wrongly, as moralistic) lets in more, not less. For Aristotle, it has a further advantage. Important in his philosophy of action is a contrast between action (*prāxis*), which has intrinsic value, and production (*poiēsis*), which has only instrumental value. Production at once brings into existence some desired end-product (whence its name), and gives concrete form (for instance, handing over cash) to an abstract conception (such as acting justly).[26] In terms of that contrast, the style and technique of B's playing, which qualify it *qua* production, belong solely to B (manifesting, say, his taste and skill); it is the value of the playing *qua* action (reflecting, say, the practical good sense of their joint decision) which belongs *in toto* to A and B. Thus part of the playing's instrumental value is to be credited to B alone, while all of its intrinsic value is to credited to A and B together. A and B may well be happy that the value of the playing in which they share without remainder is its intrinsic value.

5

It is presumably necessary, if an agent is to gain the fine in doing a virtuous act, that he should do it virtuous*ly*. For that, Aristotle laid down the following conditions: 'In the first place he must have knowledge, secondly he must choose the acts, and choose them for their own sakes, and thirdly his action must proceed from a firm and unchangeable character' (*NE* 2.4.1105a30–3). Applied to a pair of friends acting in concert, this requires that both should have achieved ethical maturity; each must ascribe an intrinsic value to the other's acting well; each must join in choosing the acts of the other; and each must know what the other is doing. The last two conditions require the friends to live together, that is to live a life in common (not particularly within four walls). If they lose all contact, then, despite any continuing personal debts, the success of one can impinge upon the *eudaimoniā* of the other no more than if the latter were dead, that is either not at all (cf. 3.6.1115a26–7), or only marginally (cf. 1.11.1101b1–9). So far I have explored various ways in which an activity may issue out of the practical dispositions of all those who minister to it, or decide upon it, or take part in it. Ideal seemed to be actual involvement in both choice and action. That preference is reinforced if we consider the first, epistemic condition upon acting well: to participate in the decision is to be aware how the activity is motivated; to participate in its execution is to be aware how it is performed. In praising such a life in common Aristotle goes still

---

[26] *Nicomachean Ethics* 6.2.1139b1–4 seem to be indicating both aspects, without separating them. They do not have to appear together: if, say, I contemplate some truths by soliloquizing in Greek, my words give my contemplation a concrete form without (unless I needed to refresh my memory) leaving behind any end-product.

further: in two ways (or rather, as I understand them, styles), one in each *Ethics*, he argues that even a grasp *of one's own activity* has to be achieved with a friend and not by oneself. Each depends in its own manner upon doing justice to both aspects of the characterization of a friend as a 'another self': his acts must be close enough to be ascribable to oneself, and yet sufficiently removed for one to be aware of them in ways only applicable to the acts of another. As is typical, the *Eudemian Ethics* is the more abstract and metaphysical, the *Nicomachean* the more concrete and empirical; each requires somewhat speculative (or constructive) expansion at a crucial point, upon which I shall focus.

A human being is a subject in search of a determinate nature, which it can achieve in two ways in perception (as also in cognition). The first is simply in perceiving the sensible forms of things: the perceiver takes on such forms himself *qua* perceiver, so that in perceiving them he is perceiving himself (*EE* 7.12.1245a5–8); and being perceived is one way of being determinate (a2–3). Quite how we understand this must be a function of how we understand Aristotle on perception in general: in the case of sight, for example, his view may be, idiosyncratically, that the eye actually takes on colour; or else, less informatively, that the eye takes on whatever form is needed for a man to be seeing colour.[27] For present purposes, the point remains that in perception we become transparent to what we are perceiving, so that perceiving it and perceiving ourselves are the same mental act (somewhat like seeing outside and seeing through a window). That is one way of being aware of oneself, yet without achieving self-consciousness. It is for the latter that one's fellows are so valuable: 'To perceive a friend must be in a way to perceive oneself' (or perhaps 'to perceive oneself in a certain manner', 1245a35–6). For as, say, I see a friend looking into my eyes, his looking is to me not transparent (as it is to him) but opaque, so that I see him looking into my eyes without thereby seeing them myself. (I speak of him 'looking' instead of 'seeing' precisely in order to capture the shift, within my perspective, out of transparency into opacity.) It is from him that I can

---

[27] Cf. Barnes, 'Aristotle's Concept of Mind', in Barnes, Malcolm Schofield, Richard Sorabji (eds.), *Articles on Aristotle 4: Psychology and Aesthetics* (London, 1979), § 7. The interpretation I favour is that the eye does take on colour, but rather in the manner of a transparent medium's receiving light (as he, not we, would understand that) than of an opaque medium's receiving a dye.

learn most easily to distinguish the perceiver from the perceived; I then generalize to my own case. All this just carries one from consciousness of one's perceiving fellows to an abstract self-consciousness *qua* perceiver. But its analogue with choice and action shared with a friend of similar character yields a richer self-awareness: in my own person, my projects are (to extend the metaphor) transparent on to their objects, so that my focus is upon the objects, not my pursuit of them; but joining in those projects with a friend I become conscious of his pursuing them, and so conscious in a new way of pursuing them myself (for we are pursuing them together). I thus become explicitly aware of myself not just abstractly as an agent, but as an agent with a certain character, thereby achieving not a bare self-consciousness but a real self-knowledge. And to retain that knowledge, I need to retain my friends.

The *Nicomachean Ethics* places emphasis upon an extended and intricate argument more impressive in structure than illuminating in detail (9.9.1170a13–b19). It is more helpful to flesh out an earlier train of thought:

If . . . the good man's activity is virtuous and pleasant in itself, . . . and a thing's being one's own is one of the attributes that make it pleasant, and we can contemplate our neighbours better than ourselves and their actions better than our own, and if the actions of virtuous men who are their friends are pleasant to good men (since these have both the attributes that are naturally pleasant)—if this be so, the blessed man will need friends of this sort, since he chooses to contemplate worthy actions and actions that are his own, and the actions of a good man who is his friend have both these qualities (1169b31–1170a4).

What does Aristotle have in mind here that could justify a thought that good men *need* friends? Two possible answers (which I shall number) might be located in the probably pseudo-Aristotelian *Magna moralia*:

(1) That we are not able to see what we are from ourselves is plain from the way in which we blame others without being aware that we do the same things ourselves; and this is the effect of goodwill or passion, and there are many of us who are blinded by these things so that we judge not aright. (2) As then when we wish to see our own face, we do so by looking into the mirror, in the same way when we wish to know ourselves we can obtain that knowledge by looking at our friend; for the friend is, we assert, a second self (2.16.1213a16–24).[28]

---

[28] John Cooper attaches great weight to this passage in 'Aristotle on Friendship', in A. O. Rorty (ed.) *Essays on Aristotle's Ethics*, § 6. It is consistent that he ascribes the

(1) is suggestive, but unclear in detail: is it 'we', or 'many of us', who need friends? If it is the latter, how are prejudice and passion to be cured by a kind of friendship of which, at least in Aristotle's opinion, the prejudiced and passionate are incapable? (2) is felicitous, but not more than suggestive: one way of explaining the mirror analogy would precisely be in the *Eudemian* terms. Briefer, but better, is a remark in the *Politics*, about the qualities relevant to a justice that respects differences, that 'most men are bad judges in their own case' (3.9.1280a15–16); however, the word 'most' suggests that, like the author of the *Magna moralia*, Aristotle has in mind variable human defects rather than a universal aspect of the human condition. Why might *all* men be better able to recognize themselves in another? Illuminating in its own way is a thought of John Cooper's: 'The presumption is that even an intimate friend remains distinct enough to be studied objectively; yet because one intuitively knows oneself to be fundamentally the same in character as he is, one obtains through him an objective view of oneself' ('Aristotle on Friendship', 322). This is sensitive and attractive,[29] but at some distance from all these texts. What in Aristotle might play the role of Cooper's 'intuition'? The *Nicomachean* passage that we are considering offers an immediate answer: co-operation. It is that which makes one's friends actions 'one's own' (*oikeiās*, 1170a3) in a justifiably extended sense;[30] and it is virtually that to which Cooper himself shifts when he writes of testing feelings of affinity 'through long experience both of the other person and of oneself' (op. cit. 323). *A* does not have to guess that *B* is a kindred spirit by 'one of those sympathies between men which, when they are not based upon physical attraction, are the only ones that are totally mysterious';[31] instead, he discovers that they share 'a single soul' through joining with *B* in deliberation and activity. Listening to *B*'s counsels, he finds that they articulate his own thoughts; observing

---

Magna moralia substantially to Aristotle himself; cf. his 'The *Magna moralia* and Aristotle's Moral Philosophy', *American Journal of Philology* 94 (1973). Others will find the author's treatment of 'goodwill' (*eunoia*) here, and more fully at 2.12.1212a1–13, typical of his 'constant botching', as Anthony Kenny has termed it; *The Aristotelian Ethics* (Oxford, 1978), 219. Cooper's own reflections on Aristotle's behalf are, of course, on a higher level.

[29] Compare Bertrand Russell's instant sense of affinity, albeit extraordinary, on meeting Joseph Conrad: *The Autobiography of Bertrand Russell: 1872–1914* (London, 1967), 207–10.

[30] It is only momentarily stumbling that the term is also applied in the same passage, in a restrictive sense, to the actions that are 'one's own' and *not* one's friend's (1169b35).

[31] Proust, *A la recherche du temps perdu*, ii. 104.

B's actions, he finds that they realize his own preferences. Many of these thoughts and preferences could not have been dictated to B from the beginning: they only become apparent to A as B speaks and acts in ways that match them, so that A owes to B his awareness of the mentality to which B answers as a perfect partner. The same should be simultaneously true of B in relation to A: each reveals the mind of the other to him in a way that he could not have achieved on his own. It is through observing the other, who is more directly visible to him than he is himself, that each discovers himself. And to maintain that discovery, even as he changes with age and develops with experience, each must maintain his friendships.

6

It is time to retrace Aristotle's transition from Vlastos's 'disinterested affection for the person we love' to his 'appreciation of the excellencies instantiated by that person' (*Platonic Studies*, 33, n. 100). Loving a person 'for his own sake' (*NE* 8.2.1155b31) I love him for the person he is (8.3.1156a17–18), that is *qua* chooser (cf. 6.2.1139b5). To love him *qua* chooser is to identify with his choices: consider the *Eudemian* concept of 'reciprocal choice' (*antiprohairesis*, 7.2.1236b3, 1237a32–3). It is above all through his choices that I try to benefit him: in a life of co-operation he partly owes his choices to me, as party both to the way of life within which they operate, and to the practical thinking out of which they issue. Consequently, his activity displays the character that we share, and the fact that we share it; it is partly in his activity that I find my own *eudaimoniā*. (In a friendship of equality, the converse holds equally of him in relation to my activity.) Notional egoism, directed at my own *eudaimoniā*, becomes practical altruism, since my *eudaimoniā* and his overlap. The phrase 'disinterested affection' becomes partly misleading, unless it simply excludes a selfish affection where there is no such overlap; but loving another for his own sake receives here an analysis that is at the same time an explanation of its possibility.[32]   .

---

[32] Of course this is not far from the lesser mysteries of the *Symposium*: here too, it has to be supposed that a man can identify with stretches of living of which he is not himself the subject, so long as they stand in the right relation to stretches of living of which he is the subject. However, there is one important contrast: Plato places weight on sequences of mental states, Aristotle on decisions and actions taken in common. Aristotle's doubts about whether the living can affect the *eudaimoniā* of the dead (*NE*

The account cannot apply if we are not at one in respect of the relevant desires and choices, both individually and jointly. If your motivations are relevantly conflicting, I can still act through your choices if you are self-controlled rather than acratic; but that will not add to my *eudaimonia*, for acting well involves not only doing the right thing, but doing it with pleasure (cf. 1.8.1099a7, 7.11.1152b6–7).[33] If, slightly differently, the goal of your choices (that is, your conception of *eudaimonia*) is relevantly at odds with mine, I may still fortuitously be able to endorse your particular choice (cf. 6.9.1142b22–6); but your activity will not fall under any conception of acting well that both of us can recognize as lending it final point. If your choice is itself at odds with mine, we shall be at odds in action.

Crucial here are two ideas:

1. Your activity may at the same time be myself in action, and your acting well part of my own *eudaimonia*;
2. I cannot count myself as benefiting you if I help you to act out a conception of *eudaimonia* that I do not myself endorse.

(1) is needed to accommodate joint action (which is more than action of my own contingent upon independent action of yours) within a formally egocentric doctrine of my own *eudaimonia* as the only final goal of my action. If Aristotle were to discard (1), he would need to revise his general theory in order to generate more than a shadow of friendship. But it is (2) that now remains problematic. Why, instead of a reciprocity of choice, where each party's choice is the mirror as well as the collaborator of the other's, should we not permit a more complex structure, whereby, enabling you to realize in some action a conception of *eudaimonia* that is not mine, I could count as myself realizing in that action a second-order motive of my own, one of tolerant benevolence? Would this not, if anything, be Vlastos's 'disinterested affection' in action? It goes deep that this was not an option for Aristotle. Consider first how, in the *Eudemian Ethics*, he distinguishes the good man as 'one for whom the natural goods are goods' (8.3.1248b26–7); these 'may be harmful for some because of their states of character' (b30). He compares the food of the healthy which

---

1.11) indicate that causal continuities impress him less than the communion of minds (though we shall find him implicitly coming closer to Plato when treating the relations of parents and children).

33 Yet it might be conceded that helping the self-controlled is helping them to approach closer to *eudaimonia*, and adding to one's own *eudaimonia* an approximation to some extra *eudaimonia* in recalcitrant material.

will not benefit the sick (b32–3). This might suggest that the foolish, unjust, or intemperate (listed in b31) need special goods to achieve their ends, just as the sick need a special diet to achieve health; but Aristotle specifies 'the natural goods' as 'things that are competed for' (b27, cf. *NE* 9.8.1169a21), giving as examples 'honour and wealth and bodily excellencies and good fortune and capacities' (b28–9), all things that the vicious need for pursuing their ends as much as the virtuous. So the parallel with the invalid's diet is inexact, for the thought is not that the vicious are benefited by receiving special goods as means to universal ends, but that they are harmed by receiving universally instrumental goods which will enable them to achieve their vicious ends. Extending a helping hand to such people is no kindness.

An underlying assumption is that a man's *eudaimoniā* is not to be assessed from his point of view, unless he is practically wise; *eudaimoniā* is not success in pursuing one's own projects whatever they may be. Aristotle already implies this assumption when he states, as a human commonplace, that people not only differ but *dispute* in specifying what constitutes *eudaimoniā* (*NE* 1.4.1095a18–21). Perhaps he feels no need to argue against a relativism which would reduce *eudaimoniā* to a function of the specific projects of the individual, for that is a position that neither he nor the common man is disposed to accept. In the terminology of Stephen Schiffer, choices of a way of life (and the wishes behind them) are 'reason-following', not 'reason-providing', guides to action.[34] 'Because I so choose' is not in itself any reason for action: resulting action will have as much point and reason as the choice itself. Some will not hold it against this view that it is deeply anti-utilitarian, or at least contrary to that variety of utilitarianism which, taking as its end the maximization of the satisfaction of desire, makes all preferences grounds of justification: to have a preference, however irrational, is to have a reason to fulfil it (and perhaps even a reason to maintain the preference as a means towards its own fulfilment). Such an attitude towards another person, translating all his preferences into positive considerations of one's own, would surely be a kind of 'disinterested affection'; but Aristotle can have none of it.

In this context one might ascribe to Aristotle a variety of cognitivism: to achieve *eudaimoniā* a man must specify it *correctly*. However, there is a way of construing this that makes its 'cognitivism' empty: if

---

[34] 'A Paradox of Desire', *American Philosophical Quarterly* 13 (1976), § 4.

the term *eudaimoniā* has prescriptive force as part of its meaning, I may well be debarred from counting as *eudaimōn* a man who realizes a conception of *eudaimoniā* that is not my own, and be able to co-operate, with a view towards their *eudaimoniā*, only with men of a character like mine. Yet from my point of view it adds nothing to require, perhaps for 'perfect' friendship, that they be good men; for within my perspective being good and having a character like mine are equivalent, and it no more underpins the perspective that it is mine than it undermines it that it may not be somebody else's. This more permissive conception of friendship (explicitly so if it replaces talk of goodness by talk of likeness, effectively so if it keeps talk of goodness but leaves notions of goodness as matters of taste or opinion) is suggested, at least to the modern reader, by two occasional features of Aristotle's presentation:

(a) He is happy to take over the popular sayings 'Likeness is friendship' (8.8.1159b3), and 'Like is dear to like' (9.3.1165b17, *EE* 7.1.1235a6);
(b) He sometimes envisages intending putative benefits (*NE* 9.4.1166a4, *EE* 7.6.1240a24–5) for supposedly good recipients (*NE* 9.3.1165b13, 9.4.1166a11, b3–4).

If Aristotle wants to demand more than this, it is a good question how he can earn it. Is 'perfect friendship' (e.g. 8.3.1156b7) more than an epithet of honour (in Hobbes's phrase) that he denies to those he does not approve of?

That this is not Aristotle's intention is already clear from the use to which he puts the slogans of (a), which is to confirm non-vacuously that perfect friendship is that of the good: 'Especially the likeness of those who are like in virtue' (that is, both virtuous) is friendship, 'for being steadfast in themselves they hold fast to each other' (8.8.1159b3–5). The same thought is more vividly expressed in his account of 'unanimity' (*homonoia*): good men 'are unanimous both in themselves and with one another, being, so to speak, set on the same things (for the wishes of such men are constant and not at the mercy of opposing currents like the Euripus)' (9.6.1167b5–7).[35] By contrast, bad men (whether thoroughly bad, or just bad, cf. 9.4.1166b5–7) have a soul 'rent by faction, and one element in it by reason of its

---

[35] Or, less colourfully, 'like a strait of the sea' (Ross and Barnes); but cf. *Meteor* 2.8.366a22–3. An unreliable tradition has Aristotle ending his life, after flight from Athens to Chalcis, studying the ebb and flow of the Euripus; cf. Anton-Hermann Chroust, *Aristotle* (London, 1973), i. 177–8.

wickedness grieves when it abstains from certain acts, while the other part is pleased, and one draws them this way and the other that, as if they were pulling them in pieces' (9.4.1166b19–22, cf. 1.8.1099a11–13). Such claims may surprise us, not least coming from Aristotle: do not they confound the wicked with the acratic in conceiving *both* as at odds with themselves? It is now even said explicitly that the bad are like the acratic (*NE* 9.4.1166b6–10, *EE* 7.6.1240b12–13). It may help to quote first one distinction that remains firm, and then two passages that are not consistent:

(I) The acratic and the self-indulgent man are also like one another; they are different, but both pursue bodily pleasures—the latter, however, also thinking that he ought to do so, while the former does not think this (7.9.1152a4–6).

(II.1) The self-indulgent man, as was said, has no regrets; for he stands by his choice; but any acratic man is subject to regrets (7.8.1150b29–31, cf. a21–2).

(II.2) If a man cannot at the same time be pained and pleased, at all events after a short time he is pained *because* he was pleased; and he could have wished that these things had not been pleasant to him; for bad men are laden with regrets (9.4.1166b22–5).

It is clear that Aristotle is stumbling through applying only two terms to three different types of misbehaviour: (a) without, or contrary to, choice; (b) according to choice but without constancy; (c) from a constant choice (a condition of fully acting *badly*, 2.4.1105a32–3). (I) above serves to differentiate (a) from (b) or (c); (II.1) and (II.2) are inconsistent between (b) and (c). When concerned to distance self-indulgence from acrasia, Aristotle ascribes to it both choice and constancy; when concerned to contrast badness of any kind with goodness, he concedes constancy only to goodness. The latter is always Aristotle's position when his topic is friendship. It has for us an important corollary: only good men identify themselves with their choices and actions over time in such a way that co-operation in thought and action can express friendship for a person who is more than a partial or transient self.

To leave the matter there would be deeply unsatisfactory. What might explain, and possibly even justify, Aristotle's association between constancy and goodness? It will not do simply to take constancy as a criterion of goodness: that, on its own, would leave open too many different ways of being good (including some quite unacceptable ones). Terence Irwin is illuminating.[36] The virtuous man

---

[36] *Aristotle: Nicomachean Ethics* (Indianapolis, 1985), ad 9.4.1166b6–25.

aims his choices at the fine, and his appetites fall into line; the vicious man aims his choices at the satisfaction of appetite. That puts the latter at the mercy of his appetites, not in the manner of the acratic man whose appetites override his choices, but in that his choices are contingent upon the fluctuating intensity of his appetites. Hence he will often later regret the intensity of an appetite which dictated a choice that would turn out expensive. As Aristotle puts it succinctly, 'He could have wished that these things had not been pleasant to him' (9.4.1166b23–4). He comes to regret not so much what he did, as that he had to do it. He makes and puts into effect his own choices, but in choosing he exercises no internal autonomy. To love such a man is to take on his ambivalence: one will too seldom be able to co-operate with him whole-heartedly, for his heart is not whole.

Interestingly, it is precisely because of the internal dissension of bad men that they can enjoy with the good an imperfect friendship that displays a degree of reciprocity and harmony: 'A good man may be a friend to a bad, the bad being of use to the good in relation to the good man's existing choice, the good to the acratic in relation to his existing choice, and to the bad in relation to his natural choice' (*EE* 7.2.1238b1–5). Why the asymmetry whereby bad men may serve good choices, but good men may not serve bad choices? We must suppose, I think, that the 'natural' choices are a proper subset of bad men's actual choices (whose necessity they have no need to regret); hence good men and bad men share some choices, in respect of which they can be of service to one another. This interpretation is confirmed by a later remark: 'A good man and a bad man may be friends . . . in so far as there is something good in all . . . or in so far as they suit each individual; for all have something of the good' (1239b9–14). The inference must be that all choose well enough to have some choices in common; these may suffice to link morally contrasted agents in fragmentary friendships.

It is, I suggest, of the essence of Aristotle's cognitivism about values that his faith that 'all have something of the good' is a special instance of an assumption about man's relation to the truth: 'Everyone has a natural aptitude (*oikeion ti*) for grasping truth' (*EE* 1.6.1216b30–31, cf. *Rhet* 1.1.1355a15–17). This has been well explored by Jonathan Barnes.[37] One remark of Aristotle's (*NE*

---

[37] 'Aristotle and the Methods of Ethics', *Revue Internationale de Philosophie* 34 (1980), § 5 ; the translation of 1216b30–1 is his (ibid. 508).

6.11.1143b6–9) he glosses to this effect: 'Human nature is so constituted that we possess a faculty for grasping truth—even if that
faculty must be refined by experience' (op. cit. 509). He then reasons:
'If nature does nothing in vain, and if we are naturally inclined
towards truth, it follows that we do, for the most part, attain the truth'
(ibid.). Such thinking underlies Aristotle's general investigative procedure: the maximal acceptance of common opinions turns out to be
not purely dialectical, in Aristotle's sense (serving to persuade those
who share them), but a propaedeutic of knowledge. What then lends
substance to a claim that there are practical truths which impinge
upon human recognition is partly that those who do pursue the fine as
a general goal tend to agree about its specification; it is also that these
truths, unlike their negations, are implicit in some of the choices
even of those who try to deny or disregard them.

So it has emerged that Aristotle was led to require of 'disinterested
affection for the person we love' that it include 'appreciation of the
excellencies instantiated by that person' (in Vlastos's phrases) not by a
failure to make distinctions, but by a train of thought that belongs
within an analysis of perfect friendship constrained by certain fundamental aspects of his ethical theory. To love another actively for his
sake is above all to identify with him in action by making his acts also
one's own as realizations of choices that one shares with him. Those
one does not think good are not candidates for such identification;
those who are not really good are poor candidates. This offers no
selfish escape from 'the active desire to promote that person's good
"for that person's sake, not for ours"' (Vlastos again), though it does
explicate that desire in a way that undermines that contrast. The
upshot is personally demanding, but not priggish (since its demands
are not gratuitous); it is not egoistic in any morally reprehensible way.
It also contains a solution to the dilemma with which this chapter
opened: the other's 'self' with which one identifies may not be unique
in character (if it were, that might be a bar to the identification); but it
is realized in a series of choices and actions over time that do identify
him, and many of which one shares with him in a common life which
is a complex particular not transferable to any other partner. Hence
one's friends contribute to one's *eudaimonia* as individuals, and not
merely as types. Aristotle's ideal of friendship, at once rich in its
philosophical content and pregnant in its practical implications, represents his moral philosophy at its best and most distinctive.

5
ARISTOTLE ON THE VARIETIES OF FRIENDSHIP

I

Aristotle's account of 'perfect' friendship amounts to an analysis of friendship as we conceive it; yet for him it is only a part, if also the focus, of a wider classification of interpersonal relations to which the language of friendship in our sense is variably appropriate. It is best to trace the interconnections by which he maps out his topic before reflecting upon its boundaries; indeed, we shall find that by its nature it requires articulation more than demarcation, and owes its unity more to a structure than to a periphery. What emerges is not a genus of friendship that forms a whole which unifies its species, but a range of relationships held together less by subsumption under a single for- mula than by reference to a single type. This pattern of definition, which falls halfway between fully 'real' and merely 'nominal' defi- nition, is distinctive and distinguishing; we may think that at its best it is peculiarly appropriate to the variability of the present subject- matter. This may console us for the intricacies and uncertainties that obstruct the path of interpretation.

2

It is characteristic of the *Eudemian Ethics* that it offers a more logical theory, or presentation of a theory, than does the *Nicomachean* about the relation between the varieties of friendship. In 7.2 Aristotle introduces them by a series of distinctions within the good and the pleasant; most relevantly, goods are intrinsic or instrumental, plea- sures are absolutely good or good relatively and apparently (1236a7– 10). The grounds of loving (*philein*) are virtue, utility, and pleasure (a12–14). There follow both a general characterization of friendship, and a denial of a genus:

A man becomes a friend when he is loved and returns that love, and this is recognized by the two men in question. There must, therefore, be three kinds of friendship, not all being so named in respect of one thing or as species of a genus, nor yet having the same name quite by mere accident ('homonymously'). For all these are spoken of in relation to one that is the primary (a14–18).

Primary (or 'first') friendship is that of good men (b2). Why is there here no genus, with three species? Why have we not just been given a definition of a genus (at a14–15)? The concision of the passage leaves us casting around for answers.

Presumably we are to take the 'for' of a18 to be indicating a reason for denying not only homonymy but also a genus. Why should the primacy of one variety preclude it from being a species within a genus? One line of answer, which at the same time contains an account of why the friendship of the good is primary, might be traced back to 1.8:

With those things that have a prior and posterior, there is no common thing over and above, and separate from, them. For ⟨if there were⟩, there would be something prior to the first thing. For the thing that is common and separate is prior because, if the common were taken away, with it would go the first thing (1218a1–5).

The argument was then applied to goodness, presumably on the ground that there is a priority among goods.[1] Such a priority has been implicitly reiterated in 7.2: intrinsic and real goodness must be prior to instrumental goodness (that is, utility, 1236a7–8), and to apparent goodness (including pleasure, a9–10, cf. 1235b26–8). If it follows that the corresponding kinds of friendship, distinguished by the goods that are their grounds, are also primary or secondary, we may here have an argument against a genus of friendship. Unfortunately, this yields only a poor argument. It is disputable whether 1.8 is making a fair point (that 'there would be something prior to the first thing', 1218a3–4) against any Platonic Form of Goodness;[2] it is not open to question that it tells not at all against a genus. For it is certainly true of genus and species, what Michael Woods alleges of Form and particulars, that their relation 'is

---

[1] One has to say 'presumably' since an explicit statement is lacking (but cf. *NE* 1.6.1096a19–23); I accept Michael Woods's supposal of a lacuna in a8 from which one has dropped out (*Aristotle's Eudemian Ethics*, 78–9).

[2] Contrast Woods, op. cit. 77, criticizing Aristotle, with A. C. Lloyd, 'Genus, Species, and Ordered Series in Aristotle', *Phronesis* 6 (1962), 70, defending him.

different from the relation between an earlier and a later member of the number series: the formula "A could exist without B but not B without A" covers a number of specific differences' (loc. cit.). If there were a generic goodness, its priority to intrinsic and to real goodness would not be of the same type as the latter's priority to instrumental and to apparent goodness; so there would be no joint assertion and denial of the priority of intrinsic and real goodness.

However, there is another way of arguing from a ranking of goods to the denial of a genus of friendship. W. L. Newman expounds an argument in the *Politics* (3.1.1275a34–b5) about kinds of citizen and constitution as follows:

Things which have to do with (or stand in relation to) objects differing in kind and in priority have little or nothing in common, and . . . constitutions, the object-matter to which the citizen is related, differ in kind and in priority; whence it follows that the citizen under one constitution is different from the citizen under another, and that we must not expect to find the various types of citizen possessing much in common.[3]

This can be applied to friendship by replacing 'citizen' by 'friendship' and 'constitution' by 'good'. The general thought must be not that in such cases there is nothing to be found in common to yield a common *characterization*, but that this cannot yield enough to provide material for a generic *definition*: the nature of friendship varies too greatly in ways that correspond to variations in the nature of its grounds. We can understand Aristotle here so long as we take his concern to be not verbal definition (which is more often possible), but the real definition of a real kind.[4] For example, Aristotle actually objects to Dionysius's definition of life as 'movement of a creature sustained by nutriment, congenitally present with it' that 'this is found in plants as much as in animals, whereas life seems to be not one kind of thing only, but one thing in animals and another in plants' (*Top* 6.10.148a26–31). He can allow himself to call soul 'substance *qua* form of a natural body which has life potentially' (*De an* 2.1.412a19–21) only so long as this is understood merely as 'a sketch or outline of the nature of the soul' (413a9–10); intended more seriously, it would fail and not succeed because it is 'peculiar to no actually existing thing' (2.3.414b26). Similarly, he is tolerant enough of general characterizations of the good, even himself calling

---

[3] *The Politics of Aristotle* (Oxford, 1887–1902), i. 242.

[4] Cf. Terence Irwin, 'Homonymy in Aristotle', *Review of Metaphysics* 34 (1980/1), §§ 6–9, to which I am here indebted.

the good of each action and art 'that for the sake of which the rest are done' (*NE* 1.7.1097a18–19); but it excludes any definition that what goodness consists in varies from case to case. The notion of a 'real kind' remains, in his hands, a vague one: it is hard to identify the degree of non-determinacy that tells not in favour of a genus as opposed to a species, but against a real genus as opposed to a notional one. But we can admit the plausibility of an argument against a real genus of friendship from the variety of its grounds.

3

Although there is no genus of friendship 'friend' is not quite homonymous, for the varieties of friendship are focally connected to a primary kind (*EE* 7.2.1236a16–18). The thought is apparently that because 'first' friendship is grounded upon what is primarily good, it is prior to other friendships grounded upon derivative goods.[5] So we would ideally explain first how utility and pleasure are derivative from goodness proper, and then how that makes the secondary friendships derivative from first friendship. Unfortunately, that task seems not worth pursuing (I have tried). It is simple to show how utility is focal upon intrinsic goodness (though it is equally focal upon pleasure, *NE* 8.2.1155b19–21); it is less easy to make out that pleasure, that is even sensory pleasure, is focal upon goodness (though Aristotle's own accounts of pleasure make it possible). But it does not follow that the secondary friendships are focal upon first friendship (though he may carelessly have supposed the contrary): I can devise no way of arguing that, because (1) the secondary friendships focus upon goodness indirectly while first friendship focuses upon it directly, thcrefore (2) secondary friendships are focal upon first friendship. What I shall set out, instead, more in illustration than in interpretation, is a proposal which tries to explicate (2) without recourse to (1); I shall then raise some difficulties, the more serious of which front (2) however it be explicated.

Within first friendship the parties are linked directly by the relation of loving for its own sake. Within the secondary friendships the same relation links the parties, but only indirectly: intrinsically valued here is not the friend himself, but the utility or pleasure he yields. To count

[5] Note 'therefore' (*ara*) in 1236a16.

the secondary kinds as kinds of friendship is to see their definitions as derivable from the definition of first friendship by addition, as follows:

Primary *Definiens*: A intrinsically loves B (plus reciprocally, etc.).

Secondary *Definientia*: (i) A instrumentally loves B (that is, A intrinsically loves the utility he gets from B); (ii) A hedonistically loves B (that is, A intrinsically loves the pleasure he gets from B).

This presentation is consistent with the text of *Eudemian* 7.2.1236a16–32 (even if it does neglect its connection with a7–10). It requires that loving another 'for being such and on account of virtue' (1236a12–13) should be equivalent to loving him intrinsically, or for his own sake in contrast at once to for one's own sake, and because of something other than himself; that was discussed in the last chapter, and is certainly in the text (cf. 1237b1–5). It is not crucial, but still indicative, that one can 'love' (*philein*) things as well as people (1236a10–12, 1237a39–40): not crucial since we might have another verb within the definitions, and yet indicative of definitions like those just proposed.[6]

A general principle is, 'First is that whose formula is present in all' (7.2.1236a20–21). Aristotle at once spells out a different instance:

Prior *Definiendum*: A man is medical.

Secondary *Definiendum*: An instrument is medical.

Secondary *Definiens*: An instrument is such as to be used by a man who is medical.

Here a derivative manner of being medical is indicated by addition to (or *prosthesis* upon, cf. *Met* 7.4.1030a32–b3) a prior manner. The latter may not, in this case, itself be primary (cf. *Met* 3.2.1003b1–2). More significant is the difference that in the case of 'medical' the prior definition will survive as a unit (inside the context 'a man who is . . .') within the secondary definition, while in the case of friendship (as I have spelled it out) new matter is inserted within the focal definition ('A intrinsically loves . . . B'); that is why, in setting out the focalities above, I was able to keep with 'medical' as a *definiendum*, but had to go beyond 'friend' (*philos*) to definitions using the verb 'love' (*philein*).

---

[6] Hence it can be a repeated complaint that lesser friends 'love' things, or properties (with a pun on *ta huparchonta*, which also means property), not people: 1237b30–2, 7.11.1244a31–2, cf. *NE* 9.3.1165b3.

Is this difference an objection to the definitional priority of 'first friendship'? Can we still apply G. E. L. Owen's characterization, 'One of these senses is primary, in that its definition reappears as a component in each of the other definitions' (cf. *Met* 7.1.1028a34–6, 13.2.1077b3–4)?[7] In a way we can, for all the elements of the primary definition reappear, in the same order, in the secondary definitions; but they do not reappear as a unit, or unitary component. More clearly of concern, and unavoidable on any exposition, is the absence of two other features. First, there is cognitive priority. While the *Metaphysics* characterizes definitional and cognitive priority separately (7.1.1028a31–b2), yet the first can appear as one form of the second (5.11.1018b30–2), or as entailing it (9.8.1049b16–17).[8] It is obscure how knowledge of first friendship can be a precondition of knowledge of the secondary kinds. Certainly experience of the former is inessential for experience of the latter; and even conceiving the latter at most unobviously depends upon conceiving the former. Secondly, there is priority in reality. It is true that this, and priority in definition, can be characterized separately (7.1.1028a32–6), and even contrasted: 'The white is prior to the white man in formula, but not in reality. For it cannot exist separately, but is always along with the compound thing; and by the compound thing I mean the white man' (13.2.1077b6–9). Yet standard examples of focal connection involve both these types of priority. Thus healthy things may preserve health, produce it, be a symptom of it, or be capable of it (4.2.1003a35–b1); medical things other than the medical art may possess that art, be naturally adapted to it, or be a function of it (1003b1–3). We could not easily imagine these things existing in independence of some related instance either of health or of the medical art.[9] Similarly, the things that are said to be with reference to substance (cf. 4.2.1003b6–10) derive their being from the being of some substance; and 'most things are called one because they do or have or suffer or are related to something else that is one' (5.6.1016b6–8). By contrast, there could well be instances of secondary friendship though first friendship was unknown.

---

[7] 'Logic and Metaphysics in some Earlier Works of Aristotle', in *Logic, Science and Dialectic* (London, 1986), 184.

[8] Cf. W. D. Ross, *Aristotle's Metaphysics* (Oxford, 1924), ii. 161; Owen, op. cit. 199, n. 54.

[9] Of course one can cite cases: the apple that Adam and Eve ate was deadly before anyone had died.

As Aristotle never defines sufficient conditions for cases of focal connection, we cannot hope for a decisive argument for or against accepting that the kinds of friendship really are focally connected. Yet we can clearly identify what is missing, and possibly even diagnose why Aristotle may have overlooked it, if we consider the focal connections that do obtain within first friendship itself. Here it is *qua* himself (or *qua* good) that one's friend is also useful (7.3.1238a3–8, cf. *NE* 8.3.1156b18– 24, 9.9.1170a5–6), and pleasant (7.2.1236b27–32, 1237a26–33, b2–5, cf. *NE* 8.3.1156b18–24, 9.9.1169b35–6). Loving the pleasure one gets from one's friend *qua* himself is fully derivative from loving him *qua* himself: his pleasantness is posterior to his virtue both in order of knowledge (to identify just how he is pleasant one must identify how he is good), and in reality (*that* pleasantness cannot be divorced from *that* goodness); equally, loving that pleasure is posterior to loving *him*, for one takes pleasure in loving him *qua* himself. The same structure is displayed by the utility of first friendship; but it is not shared by the secondary kinds of friendship, though these are friendships of pleasure and of utility. It is conceivable that Aristotle was failing to keep this last fact in mind when he asserted the focality of first friendship.

Our passage (*EE* 7.2.1236a16–32) is too rapid in any case. It provides the only evidence that Owen gives for glossing 'focal meaning' (I have followed Irwin in preferring to speak of focal connections) in terms of priority in definition (op. cit. 184). But, as Owen later observes (ibid. 198–9), that is too hospitable to examples that Aristotle would reject: the definitional priority of live to dead hands, and of real to painted animals, does not suffice to make a dead hand any kind of hand, or a painted goat any kind of goat. So it is not enough for Aristotle to remark, 'First is that whose formula is present in all' (1236a20–1): it needs further to be shown that the secondary relationships have, however vaguely, enough in common with first friendship to count as kinds of friendship. As 7.2 pursues its somewhat rambling course, it cannot but occasionally throw up material that might help (for instance, when it applies the test of time within all three kinds of friendship, 1238a14–29, *pace* 1237b9–10); but Aristotle evinces no awareness of an omission to be supplied.

4

The *Eudemian* treatment of the relations between the varieties of friendship (in 7.2) states its pattern of analysis (focal connection) unequivocally; it is its lack of detail that leaves it unclear how the pattern is to be applied (if, indeed, it is really applicable). The *Nicomachean* presentation (in 8.2–6) provides far more detail; it is less clear what pattern, if any, it is intended to fill out. Many commentators, preferring to import a pattern than either to invent or to deny one, have supposed that the focal connection explicit in the *Eudemian* account is implicit in the *Nicomachean* account also.[10] It is true that the latter presents no new data to tell against such an analysis; it also presents no new reflections to bear one out. There is nothing in it that invites a focal interpretation, and something that discourages one: the standard epithet for the friendship of the good is 'primary' or 'first' in the *Eudemian Ethics* (e.g. 7.2.1236a18), 'perfect' or 'complete' (*teleios*) in the *Nicomachean* (e.g. 8.3.1156b7). We do once in the latter meet the words 'firstly and in the proper sense' (8.4.1157a30–1); but that is in contrast to 'according to similarity' (a31–2), a phrase strikingly absent from the *Eudemian* text and consistent with, but not indicative of, focality.

A different pattern is identified by A. D. M. Walker.[11] He notes how Aristotle first characterizes friendship as involving mutual knowledge of reciprocal goodwill (8.2.1155b27–1156a3), and then alludes back to a distinction made earlier in the chapter (much in the logical style of the *Eudemian Ethics*) between the good, the pleasant, and the useful as various objects of attachment (1155b17–21) in concluding, 'To be friends, then, they must be mutually recognized as bearing goodwill and wishing well to each other for one of the aforesaid reasons' (1156a3–5). That sounds like a single state, with a variety of grounds. But Aristotle next, at the start of 8.3, restates the definition replacing the 'for his sake' of 1155b31, still implicit in the 'goodwill' of 1156a4, by a crucial qualification: 'With respect to each there is a mutual and recognized love, and those who love each other wish well to each other in that respect in which they love one another' (1156a8–10). The remainder of 8.3 so emphasizes the force of the qualification within the friendships of pleasure and utility that it is not surprising if 9.5 denies that such friends are motivated by goodwill at all (1167a12–18). So it could appear that 8.2 offers a general characterization of

    [10] Cf. W. W. Fortenbaugh, 'Aristotle's Analysis of Friendship: Function and Analogy, Resemblance, and Focal Meaning', *Phronesis* 20 (1975), 51, n. 1.
    [11] 'Aristotle's Account of Friendship in the *Nicomachean Ethics*', *Phronesis* 24 (1979).

friendship which 8.3 then refutes. There are various ways of getting round that appearance. Walker's is elegant:

While the inferior friendships may count as friendships because they do meet the definitional criteria of 8.2, they are not friendships proper because they meet these criteria only in a certain way or only with certain qualifications, whereas the friendship of good men satisfies the requirements without qualification and hence is primarily or properly friendship (op. cit. 188–9).

While I shall be adopting an interpretation quite close to Walker's, I have two kinds of doubt about his formulation. First, it does not seem verbally consistent: do the inferior friendships meet the criteria, or not?[12] Secondly, it rests heavily upon the traditional division into chapters (which is not Aristotle's): 8.2 defines friendship, while 8.3 applies the definition, with qualifications. But there is nothing clearly to signal that in the run of the text, which evolves a definition away from mere liking (*philēsis*) in a series of steps: wishing well (1155b28–9); the same, plus 'for his sake' (1155b31); the same, plus reciprocity (b32–4); the same, plus mutual knowledge (1156a2–4); the same, but (if we are to accommodate friendship in all its variety) minus 'for his sake', plus 'in that respect in which they love one another' (a6–10).[13] It seems less misleading to divide 8.2 from 8.3 at 1156a10;[14] then the final definition will be one that even the lesser friendships fully satisfy. However, the last step is special in that its effect is not to add an extra feature, but to introduce a qualification that takes something back. When the love in question is such that the effect of the phrase 'in that respect in which they love one another' is to import 'for his sake' after all, then the friends may be called 'especially friends' (1156b10); yet the phrase may also serve to exclude goodwill. Thus even if

---

[12] An earlier sentence seemed decisively negative: 'With friendships of utility and pleasure the parties do not really feel affection for each other, and so these associations are not really friendships' (ibid. 187). Given that the criteria include goodwill, and that the lesser friendships need not (in Walker's view, which I share) involve goodwill *at all*, it seems to me that the negative answer is correct.

[13] Each of the steps beyond mere well-wishing is marked by a *de* (in 1155b31, b32, 1156a3, a6); the *de* of a9 is slightly different, and marks that a9–10 clarify a8–9 in specifying the step backwards intimated at a6–8. That the *de* of a6 is slightly more emphatic than the others is implicit in my contrast between 'the same, but minus . . .' there, and 'the same, plus . . .' before; but there is no clear verbal indication that by a6 Aristotle has finished with the task of definition, and is now proceeding to a different (even if connected) task.

[14] Here I follow Geoffrey Percival, 'Notes on Three Passages from the *Nicomachean Ethics*, Book 8', *Classical Quarterly* 29 (1935), 171.

Walker is misled by the present division between chapters, he remains close to the truth as I see it. To his picture of a determinate definition in 8.2 applied with qualifications in 8.3, I prefer one of a determinable definition (that of 1156a8–10), indeterminate enough to look nothing like a real definition.

One query that Walker's interpretation raises, and mine evades, is whether he is not, after all, finding a kind of focal connection. If, as the *Eudemian Ethics* had it, 'first is that whose formula is present is all' (7.2.1236a20–1), is Walker not implying that the friendship of the good is 'first' as well as 'perfect', since on his account its definition will appear, plus qualifications, within the definitions of the lesser varieties? The best I could suggest on behalf of focal connection in the *Eudemian Ethics* was that new matter gets inserted within the focal definition ('*A* intrinsically loves . . . *B*'); is that definition any the less focal if, instead, new matter is appended at the end ('*A* wishes *B* well for his sake, etc.—subject to the qualification that . . .')? Hardly so. Indeed, it is presumably an advantage that now the original definition reappears as a unit within the derivative definitions. A greater advantage is that cognitive priority will go with definitional priority: if the lesser friendships must be grasped as the products of qualifying the best friendship, then the latter will be prior in order of knowledge. (It remains true that it fails to come out as prior in reality: only the inferior friendships might actually be realized.) Yet Walker resists reading focality into the *Nicomachean* account (op. cit. 192–4). Firstly, he notes how different it is to add to a nuclear definition *relational* clauses (not his term, but consider his examples 'productive of', 'indicative of', 'preservative of') and *qualifying* clauses (for example, 'in so far as they are mutually useful'). Qualified friendship is a borderline kind of friendship, though it still relates the same entities (pairs of human beings); by contrast, the healthiness of a complexion or of a treatment is not a borderline case of the health of a body, but a state wholly inapplicable to bodies. These are clear differences; less clear, given the obscurity in which Aristotle leaves the concept, is their bearing on focality, of which these might just be different kinds. Secondly, Walker claims that a focal reading distorts the structure of the *Nicomachean* account: the best friendship is primary because it meets without qualification the conditions for friendship set out in 8.2, not because (as an incidental corollary) its definition can be recognized as an ingredient within the definitions of the lesser kinds. He leaves this point somewhat obscure by omitting to offer any definition of the best friendship: if it is the same as that of perfect or unqualified friendship, it must be an understatement to say 'It most completely satisfies the definitional requirements of friendship *tout court*' (ibid. 194); if it is different (perhaps explicitly specifying that it can only apply to the good, cf. 8.3.1156b8–9), it would seem not to enter as an element into the definitions of the lesser kinds. Without closing options that Walker seems to leave open, we may at least say that Aristotle shows no concern to accommodate the materials of 8.2–3 within the structure of focal connection. It is certainly no objection to my variant that it does not even suggest a focal analysis.

A second query arises not from comparison with the *Eudemian* account, but from a strand of thought recurrent in the *Nicomachean* treatment itself. The lesser friendships are *similar* to the best one in that within the latter also friends are mutually pleasant and useful (8.4.1156b35–1157a3). Moreover, the lesser friendships count as kinds of friendship in virtue of this similarity (1157a31–2, b4–5). How do such remarks relate to Walker's analysis? He finds such resemblances 'too slight and superficial to do the work that is required of them' (op. cit. 189). In particular, he infers from a later passage that appeal to similarities accompanied by dissimilarities cannot settle cases of disputed classification:

It is from their likeness and their unlikeness to the same thing that they [sc., the lesser friendships] are thought both to be and not to be friendships. It is by their likeness to the friendship of virtue that they seem to be friendships . . . while . . . they appear not to be friendships . . . because of their unlikeness to the friendship of virtue (8.6.1158b5–11).

Walker comments that such similarities and dissimilarities '*generate* the problem' (op. cit. 190); hence rehearsal of them cannot yield a solution. Here, I think, he goes more seriously astray, for it seems that both his interpretation and mine need supplementation (not exactly for the same reason) by appeal to likeness to perfect friendship. It is unclear, to begin with, that Aristotle still wants a solution, if that means a decisive verdict. The *Eudemian Ethics* is straightforwardly inclusive when speaking most clearly in Aristotle's own voice (contrast 7.2.1236a23–30 with 1237b8–9), rejecting a more restrictive conception on apparently logical grounds.[15] The *Nicomachean Ethics*

---

[15] Yet, in setting the problem in 7.12 of whether the good man can need friends, Aristotle can write, 'The friend because of virtue is the only friend' (1244b16–17), no doubt because that is the kind of friendship which has point even for the self-sufficient.

inclines to be inclusive in deference to common usage, but more tentatively (8.4.1157a25–30, 8.6.1158b5–11). Further, Walker's Aristotle is in no better position to be decisive than was, in fact, the *Eudemian* Aristotle. We cannot count as friends any pair of people who are related in *some* way derivable either focally, or by way of qualification, from whatever relationship is paradigmatic of friendship. The point can be conveyed very simply: the predicate 'is not F' derives from 'is F', certainly in definition (though they are too closely related for either to be prior in cognition or in reality), also through the extreme limit of qualification (negation as an operation reversing the sense of the predicate); yet of course not being F is not a way of being F. The point made earlier about the inadequacy of definitional priority can be extended: being a dead hand is, in a sense, a qualified way of being a hand; but the qualification is *alienans*, for being a dead hand is a way of *not* being a hand.[16] So the question will arise: does adding this qualification to this predicate yield a new predicate which still specifies a kind of way of satisfying the original predicate? If there are general criteria for an answer (which need not, and perhaps should not, be expected), it remains open what Aristotle's were; but when we can identify similarities and dissimilarities (as with 'friend'), it is unsurprising if Aristotle takes them to constitute the relevant facts of the case (cf. 8.4.1157a31–2, b4–5).[17]

It may help to consider what Walker sees as a parallel: Aristotle's treatment of acrasia. The acratic in respect not of bodily pleasures, but of money, honour, or anger, are so called not 'simply', but

---

[16] Cf. P. T. Geach, 'Good and Evil', in Philippa Foot (ed.) *Theories of Ethics* (London, 1967), 64.

[17] Walker has put to me, sensibly enough, that a qualification to 'well-wishing out of goodwill' must be *alienans* if it even fails to require well-wishing. Might that save him so far from appealing to similarities? I cannot see that it does: on my account, well-wishing is simply part of a definition that all cases of friendship must fully satisfy; on his account, it would now seem to be an element of similarity to perfect friendship which, unlike any kind of goodwill, is required for imperfect friendship. (If, instead, he makes the distinction that well-wishing is rather a necessary condition of all friendship than a necessary element in the lesser friendships of similarity to perfect friendship, thus stipulating directly that well-wishing is always required for friendship while goodwill is not, he is effectively discarding the definition of 8.2.1156a3–5 for that, as I see it, of 8.3.1156a8–10.) It is true that the similarities that Aristotle cites as such are less abstract (cf. 8.4.1156b35–1157a3); in my view, as I shall shortly explain, these are needed not to subsume the lesser friendships under the general definition, but to justify the centrality of perfect friendship in a way that makes of friendship in general more than a ragbag of relationships tied together by a form of words.

'according to similarity' (*NE* 7.4.1147b32–5), or else 'with an addition' (1148a10). However, on Walker's account of them, the cases are rather different. The initial characterization of the acratic is 'those who go to excess . . . contrary to the right reason which is in themselves' (1147b31–2), and they all fully satisfy it. The effect of qualifications like 'in respect of anger' is to make a sub-classification, and not to indicate that some characterization is satisfied 'only in a certain way or only with certain qualifications' (Walker, op. cit. 188). So the characterization of acrasia is parallel less to the only partly applicable characterization of friendship in 8.2 (1156a3–5) than to the sufficiently general if not really definitional formula early in *Eudemian Ethics* 7.2 (requiring mutual love and knowledge, 1236a14–15). The question arises why any particular kind of acrasia should be singled out as a focus of similarity. Why do we not rather have a genus of acrasia, with coequal species? The answer must be, as it was for friendship in the *Eudemian Ethics*, that there is no real, as opposed to nominal, common definition. The nature of acrasia is in part constituted by its mechanism; hence it is no defect of Aristotle's central account (in *NE* 7.3) that, as it stands, it covers only acrasia in respect of bodily pleasures. If the acrasia of anger deserves to share a name with the acrasia of pleasure, and to be treated alongside it, that is so not merely because they share a general formula (1147b31–2), which might have displayed an empty verbal ingenuity (think of disjunctive formulas), but because they display sufficient similarities in detail: the full account of pleasure-acrasia, in 7.3, has only to be modified, in the light of 7.6, for it to apply to anger-acrasia also. What similarities are sufficient? There is no easy answer, perhaps no general answer. Aristotle was never closer to the concept of family resemblance.[18]

I have been arguing that, if Walker consistently takes similarities and dissimilarities to be relevant to the problem of how to define the domain of friendship but not to a solution, he will leave his Aristotle with nothing adequate to say.[19] My Aristotle could simply appeal to

---

[18] It has emerged that there are in fact three types of 'definition' to be distinguished: (i) real definitions analysing a single real nature; (ii) nominal but significative definitions applying to a variety of things that belong together by virtue of real similarities; (iii) nominal and factitious definitions applied to very dissimilar things that are only held together by a formula. We may say that definitions of type (i) capture a genus, of (ii) a class, but of (iii) nothing.

[19] There is also the anomaly that Aristotle then turns out to be prefacing a very long presentation of the problem, within 8.3–6, by a very brief presentation of the solution, within 8.2–3.

his general definition of friendship (at 8.3.1156a8–10, cf. *EE* 7.2.1236a14–15) to delimit the extension of the term without any supplementary appeal to similarities (just as the formula at *NE* 7.4.1147b31–2 may suffice to capture all and only cases of 'acrasia' without any more being said).[20] What the similarities create, in default of any real genus, is a single field of investigation that is not invented by brisk phrase-making, but unified by real connections that may justify (despite the uncertainty of 8.4.1157a25–30) the wide application of a single term and the use of a single general formula. I can now supplement my variant upon Walker clumsily but explicitly as follows: a relationship merits classification as a friendship if the parties wish one another well in the way in which they love one another, this being either for the other's sake, or in a way that bears enough resemblance to wishing another well for his sake.

About such resemblances W. W. Fortenbaugh is useful (op. cit. 54). He distinguishes two types of similarity. One is by analogy, which involves two pairs of terms, each related in the same way or similar ways. So when the badness of a poor doctor or actor is said to be 'similar by analogy' to badness proper (7.4.1148b10), and this is used to shed light on the 'similarity' between acrasia proper and the acrasias in respect of anger, honour, and gain (b10–14), the thought must be that a bad doctor stands to doctoring more or less as a bad man stands to action, while a choleric acratic stands to anger more or less as an acratic proper stands to bodily pleasure. Within Book 8 such resemblance by analogy is most clearly instanced in this passage:

There are several kinds of friendship—firstly and in the proper sense that of good men *qua* good, and by similarity the other kinds; for it is in virtue of something good and something similar that they are friends, since even the pleasant is good to the lovers of pleasure (8.4.1157a30–3).

'Something similar' here must mean 'akin to what is found in true friendship' (as W. D. Ross even translates), and not some similarity between the friends in question; for that, being common to all friendships, would be irrelevant to the primacy of one kind.[21] The last clause ('since . . .') makes clear that the similarity is one of analogy: similar are how friends in virtue stand to virtue and how lovers of pleasure

----

    [20] Walker has persuaded me in correspondence that 1156a8–10 define a clear enough boundary on their own.
    [21] Cf. M. van Straaten and G. J. de Vries, 'Notes on the 8th and 9th Books of Aristotle's *Nicomachean Ethics*', 205.

stand to pleasure, and not virtue and pleasure themselves in abstraction from human motivation. Similar analogies can be found throughout 8.3: for instance, friends for utility and friends for pleasure relate in similar ways to each other's intrinsic qualities on the one hand (they are irrelevant), and to relevant relational qualities ('in virtue of some good which they get from each other' or 'because they find them pleasant') on the other (1156a10–14). Now analogy, like similarity in general, is a symmetrical relation: if the relation of a to b is like that of c to d, so is that of c to d like that of a to b. How then can relations of similarity bear out claims to priority? Here we need to turn our attention away from resemblance by analogy to simple resemblance. To quote Fortenbaugh: 'In contrast, simple cases of resemblance do not involve four terms arranged in the manner of an arithmetical proportion. Rather two terms are related directly on the basis of some similarity or common feature' (op. cit. 54). Thus the friendship of pleasure is similar to perfect friendship in that the good too are pleasant to each other; and the friendship of utility is similar to perfect friendship in that the good too are useful to each other (8.4.1156b35–1157a3). Thus each lesser kind of friendship shares one common feature, shared pleasure or utility, with that perfect friendship which contains both. Fortenbaugh again:

This means that the friendship of morally good men can mediate a relationship between friendships based upon pleasure and friendships based upon utility . . . In the important areas of pleasure and utility direct resemblance fails. The relationship is established indirectly by reference to the friendship based upon moral goodness. Perfect friendship becomes a kind of focus of resemblance. It has the priority of mediator (op. cit. 56).

On my interpretation, the definition of friendship at 1156a8–10 needs to be supplemented by investigation of similarities to friendship involving goodwill if it is to be justified as more than a verbal feat. The notion of well-wishing is Protean: when it is wished for another for his sake (as Aristotle interprets that phrase), its goal must be his ethical goodness and *eudaimoniā*; other types of well-wishing relate to different goods, whose variety in kind excludes any genus of friendship, and may or not permit a family of friendships. It must help if we can trace similarities to a core case, but Aristotle has to justify assigning primacy so rapidly to the friendship of the good; in casting it as 'a kind of focus of resemblance' Fortenbaugh provides one justification.

Another line of justification is recurrent in the *Nicomachean* treatment, and also present in the *Eudemian*. That virtuous friends are also pleasant and useful to each other is just among the first points made to illustrate how 'this kind of friendship is perfect both in respect of duration and in all other respects' (8.4.1156b33–4). When it was first called 'perfect' (at 1156b7), that was in effect because it satisfies the definition at 1156a8–10 in a special way, that is through satisfying the stricter formulation at a4–5; but the thought is also that 'there meet in it all the qualities that friends should have' (1156b18–19). So to support his way of applying the definition Aristotle also has in mind a group of features that people expect of friendship. The most emphasized expectation is that friendship be lasting. The friendship of the good should fill that part of the bill: 'Their friendship lasts as long as they are good—and goodness is an enduring thing' (1156b11–12); it should also be lasting because it involves both absolute and relative goodness and pleasantness (b19–24). By contrast, friendships of pleasure and utility are, for various reasons, transient (1156a19–21, a33–b1, 8.4.1157a14–15, 8.6.1158b9–10). The friendship of the good is also alone immune to slander (8.4.1157a20–2, 8.6.1158b8–9); this is because it alone requires long familiarity. Further, like pleasant and unlike useful friends, good friends characteristically live together (8.5.1157b19–24, 8.6.1158a8–10).

Much the same observations are made in *Eudemian Ethics* 7.2: first friendship, as it arises from the test of time, is both stable, and safe from slander (1237b9–27); it combines absolute and relative goodness and pleasure (1236b39–1237a2, 1237a26–9); it involves not just goodwill but living together (1237b5–7). And it is an indication that these points serve to place the kinds of friendship that they are accompanied by the remark, 'This then is first friendship, which all recognize; through it the others are both accepted and disputed' (1237b8–9). (Though very concise, this is close to *NE* 8.6.1158b5–11, which are equally indecisive.) What is lacking in the *Eudemian* presentation is any clue as to how such popular points are to be put to use to supplement the logical skeleton that preceded. It is as if the *Eudemian* Aristotle is too dazzled by the pinchbeck rigour of his resort to focal connections to perceive the importance of such supplementary considerations.

In their varying treatments of the kinds of friendships we meet a contrast at least in style of presentation that is typical of the two *Ethics*. The *Eudemian* is much concerned with the logical structure of a theory. Thus the friendship of the good is 'primary', which it defines in terms of definitional priority (7.2.1236a20–1). Likewise, and more centrally, means are related to the end in the manner of a focal connection (1.8.1218b9–11). The goodness of what is healthy (in the sense of being an efficient cause of health) is focal upon the goodness of health just as its being healthy is focal upon health (b19–22). The end of things realizable by man is first among goods in that it is what makes them good (b9–11).[22] There is no such emphasis upon conceptual priority in the *Nicomachean Ethics*. It is not, in my view, that it presents a different ethical theory: there are enough indications of the same structure (for instance, at 1.12.1102a2–4) to indicate a far tighter body of theory than is casually apparent (cf. my 'Aristotle's Ethical Holism'). But the manner of presentation, at least, is different. It is symptomatic, in its treatment of friendship, that, while the term 'simply' or 'absolutely' (*haplōs*) does appear several times (8.3.1156b13, 14, 15, 8.4.1157b4), this is never in contrast to any explicit 'according to an analogy' (as at *EE* 7.6.1240a13–14), or 'with an addition'. For such clarification, Walker has to turn to the treatment of the varieties of acrasia in Book 7 (cf., all within 7.4, 1147b33, 1148a10, b6–7, 10, 13), and Anthony Kenny may have shown (in *The Aristotelian Ethics*) that *Nicomachean* Book 7 is better located as *Eudemian* Book 6. A less sparing and more studied use of technical terms might have made it possible to identify the logical structure with more confidence.

As we saw, there is one passage in the *Eudemian Ethics* that rests the claim to the priority of the friendship of the good not on logical focality, but on common expectations (7.2.1237b8–1238a10). This line becomes dominant in *Nicomachean* 8.4–6, and is typical of the *Nicomachean Ethics* in general. Familiarly, while the *Eudemian Ethics* opens with the concept of *eudaimoniā* (1.1.1214a7), the *Nicomachean* first introduces the concept of 'the practical good' (1.7.1097a23), and then argues that it is *eudaimoniā* that lives up to its popular bill (note such terms as 'evidently', 1097a28, 'is thought', b8, 'we think', b16) of being final (or 'complete', 1097a28, 33–4), and self-sufficient (b7–8, 15–16). After 1.7 has presented a functional definition of the human good, 1.8 proceeds to call as evidence 'what is commonly said about it' (1098b10–11). Later, in 10.7, contemplation is singled out as best meeting various familiar expectations of

[22] Cf. Enrico Berti, 'Multiplicité et unité du bien selon *EE* 1.8', in Paul Moraux and Dieter Harlfinger (eds.), *Untersuchungen zur Eudemischen Ethik* (Berlin, 1971).

eudaimoniā (1177a19–b26). By comparison with the *Eudemian Ethics*, the *Nicomachean* is less concerned to define a precise conclusion (so that there is much dispute about the status accorded to *eudaimoniā* in Book 1, and to contemplation in Book 10), and more concerned to be persuasive in a dialectical way, that is by appeal to the truisms of received opinion. In intention, as in upshot, the *Nicomachean Ethics* is the more popular work.

Is one to conclude that in its initial mapping of the topic 'the *Nicomachean* account of friendship reveals Aristotle at his best' (Fortenbaugh, op. cit. 62)? Ideally, it seems to me, Aristotle would have combined the rigour that is an aim of the *Eudemian* treatment with the greater amplitude of the *Nicomachean*. Yet there is surely some progress (if the latter is later): while the *Eudemian Ethics* offers an explicit statement (of focality) that is clearly less than successful and satisfactory, the *Nicomachean* offers a less explicit analysis that seems much more apt to the subject-matter. To restate my understanding of it: friendship has a single and determinable definition (that of 1156a8–10) which needs supplementing, if it is to capture more than an artificial category of relationship, by the criterion of similarity to that variety, the friendship of the good, which alone realizes the definition in a way that fully achieves what we expect of friendship.[23] This seems an interesting conception of a class, whose imprecision is its merit: 'when the thing is indefinite the rule also is indefinite', as Aristotle writes of the virtue of equity; like equitable decrees, this way of characterizing friendship resembles the 'lead rule used in making the Lesbian moulding' which 'adapts itself to the shape of the stone and is not rigid' (5.10.1137b29–32). The next step is to apply it.

5

We have found Aristotle wambling through a sequence of propositions: 'To a friend we say we ought to wish what is good for his sake' (*NE* 8.1.1155b31); 'Those who love each other wish well to each other in that respect in which they love one another' (8.3.1156a9–10); 'Those who wish well to their friends for their sake are especially friends' (1156b9–10). What was at first expected of all friendship is

---

[23] In one respect 1156a8–10 turn out too loose and are implicitly tightened, as I shall note towards the end of this chapter.

relocated as distinctive of that of 'good men *qua* good', which is friendship 'firstly and in the proper sense' (8.4.1157a30–1); other friendships are so called 'by similarity' (a31–2). How close is the similarity? Within the lesser varieties is that goodwill wholly lacking which adds a friendly motive to the wish to treat a friend well (cf. 8.2.1155b31–2)? Commentators who agree (or need not disagree) with the structure that I have adapted from Walker and Fortenbaugh can still differ interestingly in the way they apply it. I shall now shall discuss the account by John Cooper, who distinctively and refreshingly takes a minimal view of the retreat from the requirement of goodwill, and so an optimific view of the lesser friendships ('Aristotle on Friendship', §§ 1–5). Do friends in pleasure or utility wish the other well in a way for his sake and so out of goodwill (*eunoia*), or only out of self-interest and in the spirit of an exchange? One must be grateful to Cooper for giving life to the question by arguing, vigorously, for the more generous and less easy answer, even if reflecting on his reflections leads one back to one's own initial impressions.

Cooper begins by telling us to take seriously the discussion of friendship in *Rhetoric* 2.4, and in particular its definition of loving (*philein*) someone as 'wishing for him what you believe to be good things, not for your own sake but for his, and being inclined, so far as you can, to bring these things about' (1380b36–1381a1). He calls this chapter 'essential reading on this topic', and suggests of the definition that 'we cannot do better than follow Aristotle's lead here' (op. cit. 302). Cooper's purpose is at once clear: to make out that goodwill (as, in effect, it is) is present in all kinds of friendship, those of pleasure and utility as well as that of virtue. But his appeal to the *Rhetoric* is less than compelling. Aristotle proceeds there to infer that a friend must show fellow-feeling 'not because of anything else but because of the other' (1381a5), a description which the *Ethics* would apply only to the friendship of the good (e.g. *EE* 7.2.1236b30). Apparently the rhetorical Aristotle is unconcerned to draw the distinctions that will concern the ethical Aristotle; it cannot be inferred that he would assign the same general role to goodwill even after drawing them—we have to look and see. In fact, we do find the *Rhetoric* definition surfacing, in both *Ethics*, as the first in a list of characterizations of friendship prefacing discussion of self-love (*NE* 9.4, *EE* 7.6); but this is ambiguous support. The *Eudemian* definition comes closest: 'The man is thought to be a friend who wishes someone well, or what he takes to be well, not because of himself, but for the sake of the other'

(1240a24–5). However, this belongs to a set of common conceptions which are said not to be compatible (a30–1)—except within a good man's relation to himself (b11–12); and Cooper accepts (op. cit. 310) that the *Eudemian Ethics* also unambiguously denies that goodwill obtains within the lesser friendships (7.7.1241a5). The *Nicomachean* passage is similar: among the things that 'men think' is that 'a friend is one who wishes and does what is good, or seems so, for the sake of his friend' (1166a2–4); again this is true of the good man's relation to himself (a10–11, 16). A later chapter adds a qualification: 'The man is especially a friend who wishes the object of his wish well for the other's sake' (9.8.1168b2–3). The addition of the word 'especially' turns the commonplace against Cooper;²⁴ and the predicate 'wish well to those whom they love, for their sake' serves in 8.5, without the qualification, only to describe friends in virtue (1157b31–2). Of course there is also 8.2, whose deployment of 'for his sake' (1155b31) and goodwill (b32, 33, 1156a4) certainly tells in Cooper's favour. However, like Walker (as it happens), Cooper places too much weight on the traditional division between 8.2. and 8.3, and so draws a conclusion too soon: in the final definition at 1156a8–10 'wishing well' survives while 'for his sake' disappears. It is unnecessary to take Aristotle, instead, at his penultimate word.

Whatever the initial evidence, how does Cooper understand the lesser friendships? He still treats the phrase 'in that respect in which they love one another' as a qualification to the claim 'those who love each other wish each other well' (8.3.1156a9–10), but he so interprets the qualification that it permits a kind of goodwill. He construes 'because of' (*dia*) in its use to discriminate the kinds of friendship (cf. 'because of the useful', 1156a10, 'because of pleasure', a12) as signifying not 'a purpose' but 'an antecedent causal condition' (op. cit. 336, n. 12), of which a consequence is wishing the other well for his sake (ibid. 311). This suggests a single mode of friendship, with a variable causal background, and Cooper proceeds to ascribe to such friends a willingness 'to act in the interest of the other person's good, independently of consideration of their *own* welfare or pleasure' (ibid.). However, that turns out to be an overstatement: 'One's concern for the other person's good extends only so far as and as long as he remains a particular sort of person . . . and the good one wishes him to have, for his own sake, is therefore restricted to what he can

²⁴ Cf. also 8.3.1156b9–10 (though there, as I have already remarked, the commonplace is transformed).

acquire without, thereby or in consequence, ceasing to be pleasant or advantageous' (ibid. 313). The result is less rosy than we might have wished: 'Pleasure- and advantage-friendships, on Aristotle's conception, are, despite his denial that they are wholly self-centred, much more self-centred than perhaps we would be inclined to think them' (ibid. 336, n. 14). Consequently, Cooper cannot be accused of creating a genus of friendship, defined by mutual knowledge of reciprocal goodwill: what that goodwill amounts to is somewhat different within each kind of friendship.[25] Properly (I think), the upshot is indeterminate; one could play down the issue by taking a minimizing view of the goodwill that carries over into Cooper's extension of its domain. Hence his account is a possible way of filling out Aristotle's structure (as he and I agree in interpreting it) of a determinable quasi-definition taking on within each kind of friendship a different determinate form. But is it Aristotle's way? Does goodwill (a matter of motive) belong within that determinable definition along with well-wishing (at most a matter of intention)? I am not persuaded that Aristotle thinks that it does.[26]

I have already discussed occurrences of 'wishing well for his sake' (in *Rhet* 2.4, *EE* 7.6, *NE* 8.2, 9.8) that, on the face of it, support Cooper; what survived, if I was fair, was a little evidence (the absence of 'for his sake' from *NE* 8.3.1156a8–10, the addition of 'especially' in 9.8.1168b2–3) that tells against him. Another preliminary issue is linguistic: is Cooper right to construe 'because of' (*dia*) in its use to discriminate the kinds of friendship as signifying not 'a purpose' but 'an antecedent causal condition' (op. cit. 336, n. 12)? His simplest argument is that if Aristotle had meant purpose, he would have used 'for the sake of' (*heneka*). In fact, *dia* and *heneka* can easily occur interchangeably.[27] However, the best alternative construal is not the opposite of Cooper's, that 'because of' means goal and not ground, but that ground and goal here go hand in hand, so that goodness, pleasure, or utility are at once attributes of the friends, and purposes of

[25] On this, cf. one of Cooper's original articles, 'Aristotle on the Forms of Friendship', *Review of Metaphysics* 30 (1976/7), 644.

[26] A brief reminder: we must not presume that his *philia* is precisely our friendship; goodwill may be a necessary aspect of the latter (as surely it is), yet not of the former. I shall consider the relation of *philia* to friendship at the end of this chapter.

[27] Compare *Rhet* 1.5.1361b37 or *EE* 7.6.1240a25 (*dia*) with *Rhet* 2.4.1380b37 (*heneka*), *NE* 8.4.1157a26 (*dia*) with 1157a27–8 (*heneka*), and 9.1.1164a8 (*dia*) with a10 (*heneka*); also 8.3.1156a31 (*dia*) with a33 (pursuing pleasure), and 9.5.1167a18 (*dia*) with a16 (hoping for utility).

their friendship. It fits this that *dia* is not ambiguous, but a general term to convey any of the four causes, of which the final cause is one (cf. *Phys* 2.7.198a14–21): *dia ti?* is simply the indeterminate question 'Why?' It confirms this that the phrase 'because of virtue' (of which Cooper's treatment, op. cit. 310–11, is a priori) can signify either a quality of the person loved (*EE* 7.2.1236a13, cf. *NE* 8.3.1156a12–13), or the goal of the friendship (8.13.1162b7).[28] Though an argument dies, Cooper's conclusion survives; for he is not maintaining that the kinds of friendship differ only in ground and not in goal (cf. op. cit. 334–5, n. 6). Even if 'for pleasure' as the label of a kind of friendship signifies a goal as well as a ground, it does not follow that that is its only goal: Aristotle might choose to refer to it by anything which is differentiating, whether by its ground or by one among its goals; hence goodwill is not excluded by the mere label. But we have found nothing yet that really bears Cooper out.

We might not expect to find anything until we turn to the treatments of goodwill in *Eudemian Ethics* 7.7 and *Nicomachean Ethics* 9.5.[29] Cooper admits that *Eudemian* 7.7 unambiguously excludes goodwill from the lesser friendships (632, 641–2); this is explicit in the sentence, 'Neither in useful friendship nor in that according to pleasure is there goodwill' (1241a5). He tries to neuter this concession by suggesting that the *Eudemian Ethics* in general has 'no clear and consistent theory on this point', on the ground that 7.11.1244a21–3 admit well-wishing within those friendships; but well-wishing does not include goodwill, in either *Ethics*.[30] *Nicomachean* 9.5 is not equally forthright:

One might by an extension of the term say that goodwill is inactive friendship, though when it is prolonged and reaches the point of intimacy it becomes friendship—not the friendship based on utility nor that based on pleasure; for goodwill too does not arise on those terms (1167a10–14).

    [28] As I argued in Chapter 4, these come together in that the goal in friendship distinctive of the good man can only be achieved if his friend is himself good.

    [29] It is therefore regrettable that Cooper's only discussion of these (after a brief mention, and a promise to return, 'Aristotle on Friendship', 310) is omitted from the A. O. Rorty version; my references to him in this section will now be, except where indicated, to 'Aristotle on the Forms of Friendship'.

    [30] Cooper asserts that it does in the *Nicomachean*; that fits 8.6.1158a7–8, but not 8.2.1155b31–2 (where 'for his sake' and 'thus' surely add something to 'wish well'), nor 9.5.1167a15–17 (to be put to use later). Cooper does not reflect upon the implications of his concession (perhaps because he hopes to have neutered it). If the view that he is opposing is 'harsh' and 'depressing' (Rorty edn., 305), contradicted by the *Rhetoric* and excluded by the meaning of *dia*, how much is gained by expunging it from one *Ethics* if it keeps a place within the other? Of course Aristotle's views can change, and for the better; but even a discarded view must have a home somewhere in his thought.

The last clause (a13–14) might be taken (as I shall take it) as equivalent to the plain exclusion of goodwill in *Eudemian* 7.7.1214a5. But Cooper understands Aristotle otherwise: 'Spontaneous goodwill of the kind here under discussion can only be based on admiration for goodness of character; one can feel goodwill towards someone whom one *thinks* is a good person even though one has no deep personal knowledge of his character and has not personally been affected by any noble action of his, but no one feels goodwill for someone else on the mere ground that he *might* be a pleasant companion or useful business partner' (642). How then are a13–14, and in particular the phrase *epi toutois* (translated as 'on those terms'), to be understood? Cooper comments on these two lines, 'It is the expectation of pleasure or profit that brings one to develop such friendships as these, and there is no such thing as unself-interested well-wishing for the sake of one's own pleasure or profit' (ibid.). It seems to me difficult to translate *epi toutois* as 'for the sake of these things' here (though it might be easy elsewhere): the motive of goodwill is not itself a thing to which it is natural to ascribe, or deny, further motives. In any case, the point that Cooper's Aristotle needs to be making is not that, of course, goodwill cannot itself have an ulterior motive, but that (as I quoted above) goodwill can arise out of detached admiration for goodness (cf. 1167a18–21), but only from personal gratitude for benefit or gratification. However it is unlikely that Aristotle is making this second point: it puts too much strain upon *epi toutois* if (as would fit) we translate it as 'on those terms' but take those terms to be not simply utility or pleasure (picking up 'utility' and 'pleasure', a12–13), but utility or pleasure *to another*; and besides, even if the point would be 'very acutely observed' (Cooper, 643), it contradicts an earlier remark: 'Many people have goodwill to those whom they have not seen but judge to be good or useful' (8.2.1155b34–1156a1). That 1167a13–14 are excluding goodwill from the lesser friendships is confirmed, I think, by the lines that follow:

For the man who has received a benefit bestows goodwill in return for what has been done to him, and in doing so is doing what is just; while he who wishes someone to prosper because he hopes for enrichment through him seems to have goodwill not to him but rather to himself, just as a man is not a friend to another if he cherishes him for the sake of some use to be made of him (a14–18).[31]

---

[31] A little tribute: by changing a 'but' into an 'and', and omitting an inserted 'only', Barnes rescues from impenetrability a passage that had fazed me.

Here Aristotle contrasts two agents: the man who, through intimacy, advances beyond mere goodwill and has a benefit to repay, which he repays; and the man who, motivated by hope (or perhaps expectancy) of future benefit, wishes the other well, but has no real goodwill towards him. What suits me here is not only the second clause (a15–18), but the little word 'for' (a14): if the whole sentence is supporting a13–14, those lines can only be denying (like *EE* 7.7.1241a5) that goodwill is present in the friendships of pleasure and utility. Hence *Nicomachean* 9.5 is to be understood as siding with *Eudemian* 7.7, and against Cooper.

So far, then, it seems to me that Cooper is correctly understanding the structure of Aristotle's treatment, but applying it against the grain of the text. Aristotle's general characterization of friendship was itself abstract, and to be enriched by reference to one kind, that of perfect friendship. Cooper supposes that it is the notion of goodwill that has to adapt itself to the shape of the facts; I suppose that it is well-wishing. His idea is that goodwill carries over, but is circumscribed; my idea is that Aristotle primarily locates the well-wishing that helps to constitute friendship within wishing to forward another's *eudaimoniā* as an extension of one's own, and finds it more than notionally present in the forms of wishing him pleasure or advantage on the ground that those too are served by perfect friendship, in its own way. The 'well' of wishing another well becomes multifarious when the nature of the good things one wishes him is left open; it recovers enough unity through its application within the paradigm of friendship focused upon *eudaimoniā*. Very conscious of a debt to Cooper for instilling life into what before seemed cut and dry, I do not wish to exaggerate the difference between our positions. It seems further just to close this section on a note of uncertainty: no one could have expected that a view of the friendships of pleasure and utility generous enough to contradict every reader's initial impression (especially of *NE* 8.3) would stand up to critical scrutiny for so long. Within the *Nicomachean Ethics* only one of the passages (9.5.1167a10–18) that Cooper cites in its favour has yet appeared to tell at all decisively against it; and such appearances can deceive. As Simmias remarked after a more famous (but I hope more fallacious) stretch of argument, 'Having a low regard for human weakness, I am bound to retain some doubt in my mind about what has been said' (*Pdo* 107b1–3).

6

Too complex to resolve that doubt into confidence, but both important for Cooper and intriguing in itself, is Aristotle's discussion of a
distinction that he makes in both *Ethics* (at *NE* 8.13.1162b21–
1163a9, and *EE* 7.10.1242b31–1243b14) between two subspecies of
friendship for utility, the one 'legal', the other 'moral' (1162b23,
1242b32). Cooper (Rorty edn., 337–8, n. 16) finds a contrast to suit
him between the two *Ethics*: the *Nicomachean* should only count the
moral type as really a friendship, for only it involves goodwill and
giving to the other 'as to a friend' (1162b31)—though Cooper concedes that Aristotle could grasp the point more firmly; the *Eudemian*
counts only the legal type as really a friendship of utility, criticizing
the moral type as a confusion between utility-friendship which is
wholly self-interested and character-friendship which expects no
return. Thus, for Cooper, the *Nicomachean* treatment is 'a distinct
improvement', though not consistently thought through. I think that
Cooper is right to find the *Eudemian* treatment a correct (I would add
a subtle) application of its view of utility-friendship; I think that he is
wrong to find a different account in the *Nicomachean Ethics*. So I
shall expound them together.

The legal type of utility-friendship is on written terms (*NE*
8.13.1162b25–6) that define either an immediate exchange or else a
fixed repayment (1162b27–8, *EE* 1242b35); the former is wholly
commercial (1162b26), the latter more generous (b27) in permitting a
postponement, which is a 'friendly' feature (b29). The moral variety
is not on fixed terms, but 'as to a friend' (1162b31); what does that
phrase signify? Cooper supposes that it implies goodwill: 'Aristotle
says the parties give to one another *hōs philō(i)*, i.e. in the spirit in
which true friends do, without looking for or soliciting any particular,
exact return' (loc. cit.). It is indeed definitive of this subspecies that
the return is not defined in advance. But its spirit is far from that of
true friends (in the restrictive sense of e.g. 9.5.1167a18), as Aristotle
at once makes clear: 'But one expects to receive as much or more, as
having not given but lent; and if a man is worse off when the relation is
dissolved than he was when it was contracted he will complain'
(1162b32–4). At least the overriding motive of utility-friendship is
self-interest: 'The friendship of utility is full of complaints; for as they
use each other for their own interests they always want to get the

better of the bargain, and think they have got less than they should' (b16–18). One may compare the contrast in 9.1 between 'those who offer something for the sake of the other party' (who are practising the friendship of virtue), and cases where 'the gift was not of this sort, but was made with a view to something' (1164a34–b1, b6–7).[32] How then can the moral variety be 'as to a friend' (1162b31)? The *Eudemian* analogue is clearer (though not, I shall argue, divergent):

There is recrimination especially in this friendship; the reason is that it is unnatural. For the friendships in respect of utility and of virtue are different; but these wish to have both together, and while they associate for the sake of utility they make out the friendship to be moral, as being good men; therefore as trusting one another they make it out to be not legal (1242b37–1243a2).

'As' (*hōs*) is ambiguous here: no doubt the parties really are trusting one another in that they are eschewing fixed terms ('they make an exchange as good and trustworthy men', 1243a11); but in context 'as being good men' clearly imputes a pretence—that of virtue-friendship. If we return to the *Nicomachean* phrase 'as to a friend' (1162b1) we find a multiple ambiguity, between *real* friendship (cf. 8.4.1157a30–31), an element of real friendship, and a pretence of real friendship. The first is already excluded, but to pin the phrase down further we need to read further:

All or most men, while they wish for what is fine, choose what is advantageous; now it is fine to do well by another without a view to repayment, but it is the receiving of benefits that is advantageous. Therefore . . . we must recognize that we were mistaken at the first and took a benefit from a person we should not have taken it from—since it was not from a friend, nor for one who did it just for the sake of acting so—and we must settle up just as if we had been benefited on fixed terms (1162b34–1163a6).

The words 'not from a friend' (a4) at last make clear that 'as to a friend' signified pretence (thus intimating what is more fully described at 9.3.1165b4–12). Moreover, the whole passage (which is close to *EE* 1243a34–b1) is only interpretable as excluding the existence of any open and secure alternative between the legal friendship of utility which is on fixed terms, and the full friendship of virtue within which beneficence is not for the sake of any return. Thus the two *Ethics* agree that the moral friendship of utility is 'unnatural' (1242b38).

---

[32] Barnes translates the last phrase by 'on conditions'; that is all right, so long as they left open the size of the return (cf. b7–12).

The *Eudemian Ethics* deems it, for that reason, especially liable to recrimination (1242b37–8); the *Nicomachean*, in effect, agrees (1162b23–5). Nor do they diverge over the basis for calculating the return. In a real friendship of virtue the measure of the proper return is the choice of the original agent (1163a22, 1243b2–3, cf. *NE* 9.1.1164b1–2), that is (as it would seem from the whole passage 1163a9–23) the cost which the agent considered worth while when making his choice. However, this should not be a source of recrimination, as the agent was not acting in the spirit of an exchange; indeed, reciprocation might be viewed not as the repayment of a debt, but rather as an act of retaliation, of getting one's own back by acting finely oneself (1162b6–13). Further, the same measure applies to the act of reciprocation, so that it is enough to reciprocate as best one can, not by choice doing less than is appropriate (1243b9–12). By contrast, in the friendship of utility it is the benefit of the recipient that is the measure (1163a16–17). In the legal variant, the return is fixed by explicit agreement (1162b25–8, 1243a32); in the moral variety, the return should be that on which the parties would rationally have agreed (1243b4–5), that is, in effect, in accordance with the benefit to the recipient (cf. 9.1.1164b6–21). Here, inability to pay fully will not be a satisfactory excuse (1243b12–14).

Thus it appears that in both *Ethics* a variety of the friendship of utility in which at least one party purports to be benefiting the other for his own sake is not allowed to be anything but a pretence or confusion, clearly on the assumption that, if it were anything more, it would belong within a different kind of friendship, that of virtue. If so, goodwill cannot be part even of a determinable definition of what counts as friendship.[33]

7

Or rather, it is now clear that Aristotle's *philiā* falls far short of our friendship. It does not follow that he is more cynical about the springs of friendship than we are, and sees mere well-wishing where we see

---

[33] It is true that the analogous point is not made out for the friendship of pleasure; but even when making the observation that lovers who are mutually pleasant are more friends and more constant than lovers who are mutually useful (unless he really means lovers of whom one is pleasant and the other useful), Aristotle keeps the language of an exchange (*NE* 8.4.1157a12–14).

goodwill;[34] instead, he may simply be analysing a term with a wider extension than ours. Cooper finds the upshot of the interpretation that I have been defending 'harsh' and 'depressing' (Rorty edn., 305); that is because he supposes that only 'paragons of virtue' are capable of perfect friendship. I have already implicitly taken a different view: it is true that, on Aristotle's assumption of a natural human tendency towards what is really good, any taints of vice are liable to conflict with a tincture of virtue, and so exclude that ideal of friendship that presupposes a unity of purpose intrapersonal as well as interpersonal; but, just as men form a spectrum from the very good to the very bad, so examples of friendship in virtue vary from the total to the very fragmentary (as I argued in the last chapter from *EE* 7.2.1238b1–5). When Aristotle remarks early in the *Nicomachean* treatment, 'We may see even in our travels how near and dear every man is to every other' (8.1.1155a21–2), he must have goodwill in mind: the term 'near' (*oikeios*) expresses a relation of identification (cf. 9.9.1170a3). According to his account of the origin of goodwill (in 9.5), the cause must be not bare human sympathy (though he may have a pre-theoretical awareness of that, cf. 9.4.1166a7–9), but the fellow-feeling which presupposes shared values.[35] Even beauty, whose mention here (9.5.1167a20) might seem excessively Greek, presumably only inspires goodwill, in addition to other responses, as a bloom upon the face of virtue (to borrow a metaphor disputedly present at 10.4.1174b33), say the endurance of an athlete (a20–1). What is needed is a community of values (and that may only be partial), not a community of saints. So we need not fear that goodwill has become the prerogative of a club from which 'most people, including virtually all of Aristotle's readers' are excluded (Cooper, op. cit. 305, apparently regarding the latter as below par).

Besides, well-wishing does not only deserve respect when it is generated by identification with another. Most of us feel an undifferentiating and usually idle goodwill towards virtually all of our fellow-humans (and many of our fellow-animals as well); but that

---

34 Cf. La Rochefoucauld (*Maximes* 83): 'What men have called friendship is only an association, a reciprocal arrangement of interests, and an exchange of services; it is in short only a transaction by which self-love always intends to gain something.'

35 It is a familiar feature of travelling that it brings us into dealings with strangers over simple matters (like food and comfort) in respect of which there are variations in tastes and traditions, but also a large measure of agreement in attitude.

may not be what motivates us *qua* colleague, customer, or conversa-
tionalist. I do not mean that goodwill withers in those connections
(though goodwill towards one's colleagues has its intermissions), but
that the casual or professional relationship may depend not upon any
increase in that basic goodwill, but upon the separate, if often not
dissimilar, interests of each party. Among all the varied instances of
human association, those permeated by goodwill may be a small
minority. Within the others, well-wishing between associates is no
expression of friendship (in our sense), but it may be more than 'stop-
go': the man 'who wishes someone to prosper because he hopes for
enrichment through him' (9.5.1167a15–16) is making a general
investment in an individual, and not just particular calculations from
occasion to occasion. To the extent that goodwill remains as an
undertow, linking the parties *qua* human beings, no total relationship
between persons falls wholly within either of the lesser friendships.
Aristotle's description of these must be understood as schematic and
abstract; instantiations of them will almost always involve what he
calls 'mixed friendship', so long as we think of that with reference not
just to roles (as he tends to) but to persons.[36]

   What then, if not friendship in our sense, is Aristotle's topic? It is
one to which it is right to devote about a fifth of a course in practical
philosophy. (A modern work on ethics and moral psychology which
gave that much space to friendship would seem quaint; that is only in
part because modern moral philosophy has become obsessed with
one's obligations towards people one does not know.) The width of
the topic is indicated by this passage:

To inquire how to behave to a friend is to look for a particular kind of justice,
for generally all justice is in relation to a friend. For justice involves a number
of individuals who are partners, and the friend is a partner either in one's
family or in one's life (*EE* 7.10.1242a19–22, cf. *NE* 8.9.1159b25–32,
8.11.1161b11, 9.12.1171b32–3).

Thus Aristotelian *philiā* is partnership, or association (*koinōniā*), and
partnerships are as diverse as friendships. To the extent that a partnership serves utility, it must consist of at least two persons diverse

---

[36] To be precise, partnerships that do not increase the initial goodwill may still make
it active instead of idle; the partners may then be described as *feeling* mutual goodwill
qua fellow-men, but *bestowing* it *qua* fellow-men in partnership with one another. This
pinpoints the difference, which has become a fine one, between myself and Cooper:
within the lesser friendships, what he ascribes to men *qua* partners, I ascribe to them
qua human (or humane) partners.

from each other, who exchange goods commensurable with one another (*NE* 5.5.1133a16–19). More generally, all its members must have something in common in which they all share, equally or unequally; none must simply have the role of subserving the interests of the others (*Pol* 7.8.1328a25–30). The effect is significantly to tighten the determinable definition of *philiā* as mutually recognized mutual well-wishing (*NE* 8.3.1156a8–10, *EE* 7.2.1236a14–15): the well-wishing must not be idle, as even goodwill can be (*NE* 9.5.1167a1–2, 9–10, *EE* 7.7.1241a10–12); there must, in effect, be an actual partnership.[37] So we have an instance of *philiā* whenever a pair or group of human beings is interacting in a way intended to benefit one another through beneficence or co-operation according to some shared conception of benefit. *Philiā* as positive interaction between human beings must be the largest concern of any practicable morality; it deserves all the pages devoted to it in Aristotle's two surviving works on ethics.

And yet Aristotle betrays signs of an ambivalence about this conveniently broad use of the term *philiā*.[38] The *Rhetoric* definition incorporating 'not for your own sake but for his' (2.4.1380b36–1381a1), which surfaces in the two *Ethics* as a commonplace (*NE* 9.4.1166a2–4, *EE* 7.6.1240a24–5), captures an ideal that clearly coloured the popular conception of *philiā*. I gave as one ground for the centrality of friendship in virtue that it alone has all the features that people expect of *philiā* (8.3.1156b18–19); it is apparent that goodwill was among those features. The more restrictive conception leaves its trace in an uncertainty which Aristotle alternatively ascribes to others (*EE* 7.2.1237b8–9, *NE* 8.6.1158b5–11), or admits to himself (8.4.1157a25–30), about whether the lesser friendships truly are types of *philiā*; also in occasional restrictive uses of *philos*, often in abrupt juxtaposition to the wider use.[39] A kind of compromise is achieved in talk of degrees of *philiā* (8.3.1156b10, 8.4.1157a13,

---

[37] Alternatively, it may be enough that there has been a partnership, interrupted only by distance; at one point Aristotle distinguishes the activity of friendship from friendship itself as a disposition to such activity (*NE* 8.5.1157b5–11). However, *pace* Walker (op. cit. 186), this is still a narrowing (though doubtless always intended): well-wishing need not even involve the disposition, but can be idle by nature (9.5.1167a8–10).

[38] What follows amounts to a concession that Walker and Cooper, even where I diverge from them, are sensitive to an aspect of Aristotle's attitude.

[39] Contrast 9.5.1167a16–18 with a12–13, *EE* 7.2.1237b31–2 with a33–4, and 7.7.1241a12–13 with a4–5; Aristotle can even write, 'Of these [sc. friendships], that because of pleasure is more like friendship' (*NE* 8.6.1158a18).

9.6.1167b10, 9.8.1168b2) or of 'real' *philiā* (*EE* 7.2.1238a19–20); the role I ascribed to similarities is bound to produce differences in degree. Aristotle finds common views contradictory: though they demand goodwill, they also apply the term *philos* widely (*NE* 8.4.1157a25–9). He blames those who mistake the primary for the universal for being unable 'to do justice to all the phenomena concerning *philiā*' (*EE* 7.2.1236a25–6); and yet the 'phenomena' (or common views) are themselves inconsistent (7.6.1240a30–1). Aristotle is one among many philosophers who, confronted with vagueness and even incoherence in common conceptions and even usages, opt for the most general and convenient; but it is his habit to prefer consensus to stipulation, and here the strain shows. This, I would finally suggest, explains his wambling within *Nicomachean* 8.2–3: he is not gratuitously inserting a requirement of goodwill in order to take it back, but acknowledging (he writes literally not 'we' but 'they say', 8.2.1155b31, 32), and even initially endorsing (1156a3–4), a familiar expectation before he puts it in its place (by his own determinable definition at 8.3.1156a8–10). The divergences between myself, Cooper, and Walker are of nuance: Walker finds a definition of friendship (within 8.2) which the lesser varieties only satisfy qualifiedly, since goodwill is absent from them; Cooper thinks that goodwill is present in those varieties, though qualifiedly; I have argued that all the varieties satisfy the final initial characterization, but that the lesser varieties only earn inclusion within a single class of relationships to the extent that they resemble perfect friendship, which does require goodwill. It is not surprising that different interpreters should resolve Aristotle's ambivalence in slightly different ways, each of which reflects from its own viewpoint the cross-currents of the text.

6

THE HOUSEHOLD

I

Our word 'friend' has an honorific but restricted sense: one's friends fall outside the necessities and importunities of home, workplace, town, or country. One can imagine a working and married adult leading a happy and responsible life, only arguably (even if one would argue it) at some cost, without any real friends, while for a Greek like Aristotle to ask whether a man needs friends is to ask whether one could be a happy hermit (cf. *NE* 9.9.1169b16–18). If we are to respect Greek conceptual boundaries rather than imposing our own, we need to consider the relationships that constitute a family and a state, more precisely in their terms, a household and a city. That may sound a wild extension of topic, but the focus of our interest in it can be narrowed: what development and variations do Plato and Aristotle impose here on the themes that I have already traced in their treatment of love and friendship? The very fact that they can apply the same term *philiā* in these further areas must encourage them to extend their theories, or rather to devise theories that are extendible, to explain family and social relationships in ways not alien to their analysis of the closest personal relationships. By determining the domain of a theory, concepts influence its content; to understand what Plato and Aristotle have to say about our friends, we need to explore what they do say about their *philoi*.

2

Plato, notoriously, had radical proposals to make about the dissolution of marriage and the family, and their replacement by a communality of spouses and children. Those come in the *Republic*, and are summarily endorsed at the start of the *Timaeus* (18c6–d5); by the *Laws* they have become an ideal that is not to become a reality (5.739b8–e4, 7.807b3–c1). But rather as Socrates' first speech in the

Phaedrus reveals that the transfiguration of pederasty in the second was not the product of a blindness to actuality, so Plato betrays a sensitivity to the actual relations of parents and children, even if he lacks an interest in them to yield an account as elaborated as that of Aristotle.

Of course parents are partial to their offspring (which may be part of a problem). Just as poets are fond of their own poems, so fathers are fond of their own children: each is their own creation (*ergon*, *Rep* 1.330c3–6). Despite his agreement with Diotima that one loves not one's own, but the good (*Symp* 205e5–206a2), Socrates in metaphorical talk with Theaetetus shows Plato quite aware that parents, perhaps especially mothers, are reluctant to have a first-born exposed, even if it is defective (*Theaet* 160e–161a). The biological link to their children strengthens the attachment of the parents (cf. *Symp* 209c5–6). When a child is only adopted, as in the case of an orphan, his guardian is likely to look after him less carefully than he would his own son (*Laws* 11.929e7); laws are needed to guard against that (11.928).

What is it that children offer their parents? We evolutionists might hesitate to assume that there must be an answer: wanting children would be favoured by natural selection even if it had no grounds. Plato, of course, is rich in rationalization. In the schematism of the *Symposium*, children offer parents a physical extension of themselves, while boys offer lovers a mental extension (208e1–209c7); but the thought was always available to him that children can offer both. If the individual person is immortal, that can only be in virtue of the immortal soul that he is (e.g. *Laws* 12.959b3–4). In the *Symposium*, as we saw, it is a life, physical or mental, that can be prolonged with another as its subject (207c9–208b6). In the *Laws*, it is the human race that is, through reproduction, 'a companion of eternity' (4.721c2–6); in a way that is not explained, that yields a desire in each member of the race for that kind of immortality among others (b8–9). If children can inherit their parents' physiology, how may they inherit their minds? There are two ways. Plato believes in the inheritance even of acquired characteristics: fathers who behave insolently or unjustly, especially around the time of conception, will stamp their vices upon the souls and bodies of their children (*Laws* 6.775d4–e1). The other way is that of education: it should be the task of parents, as of educators in the *Republic*, to foster the best element in their children with the aid of the like in themselves, so as to set up a guide and ruler, on its model and in its place, in the mind of the child (*Rep*

9.590e8–591a2). That will equip the child for the autonomy (cf. a2–3) that will never be enjoyed by someone who remains the 'slave' of another's reason (590c8–d6).[1]

Aristotle's account is a conceptual and psychological elaboration of Plato's. Parents love their children as poets love their poems (*NE* 4.1.1120b13, 9.7.1168a1–3). Existence counts as a benefit (8.11.1161a16–17, *EE* 7.8.1241b1–3), but it is indeed 'the greatest' of benefits (1161a17) in a way that modifies the usual pattern of beneficence (for which cf. *NE* 9.7): the beneficiary is valued by his benefactor not as the recipient (one might say, the receptacle) of the benefit, but as the benefit; the child is himself his parents in action (cf. 9.7.1168a7). That 'every man loves his own handiwork better than he would be loved by it if it came alive' (9.7.1167b34–5) is a somewhat bizarre generalization from an allegedly familiar fact: 'The originator is more attached to his offspring than the offspring to their begetter' (8.12.1161b21–2). Love of existence is the source of parental devotion (cf. 9.7.1168a7–8) as well as of filial gratitude (8.11.1161a16–17); but the former is the stronger. Aristotle adduces various reasons why parents love children more than they are loved by them (8.12.1161b19–26), and why, further, mothers love children more than fathers do (8.12.1161b26–7, 9.7.1168a24–6, *EE* 7.8.1241b7–9): parents, and mothers especially, know their children better than they are known by them, and better know that they are their children; mothers think the children more their own work, because they have put more pain into producing them.[2]

Yet neither the fact that the beneficiary is the benefit, nor these further psychological observations, exhaust the significance of Aristotle's most striking claim: 'Parents love their children as themselves (for their issue are by virtue of their separate existence a sort of other selves)' (*NE* 8.12.1161b27–9). Child as 'other self' (*heteros autos*) is no mere verbal variant upon child as 'part of oneself' (5.6.1134b11): a proper part of myself is only a fragment of myself, like my hair and

---

[1] Historically, however, the incapacity of mothers and the failure of fathers to perform this task appear to have left pederasty to fill the gap. Cf. George Devereux: 'The Greek father usually failed to counsel his son; instead, he counseled another man's son, in whom he was erotically interested'; 'Greek Pseudo-homosexuality and the "Greek Miracle"', *Symbolae Osloenses* 52 (1967), 78.

[2] An Aristotelian point that Aristotle does not make here is that forward-looking identification is likely to be stronger than backward-looking, just as—as I once heard David Rees remark—future well-being is crucial for *eudaimonia* in a way that past well-being is not (cf. *NE* 1.11.1101a16–17).

teeth (cf. 1161b23), while another self must resemble the whole of me. A child who never grew up would never become a copy of its parents: it would continue to depend upon them, and they would hardly be alive in it. That children *grow up* to be their parents' 'other selves' is implicit in a description of the child as part of its father 'until it reaches a certain age and is separated' (1134b11). If we put that and 1161b28–9 (quoted above) together, it becomes clear that it is the adult offspring that is 'another self'. This relation is partly biological, partly moral. It is appropriate that parents should impress their character, by instruction and example, upon their children; out of prior affection and gratitude these are naturally obedient (10.9.1180a31–2, b4–7). When the child's virtue is said to be 'not his own in relation to himself, but in relation to his goal and his guide' (*Pol* 1.13.1260a32–3), his goal, which is his adult self, is also his guide's other self; his father is in person an efficient, in proxy a final, cause.

Biologically speaking, physical procreation preserves specific but not numerical identity: 'In some cases it is even obvious that the producer is of the same kind as the produced (not, however, the same nor one in number, but in form), e.g. in the case of natural products (for man produces man)' (*Met* 7.8.1033b29–32). The resultant immortality is specific and not particular (*De gen corr* 2.11.338b5–19; *De an* 2.4.415a26–b7). But talk of 'another self' conveys a closer relation between individuals. Its connotation of sameness in diversity amounts to a paradox that becomes intolerable if the sameness is construed as actual identity. That this is not Aristotle's intention is clear from the formal properties that he assigns to the relation. It comes in degrees, and is not fully symmetrical: thus 'the originator is more attached to his offspring than the offspring to their begetter' (*NE* 8.12.1161b21–2, already quoted). Clearly the reality of the situation is not a relation of identity, but attitudes of identification that vary in intensity (as between fathers and mothers), and may be wholly unreciprocated (as by a child who cannot even identify his mother, 8.8.1159a28–33). It is not a coincidence that Aristotle most transparently uses the language of identity when he is alleging a kind of transitivity:

Brothers love each other as being born of the same parents; for their identity with them makes them identical with each other (which is the reason why people talk of 'the same blood', 'the same stock', and so on). They are, therefore, in a sense the same thing, though in separate individuals (8.12.1161b30–3).

Yet the actual identity here is one of the family, and not of its members. The last sentence quoted is Janus-faced, looking back towards family identity, forward towards psychological connections that come close to those between perfect friends: 'Two things that contribute greatly to friendship are a common upbringing and similarity of age; for "two of an age take to each other", and familiarity makes for comradeship; whence the friendship of brothers is akin to that of comrades' (1161b33–1162a1). In similarity of character, and equality (8.11.1161a25–7, 12.1162a9–15, *EE* 7.10.1242a35–40—though, as with comrades, seniority in age gives certain privileges, 7.10.1242a5–6), brothers can exemplify the best kind of friendship in virtue, if the character they share is good.

More problematic is how the relations of parents and children stand to Aristotle's threefold categorization of friendship. Until one's children have achieved independence, thus becoming another self instead of part of oneself, it is only in a qualified sense that there can be justice towards them (*NE* 5.6.1134b9–11), or friendship (cf. *EE* 7.10.1242a19–22). Once there is unqualified friendship, it would seem to fall outside the categorization to the extent that it is grounded on love of mere existence (cf. *NE* 9.7.1168a7–8), to which even in abstraction there is something 'fine' (here equivalent to intrinsically desirable, *Pol* 3.6.1278b25–6). Yet the indications are that Aristotle would wish to classify it as an unequal friendship according to virtue. To an extent, this works well. Father and child are related by *philiā*, but it would be out of place for them to be *philoi* (*EE* 7.4.1239a4–6); the same is true of the analogous relations involving great moral inequality of king and subject, and god and man (*NE* 8.7.1158b33–1159a2, 8.11.1161a15, 8.12.1162a4–5.). The friendship of children to parents is a relation to them 'as to something good and superior' (12.1162a5); but, as in perfect friendship, there is pleasure and utility too, through a life lived in common (1162a7–9). Yet Aristotle does not tailor his perceptions to fit his model. On neither side need the relationship involve pleasure in the other's company: fathers wish their children to exist, but consort with others (*EE* 7.6.1240a29–30); benefactor and beneficiary both desire the other's existence, but the company of the pleasant (7.11.1244a28–30). Nor are the intensities of their feelings such as the model might demand and predict: the better should be more loved than loving (*NE* 8.7.1158b25), and the friendship of parents and children is according to merit (8.11.1161a21–2); and yet, as we saw, it is the parent who is fonder of the child.

However, even if pleasure is a corollary of a friendship of goodness, where the goodness is very unequal we may suppose pleasure to be taken rather in forwarding the other's *eudaimoniā* than in sharing it (a picture which preserves a structure from Plato while discarding Aristotle's usual emphasis upon mutual perception). And it is a familiar problem with beneficence that, despite the demands of gratitude, we love those to whom we give more than those from whom we receive; Aristotle's solution (as we saw in Chapter 4) is that in loving his beneficiary the benefactor is loving himself in action. In loving and serving their children parents are leading and serving their own lives.

3

Plato's and Aristotle's attitudes to the relations between men and women are functions of their beliefs about the female mind, but not the same function. Aristotle's attitudes make the best of his disparaging beliefs; Plato's beliefs are more ambivalent, but his attitudes less sympathetic. Aristotle clearly welcomes women, but restricts their status; Plato elevates their role, but apparently regrets their necessity. Aristotle endorses a repressive reality which only allows women to be women; Plato proposes a coercive phantasy which would transform them into men. If Aristotle is here a Procrustes, Plato is a Pygmalion.

Unlike Aristotle, Plato was alert to a possible mismatch between women as he perceived them in Athens, creatures of darkness and seclusion, quite unready to be dragged into the light of day (*Laws* 6.781c4–7), and women as they might be, educated and emancipated for their own good and the good of the city. Julia Annas complains, 'He accepts and even exaggerates offensive contemporary sexist stereotypes.'[3] That may be true; it is the habit of radicals to traduce the status quo. At least Plato was intending to describe a scandal, and not a fact of nature. The picture is certainly displeasing: it is of a nature dizzy (*Rep* 4.431b9–c3, 8.557c7–9), nasty (5.469d7–8), weepy (*Pdo* 117d3–e2, *Rep* 3.395e1–2, 10.605d7–e1), and uppity (3.395d6–e1, 8.549c8–d3). In practice, no doubt, Plato was a misogynist; in theory, he dreamed a dream, but perhaps a misogynist's dream.

To escape from actuality, Plato repeatedly invokes nature or *phusis* (in fact, twenty-four times from *Rep* 5.453a1 to 456d1). He supports his appeal by citing the lower animals (5.451d3–9, 466d7), and

---

[3] *An Introduction to Plato's Republic* (Oxford, 1981), 184.

primeval or remote peoples (*Critias* 110b5–7, *Laws* 7.804e4–805a3,
806a7–8). His interpretation (it would be hard to say of what data) is
that the same nature is exemplified in men and women, but that it is
better exemplified in men (*Rep* 5.456a10–11). Thus the average man
is in all ways superior to the average woman, though many women are
better than many men in many things (455c4–d4, cf. *Crat* 392c6–9).
This is a view that can take on a variety of emphases. It is inferred that
women should be educated to serve as guardians (in the *Republic*), or
in the assembly and dicasteries (in the *Laws*); but it need not be
excluded that the souls of morally defective men deserve to be reincar-
nated in women (*Tim* 42b5–6, 90e6–91a1). For we are not to think
merely that, in modern terms, the average woman's IQ is a few points
lower than the average man's. Qualities of mind other than intellectual are close to those of the body (*Rep* 7.518d9–10, cf. *NE*
10.8.1178a14–16); so women's physical weakness must have pointed
for Plato to a moral inferiority (cf. the extended use of 'weak' at
5.455e1, 456a11). It is to compensate for this 'weakness' that women
take to secrecy and craft (*Laws* 6.781a3–4). Plato does acknowledge
some good qualities as naturally feminine, namely moderation and
caution in contrast to magnificence and courage (7.802e5–11); but
the former sound the lesser virtues. Even equal education for men and
women can be urged on the ground that, since a woman's potential for
virtue is less than a man's, to neglect it is perhaps to run twice the
danger (6.781b1–3). So even by nature women are on average (not in
every case) more than marginally worse off than men—if not so
disagreeably as in Plato's actual experience. How was the best to be
made of that? Of the utopian in Plato we expect solutions; what we
receive is more of an evasion.

   To give focus to a disappointment I shall start by sketching two
analogous solutions that Plato does not in fact propose, but could have
proposed had he wished. Suppose that one accepts that there are
feminine qualities, that is qualities characteristic of women as
opposed to men, desirable as well as (though not, if they really derive
from some inferiority, as much as) masculine qualities; one will then
look for a blending in life of the two classes of qualities. There should
be two ways of achieving that: one is to respect, even to emphasize,
the differences between the sexes, and to look to marriage as an
institution that brings together the qualities of man and woman in a
human partnership; the other is to encourage a kind of androgyny by
which individuals attempt to combine those qualities, if often

unequally, within themselves. The aim of both policies is to achieve a union of complementary qualities; in one case the unit is a pair of people, in the other the single person. The first policy looks to marriage not just to define one's private life, but to direct one's life; the second aims at a marriage of temperaments within one's own mind.[4] But what do we find in Plato?

For Plato's provisions on behalf, and not in place, of marriage, we look to the *Laws* and *Politicus*. Both recommend marriage between complementaries, not like and like. The *Laws* looks to the interests of spouses, children, and city: while everyone is always naturally attracted to the person most similar to himself, it is better for the virtue of the spouses (6.773a6–7), the blending of their children (d4), and the balance of society (b7–c3) to marry someone of contrasted fortune and temperament. If man and wife become estranged, presumably by their ungentle temper, each will ideally be found a more gentle mate, whether for the procreation of children, or for mutual care and companionship in old age (9.929e9–930b3). The *Politicus* also deprecates being governed by the affection of like for like (310c4–7) instead of the eugenic need to mix courage with restraint (e8–9). To an extent, Plato is displaying a concern to make the best of marriage in the way sketched above. But there is a crucial divergence: about differences between the sexes he is silent. Indeed, it is implicit in the genetic argument as he presents it that men and women are not naturally complementary, so that we must rely upon explicit principles and 'charms' (*Laws* 6.773d5) to discourage, say, a daring man and daring woman from uniting to produce a headstrong son or daughter. This is the more surprising in that the contrasts he instances, between the hasty and the steady (773a7–b2), and the adventurous and the circumspect (*Pol* 319d6–7), could be used to differentiate the natures of the sexes (cf. *Laws* 7.802e5–11). There is no suggestion that a homosexual liaison is liable to be less successful, because less complementary, than a heterosexual one.

In the *Republic* marriage is abolished. Since sexual reproduction is not, at least the eugenic argument for the copulation of complementaries should have the same force. In fact, it is absent; instead, we are told 'to mate the best of our men with the best of our women as often as possible' (5.459d7–8), that is with women 'akin to them by nature'

---

[4] Most attractively, no doubt, one may pursue the second policy within the first, absorbing within a married life those qualities of one's spouse that complement and can complete one's own.

(456b3). Why this discrepancy? It is not that Plato has yet to conceive the notion of complementary characteristics; rather, as James Adam well remarks, 'The opposite qualities of strength and sensibility are already united in the character of each of the parents' (*The Republic of Plato*, ad 5.456b10). In fact, the training and education of the guardians involve the reconciling of two contrasts: between the toughness of spirit and the tenderness of reason (3.410c8–e9, summarized at *Tim* 18a4–7), and between facility and stability within reason itself (6.503b7–d12). This is explicitly a policy of combining opposites within a single mind. Intriguingly, each of the oppositions is, according to a perennial typology, of a masculine quality to a feminine; that makes it striking that Plato does not conceive them in that light. No doubt he would have wanted to revise them had he done so: otherwise a tension would have shown up between the superiority of reason to spirit, and the presumed superiority of man to woman. Plato is unaware of that danger; to be recommending a kind of androgyny is far from his intention. He is willing to pretend, unseriously, that the philosopher should resemble a well-bred dog (2.375d4–376c2), but not seriously to propose that the philosophic mind should be half feminine.

Thus Plato was in a position to offer women some consolation for a supposed basic inferiority: out of it, he could have conceded, arise certain good qualities, characteristically feminine, that are essential to achieving balance both within human relationships, and within the individual mind. That is not the consolation he offers. Instead, the best prospect he is willing to hold out to women is of a transformation into he-men. It is as true of the *Laws* as of *Republic* 5 that, as Annas well complains (op. cit. 185), Plato 'spends his time claiming, irrelevantly and grotesquely, that women can engage in fighting and other "macho" pursuits nearly as well as men'. One revealing detail is that Plato applies the very same terms 'noble' and 'virile' (*gennaios* and *blosuros*) to future guardians (7.535b1–2), that is in effect (in the context of a10–b1) to the finest of young men, and to the one woman (if we set aside the fictional Diotima) whom Socrates is willing to take as his model, his midwife mother Phainarete (*Theaet* 149a2). The best that can be said of Sarmatian women, and the worst of Spartan, is that the latter make the former seem like men (*Laws* 7.806b7–8). Women are to be admitted on terms of virtual equality into the ideal utopia of the *Republic*, or the second-best utopia of the *Laws*, on one condition: they are to turn themselves, so near as possible, into men.

Plato's masculine stereotype is never so pronounced as when he is imposing it on women; here, we may feel, idiosyncrasy is taking over from philosophy.[5]

Aristotle's predilection was different: at least on stage, 'it is not fitting for a woman to be brave or clever' (*Poetics* 15.1454a23–4). More precisely, she should only be a brave woman, and so brave in a way that would be cowardly in a man (*Pol* 3.4.1277b21–2). The courage of a man is not that of a woman: they differ as that of a commander from that of a subordinate (1.13.1260a23). This contrast holds between male and female virtue in general (1.5.1254b13–14, 1.13.1260a21–4). The ground would seem to be that women have a deliberative capacity, but an ineffectual one (*akūron*, 1.13.1260a13), whether because, being more emotional than men (*Hist an* 9.1.608b8–11), they are acratic, or because they keep changing their minds (cf. *NE* 7.9.1151b15). Consequently, women need the decisions of others to act upon. Their acts will then be more than 'as if' virtuous, not just matching the content but manifesting the presence of correct judgement (cf. 6.13.1144b26–7); but that must be the firm judgement of a man. Accordingly, silence is the salient female virtue (*Pol* 1.13.1260a30, 3.4.1277b23).[6]

Thus the relation of husband to wife is as ruler to ruled (*EE* 7.3.1238b24–5). Aristotle vacillates about how to label it in political terms. Most often he calls it 'aristocratic' (e.g. 7.9.1241b30), on the ground that the man rules according to merit, entrusting to the woman those tasks that 'befit' her (*NE* 8.10.1160b32–5, 8.11.1161a22–5); otherwise his rule becomes 'oligarchic' (8.10.1160b35–1161a1). But once the rule is called 'political' (*Pol* 1.12.1259b1). However, he effectively glosses the terms as equivalent here by adding that, whereas political rule usually involves equal citizens ruling and being

---

[5] This complaint is not new; it was first made, to my knowledge, by Ulrich von Wilamowitz-Möllendorf (*Platon*, i. 398–9), who illuminatingly compares female figures in archaic sculpture as combining a male physiognomy with female sexual characteristics. Plato's female gymnasts and warriors have become the ancestresses of Michelangelo's Leda, and Betjeman's Joan Hunter Dunn. Perhaps he would have been happy to dispense with them altogether if he could have allowed himself Ursula Le Guin's phantasy (to which Alethea Hayter has referred me) of a species of neuter humanoids who reproduce themselves by temporarily assuming a sex; *The Left Hand of Darkness* (London, 1969).

[6] It will be apparent later that this risks confounding women with slaves (which is un-Greek, 1.2.1252b5–6). Aristotle would better have envisaged domestic decisions owing their content to the consultation of man and wife, their efficacity to the man's decisiveness and strength of will.

ruled by turns, the woman is always subordinate to the man (1259b1–
10). If the woman is dominant, that is contrary to nature (b2–3), and
owed not to virtue, but, say, to the power of a dowry (*NE*
8.10.1161a1–3). Where husband rules and wife is ruled, they enjoy
that equality which is not arithmetical but proportional (*EE*
7.3.1238b21–5), living a life unequal to the other's but equal to their
respective merits; and political justice holds among men who are 'free
and either proportionally or arithmetically equal' (*NE* 5.6.1134a25–
8). The concession is that there are tasks for which the woman is
better fitted; so each is to supplement the other, pooling their distinct
capacities (8.12.1162a22–4). In inferring an identity of role from the
example of animals Plato was neglecting the household (*Pol*
2.5.1264b4–6, cf. *Rep* 5.451d4–e1). Here, man and wife serve one
another as opposites (*EE* 7.5.1239b23–5), loving each other as tallies
which, put together, achieve a single mean (1239b30–2, cf. *NE*
8.8.1159b19–23); for instance, she preserves what he acquires (*Pol*
3.4.1277b24–5). The limitations are two: the wife remains subordinate, and her sphere is the home (cf. *NE* 5.6.1134b16–17, *Pol*
2.5.1264b6).[7]

Aristotle's depiction of the marital relation is redeemed, to an
extent, by his enthusiasm for it. He places it biologically as a natural
corollary for human beings of that instinct to reproduce which we
share with animals and plants (*NE* 8.12.1161b16–19, *Pol*
1.2.1252a26–30); for, unlike other animals (so he asserts), who perform occasional couplings, we form lasting couples (*EE*
7.10.1242a22–6). This is one answer to a difficulty that Stephen
Clark has raised about the appeal to man's characteristic activity
(*ergon*): 'Man is one of the few animals to be permanently in rut (*Hist
an* 5.8.542a26–7) . . . It is not therefore immediately obvious, least of
all to Aristotle, that Don Juan was right' (*Aristotle's Man*, 17).
Aristotle, quite sensibly, associates a steady sexual drive with con-
nubiality, not promiscuity (whose source is rather boredom).[8]
Human sexual differentiation falls under a general principle that it is
better for that which imposes the form to be separate from that which

---

[7] There is a way of neutralizing this relegation: the wife's—and indeed the husband's—place might be in the home in the sense in which the barber's place is in the
barber's shop, the banker's in the bank, etc. But I take Aristotle to assume that to be a
good woman is to be a good wife and mother in a way that to be a good man is not to be a
good husband and father, but also, say, a good citizen.

[8] He also, common-sensibly, recognizes the value of children in cementing a
marriage (*NE* 8.12.1262a27–9).

supplies the matter (*De gen an* 2.1.732a3–7); furthermore, the sexes differ most in character where the species is most developed (*Hist an* 9.1.608b4–8). Morally, Aristotle places the relation of man and wife, if they are good, within the friendship of virtue; for each will delight in the proper virtue of the other (*NE* 8.12.1162a25–7). That is, of course, an unequal virtue, of ruler and of ruled; but the partnership still depends upon a shared perception of moral values (*Pol* 1.2.1253a15–18). Like all friendships in virtue, this one also yields pleasure and utility; but here, no doubt, those do not only arise as corollaries. To the extent that the utility is independent of the virtue, the friendship can also be mentioned as one of utility (*EE* 7.10.1242a31–2); indeed Aristotle, rather restrictively, explains the attraction of opposites by utility (7.5.1239b23–34). But that is an aspect, not the focus.

Unlike Plato, Aristotle was a married man, and apparently a devoted one.[9] His style here, even so, remains undemonstrative;[10] yet the appreciation that he evinces of an institution in our eyes shackled and blinkered seems unselfish and sincere. Whether it disconcerts us more or less, we may surmise that Aristotle's complacency was the product of a greater personal perceptiveness, untrumped by utopian ideals, than Plato's abstract if more imaginative discontent.

4

Unforgiving of slavery, we tend to think of slaves in large groups, in Athenian or Syracusan quarries, on Roman latifundia, in slave-ships or on southern plantations, in (effectively) Siberian labour-camps. Apologists of slavery prefer to dwell upon family retainers, partners in domestic life, happy parasites upon the happiness of others. When A. E. Housman and Robert Bridges shook hands on the proposition that civilization without slavery is impossible,[11] we may presume that the great good they had in mind was not collective forced labour, but freedom for poets from household chores. It is largely true of Plato

---

[9] Cf. Anton-Hermann Chroust, *Aristotle*, i. 81.

[10] As, despite the impression made by levelling translators, it ceases to be in his ethical writings at moments of conscious moral eccentricity (e.g. *NE* 9.8.1169a18–25, 10.7.1177b26–1178a2).

[11] *The Letters of A. E. Housman*, ed. Henry Maas (London, 1971), 217.

and Aristotle that they treat slavery within the ambit of the household; both see its acceptable form as an intimate relation between persons in which the master supplements the infirm understanding of the slave by his own intelligence.[12]

In the *Republic*, Plato's interest in the institution of slavery is so minimal that it is disputed whether he intends it at all.[13] In the *Laws*, slaves are subjected to legislation that seems harsh even by the standards of his own time.[14] His attitude towards slaves seems ambivalent. On the one hand, slaves are to be punished rather than admonished (*Laws* 6.777e4–6), and, when needing medical treatment, to be given instructions without an explanation (4.720b8–e6); indeed, because of the connection between friendship and equality of a kind, masters and slaves will never be friends (6.757a1). On the other hand, the master who treats his slaves justly is sowing the seeds of virtue (6.777d7–e1). The relation of master and slave is analogous to that of soul to body in the *Phaedo* (79e8–80a2), and of head to other bodily members in the *Timaeus* (44d6–7); in both works, in effect, that relates master to slave as reason to the irrational. That confirms the ambivalence, for there is an optimism and a pessimism to Plato's view of the irrational.[15] At worst, appetite is insatiable, keen to enslave and dominate the soul (*Rep* 4.442a5–b2); reason must prune it coercively like a farmer, 'nursing and cultivating its tamer elements and preventing the wilder ones growing' (9.589b2–3). At best, there is scope for persuasion and agreement: Plato can write of 'concord' (*sumphōnia*, 4.432a8, 442c10, 9.591d2), 'agreement' (*homodoxiā*, 4.442d1), 'unanimity' (*homonoia*, 4.432a7), and even 'friendship' (4.442c10,

---

[12] There is a rare reference to 'city menials' at *Laws* 7.794b7; but even they are described as acting as individuals on the specific instructions of another individual.

[13] Contrast Gregory Vlastos, 'Does Slavery Exist in Plato's *Republic?*', *Platonic Studies*, 140–6, with Brian Calvert, 'Slavery in Plato's Republic', *Classical Quarterly* 37 (1987), 367–72. Vlastos takes mention of 'child and woman and slave' (4.433d2–3) as decisive; but there Plato must be nodding, for they constitute the subordinate elements in the traditional household which he has abolished. However, Vlastos is right to reject any argument from silence (op. cit. 141, n. 6). Calvert claims that there is no category of work for slaves to perform that could distinguish them from artisans; but, while both groups are parasitic on the reason of others (cf. 9.590c8–d6), slaves may be distinctive in needing a constant and detailed supervision unworthy of guardians and even of auxiliaries. Artisans and slaves would belong *together* as representatives of appetite; Calvert is wrong to argue that psychic parallelism would demand a fourth part of the soul. That artisans should at once be metaphorical 'slaves' (ibid.) and literal masters is a complication, but not an incoherence.

[14] Cf. W. K. C. Guthrie, *A History of Greek Philosophy*, v. 348–9.

[15] I have learnt here from Christopher Gill, 'Plato and the Education of Character', *Archiv für Geschichte der Philosophie* 67 (1985), 11–12, 15, 21–2.

9.589b5).[16] These tensions need amount not to a contradiction, but to an alternation of hopes and fears: desiring slaves, and slavish desires, are to be brought in line now by force, now by persuasion. The ideal is a slave more virtuous, and therefore even more devoted to his master, than brother or son (*Laws* 6.776d7–e1); such virtue is at once to slave's and master's benefit (777d2–3).[17] The danger is a slave loyal instead to his fellows; it is best if slaves share neither homeland, nor home language (c8–d2). We may be reminded of the jealous lover described by Lysias and Socrates in the *Phaedrus*, selfishly concerned to exclude his boy from any company and influence but his own (232c5–d2, 239e2–240a2); for Plato there is the difference that a good master is the best, the sensual lover the worst, of guides. Plato's ambivalence arises, it must seem to us, out of a prejudice, and an observation: he assumes that there is a natural distinction between slave and free man; he observes that it does not come easily to slaves to respect it (6.777b4–c1). Hence slaves are to be fostered like friends, and distrusted like enemies.

The notion of a natural slave, implicit in Plato, becomes explicit and elaborated in Aristotle. He is a man by a nature not his own but another's (*Pol* 1.4.1254a14–15, 1.5.1254b20). His subordination, unlike his master's authority, is a matter not just of role, but of personhood: 'The master is only master of the slave, and is not his; the slave is not only slave of the master, but also wholly his' (1.4.1254a11–13). The point is not simply and tautologically that the master owns the slave, not vice versa: it is that a master is one thing that a man may happen to be, while being a slave is one way of being a man. A man may become a slave through ill fortune (notably captivity in war), but only a conventional slave; Aristotle approves no more of purely accidental slavery (*Pol* 1.6) than Plato of Greek enslaving Greek (*Rep* 5.469b8–c7). It is true than not all mastery is conventional either; for a man may deserve to be a master (unlike a natural slave who makes slaves of others). But while a man may deserve mastery, at least in relation to others who deserve slavery, he never needs it in order to be a man of the kind he is; a slave who deserves slavery is, in himself, incomplete as a man. A slave has the

[16] The ambivalence continues after the *Republic*: the *Phaedrus* describes a process of breaking in the lover's appetite so that it is silenced by reason (253e5–255a1), the *Laws* one of inculcating feelings in the child that will harmonize with reason (2.653a5–c4).

[17] Plato actually recommends it as benefiting master more than slave; that probably over-corrects the opposite error, as does his recommendation that masters should harm their slaves even less than their equals (d3–5).

status of a part (1.4.1254a8–11), more exactly, of a 'separated part' (1.6.1255b12). However, in specifying the manner of dependence further Aristotle fluctuates in effect between two individually coherent alternatives which he never explicitly separates. While Plato is ambivalent, Aristotle risks being inconsistent. I shall try to make out that the inconsistency is only apparent; but the appearance needs to be noticed.

There is first what we may call the lower slavery, with master as tyrant. The slave is his master's tool (*NE* 8.11.1161b4, *EE* 7.9.1241b23, *Pol* 1.4.1254b17); thus he is analogous to the body as tool of the soul (*De an* 1.3.407b26, 2.4.415b18–19, *EE* 7.9.1241b22). Whence a threefold analogy: master to slave is as artisan to tool or as soul to body (*NE* 8.11.1161a34–5, *EE* 7.9.1241b17–19, 1242a28–9). It is primarily the master who benefits from the slave, as a tyrant benefits, though unjustly, from his subjects (*NE* 8.10.1160b29–30, *Pol* 5.10.1311a2–4). If it can be added that they share the same interests, this is because the master's benefit is *ipso facto* that of master-cum-slave (*EE* 7.9.1241b21–2, *Pol* 1.6.1255b9–10); it forms the focal goal of a single active unit. The slave assists his master's actions (*Pol* 1.4.1254a8), but just as a means to the other's ends: ends and means have nothing in common (*Pol* 7.8.1328a28–33), and the goal is the master, not the slave, in action. Consequently there can exist between them no community, no partnership (*koinōniā*, *EE* 7.9.1241b19); nor any kind of friendship beyond one 'by analogy' (7.10.1242a28–31), surely remote.

There is secondly the higher slavery, with master as king. The analogy here is between the dependence of the slave and that of the child: 'Since the child is undeveloped, it is clear that his virtue is not his own in relation to himself, but in relation to his goal and his guide; likewise, the virtue of a slave is in relation to his master' (*Pol* 1.13.1260a31–3). The rule of father over son is not despotic, but regal (*NE* 8.11,1161a15, *EE* 7.9.1241b29, *Pol* 1.12.1259b1); its internal analogue is the control not of body by soul, but of desire by reason (*NE* 1.13.1103a3, *Pol* 1.5.1254b4–6). It is to reason and desire that master and slave, on this conception, are most precisely akin. The natural slave is 'he who participates in reason to the extent of apprehending but not possessing it' (1.5.1254b22–3); the desiring element in the soul, unlike the vegetative which in no way participates in reason, 'shares in it, in so far as it listens to and obeys it' (*NE* 1.13.1102b29–31). That 'the irrational element is in some sense persuaded by reason' is indicated by the giving of advice (1.13.1102b33–4); analogously, it is a mistake to 'deprive slaves of reason and say one should employ command only; for slaves need admonition more than children' (*Pol* 1.13.1260b5–7). Thus a slave is capable of virtue of character (1.13.1260a32–3, b3), if 'only a little, viz. so much as not to fail in his function through intemperance or cowardice' (1260a35–6, cf. a1–2). This amounts to an executive virtue in need of externally supplied goals. Being essentially obedience, it operates not only in accord with, but in the presence of, reason (cf. *NE* 6.13.1144b26–7); the incapacitating factor is that the slave's virtue is, and must remain, at the service of another. Moreover, if the slave really stands to his master as the child to 'his goal and his guide', that is not only to his director but also to his adult self (*Pol* 1.13.1260a32–3), it must be the master's benefit that is the *criterion* of the slave's virtue; yet it need not follow that the *value* of that virtue is purely instrumental.[18] In that the slave is 'able to participate in law and agreement' (*NE* 8.11.1161b7–8), and in that he also benefits from the relationship (*Pol* 1.6.1255b12–13), there can be friendship between him and his master (*NE* 8.11.1161b7–8). Friendship of what kind? One in part, no doubt, of mutual material utility (e.g. 'The master's rule cannot survive when the slave is perishing', *Pol* 3.6.1278b36–7); also one that involves an extreme and lasting inequality; yet also one that might be titled 'because of virtue' in that the parties respect and forward in one another the virtues proper to the capacity of each.

How, if at all, are these two different conceptions of natural slavery, higher and lower, to be reconciled? The easiest thought is that they discriminate two categories of natural slave; Aristotle's failure to separate them makes it unlikely that he meant that. A harder thought may lie behind an otherwise cryptic distinction: '*Qua* slave one cannot be friends with him; but *qua* man one can' (*NE* 8.11.1161b5–6). Perhaps the two kinds of slavery are different aspects of the same relationship, the lower slavery relating master to slave *qua* slave, the higher relating master to slave *qua* man.[19] If this is right, it also

---

[18] For a related distinction between the measure and the motive of virtuous action, cf. Anthony Kenny, *The Aristotelian Ethics*, 208.

[19] Martha Nussbaum applies 1161b5–8 instead to the conventional slave, 'Shame, Separateness, and Political Unity: Aristotle's Criticism of Plato', in A. O. Rorty (ed.) *Essays on Aristotle's Ethics*, 434, n. 54; that involves, I think, too great a change of topic, and conflicts, as she notes, with the sensible point that master and conventional slave are less likely to be related by friendship than master and natural slave (*Pol* 1.6.1255b14–15). In fact, a master's relation to a conventional slave resembles his relation to a natural slave *qua* man less than it resembles his relation to a natural slave *qua* slave.

disarms Aristotle's most chilling phraseology: a slave will be 'a living tool' as a tool is 'a lifeless slave' (8.11.1161b4, cf. *EE* 7.9.1241b23–4) only *qua* slave; he will never be simply a tool, for he is also a man (if an incomplete one).[20] We have seen that Aristotle holds that slaves *qua* slaves can be party to friendship only in a sense, but *qua* men to a variety of friendship even of the best kind. We may think it unduly artificial that the abstractions ('*qua* man' and '*qua* slave') are pursued so far as to be both treated as possible focuses of friendship; but the distinction itself is crucial and recurrent. The remark (quoted earlier) that the slave is wholly his master's while the master is not his slave's (*Pol* 1.4.1254a11–13) is equivalent to an observation that the master is only a master *qua* master, while the natural slave is even a slave *qua* man. The condensed thought at *Nicomachean Ethics* 8.11.1161b5–6 must be not that slavery itself is an unfriendly relation though master can befriend slave *qua* man (which would be true of conventional slavery), but that it can be a friendly relation in one way (with slave *qua* man) though only barely in another (with slave *qua* slave). Slavery in accordance with nature is a human relation, and a form of friendship.

In assessing the acceptability of Plato's and Aristotle's similar (though not equally elaborated) justifications of slavery we have to distinguish justice of content from justice of application. Whether a doctrine advocating natural in contrast to conventional slavery can justify actual slavery is in part an empirical question; false assumptions about fact may make the doctrine dangerous but they do not prove it wrong, while true factual beliefs may make the doctrine beneficial without proving it right.[21] What is significant for us is that attention to the relation of slavery to friendship is not a marginal eccentricity in these accounts, but a central feature.

[20] George Huxley nicely compares 'the old Russian view of serfs as "baptized property"', *On Aristotle and Greek Society* (Belfast, 1979), 8; that phrase constitutes a harsh paradox precisely because it fails to make the distinction that I am ascribing to Aristotle.

[21] There is a brief but fascinating account of an historical and historically important debate about slavery conducted in Aristotelian terms in Huxley, op. cit. 10–12.

7
THE CITY

I

What I have been describing in the previous chapter represents for Plato a 'second-best' (*Laws* 7.807b7): ideally, as the *Laws* still agrees (5.739b8–d5, 7.807b3–c1), the private household would be abolished, and the proverb 'Friends share all' (*koina ta philōn*) fully realized (739c2–3, cf. *Rep* 4.424a1–2, 5.449c5), not only of possessions, including slaves, but even of spouses and children.[1] However, even in the *Republic*, such communism is restricted to the guardians (who represent reason in the state) and the auxiliaries (who represent spirit, and some of whom will become guardians), perhaps for a reason suggested by E. Bornemann: the imposition of communism on the artisans would undermine that motivation, appetite, which they represent, since property is an object of appetite (cf. 4.436a1–3, 8.553c5, 9.580e5–6).[2] So we have to consider both how Plato intends communism to transform the guardians, and how he expects that effect to carry through to the artisans so that the whole city becomes a community of friends.

The guardians (men and women, and including the auxiliaries) 'will live and feed together, and have no private home or property'

---

[1] Plato repeatedly talks of sharing 'wives' or 'women' (*gunaikes*) when he means spouses: 4.423e7, 5.451c6, 457c10, d7, 460b3, 464a9. W. K. C. Guthrie's comment 'Old habits die hard' (*A History of Greek Philosophy*, iv. 480, n. 1) is plausible enough; but it is hardly surprising, when Plato's starting-point was the Greek custom of 'having women and children apart' (5.464d1–2), that his endpoint should be expressed, especially for a male audience, as having 'women and children' in common. He does also speak of sharing 'marriages' (4.453e7, *Tim* 18c8), which attempts to get round the lack of a Greek equivalent of the neutral 'spouse'. Some translators suppose that he even lapses into speaking of 'the wives of the guardians' (5.454e3–4, 457a6); but, like Desmond Lee, I take the phrase to mean 'the women among the guardians', with not a possessive but a partitive genitive.

[2] 'Aristoteles' Urteil über Platons politische Theorie', *Philologus* 79 (1923–4), 123. Possibly confused by the absence of any such qualification in the reminiscences of the ideal in the *Laws*, Aristotle complains (*Pol* 2.5.1264a11–13) that the restriction is unclear in the *Republic*; unfairly, as Bornemann argues (op. cit. 113–18). The restriction is most explicit in the recapitulation at *Timaeus* 18b1–4.

(5.458c8–d1). Plato realizes that the free mixing of the sexes will increase the opportunities for acting upon 'sexual necessity' (d5), and recoils from any absence of regulation (d8–e1). Sexual intercourse is to be restricted, when the parties are of the right age to have children, to 'sacred marriages' (e3), or 'statutory festivals' (459e5). By means of a pretended lottery (460a8–10), the best are to mate with the best, the worst with the worst as seldom as possible, and only the children of the best to be brought up (459d7–e1).³ Mothers are to be prevented from recognizing their own children (460c9–10). That produces a problem once, past the age of breeding, men and women are free to mate as they please (461b9–c1). To preclude intercourse between father and daughter or mother and son even after deregulation, a new kind of group family is invented: those born as a result of some festival will call 'mother' or 'father' whoever bred then, and 'brother' or 'sister' whoever was conceived then (461d2–e2). It seems significant (and not just 'for completeness', as Desmond Lee suggests, ad loc.) that Plato gives a definition of 'brother' and 'sister', even though he is not concerned to prevent incest between siblings (461e2–3). One remembers an earlier, if incompatible, myth: that all the citizens were really conceived and reared by Mother Earth (3.414d2–7). That was intended to encourage them to fight for their country (though that could be relevant now only to the auxiliaries or soldiers), and to view their fellow-citizens as 'brothers' (e3–6). Presumably Plato expects this later, narrower extension of 'brother' and 'sister', taken together with the extension of 'father' and 'mother' of which it is a corollary, to serve a fragment of the same purpose, enlarging the domain of quasi-familial affections.⁴ If so, we may doubt its success. Why should the

---

³ Are we to take the implication that the worst will mate with the worst occasionally as an admission that the authorities can be mistaken about the quality of the parents until they have produced a child, or as a humane concession to spare them a prolonged virginity? If they too are subject to 'sexual necessity', it should be the second.

⁴ A wider fragment if, as James Adam supposes (*The Republic of Plato*, ad 461d8), a child will count as its 'parents' not merely those who were breeding at the festival when it was conceived, but all who were then of breeding age. That is a possible reading of 461d8, and an easier one of *Timaeus* 18d2: but it seems incompatible with the precision of 461d2–5. It would restrict matings far more severely than is needed to prevent incest, which is the explicit purpose of the passage; yet it would seem a welcome aid to social solidarity, which I am now suggesting to be a subsidiary goal, and come close to bearing out the large claim at 463c5–7 (which even Adam finds 'a slight exaggeration', ad loc.) that every guardian will view every other as a relation. However, suppose that the best adults were scarce enough that at every festival during the maturity of any pair of parents at least one of them would be called upon to breed: then the effect would be precisely the same. It is true that, within a generation, that supposition would entail

phrase 'my brother', for instance, retain any emotive force in the mouths of speakers who can never apply it literally? Perhaps Plato supposes that its force is purely conventional, and can accompany the phrase, if we so wish, whatever sense it assumes (cf. 463c9–d8); or that its force is determined by belief about biology, so that a man will have brotherly feelings for anyone with whom he may, for all he knows, have a parent in common. If so, he was surely mistaken: more plausibly, the power of the phrase is parasitic upon personal familiarity with family life.[5] In effect, Plato is attempting not to abolish ordinary feelings, but to expropriate them. So far, they seem unlikely to survive the process, and his communism more likely to dissolve old ties than to create new ones.

However, Plato has a justification, which follows. In abolishing (among the guardians) the private household and family, he expects also to abolish private joys and sorrows (464c7–d3). His goal is the collectivization, so to speak, not only of externals, but of emotions.[6] The ideal is a community in respect of pleasure and pain, in which all citizens grieve and rejoice at the same things (462b4–6). That is expressed in their using 'mine' and 'not mine' together (c3–5). Everyone is to identify with everyone else's success and failure: 'In this city more than in any other, when one citizen fares well or ill, men will pronounce in unison the word of which we spoke: "It is *mine* that is faring well; it is *mine* that is faring ill" ' (463e3–5). That 'way of thinking and talking' (464a1) will generate a sharing of pleasures and pains; and the precondition is the sharing of spouses and children among the guardians (464a1–10). This extension of the notion of 'mine' is more dramatic than that of 'brother' and the like. It is also safe from the objection which that faced: whereas 'brother' borrows its force from family life, which is to be abolished, 'mine' takes its force from the interests of the individual, and the individual is not to be abolished, though his interests are to be extended.

either a population explosion, or an infrequency of festivals, or an increasing number who would have to remain chaste until past the breeding age. I mention the supposition to bring out that the practical difference between Adam's reading, and the one in my text, must vary according to factors of which Plato does not inform us.

[5] Even if Plato could have conceived it, it would hardly be sufficient, instead, for the guardians to play the sociologist and study the model among the artisans.

[6] I intend 'collectivization' as the converse of Gregory Vlastos's 'privatization', which in the political world of 1969 when he was writing he could suppose himself to be coining ('The Individual as Object of Love in Plato', 17, n. 48).

It is not easy, however, to follow Plato's meaning. On one interpretation he will liable to a variant of the same objection. R. M. Hare
has suggested that, in addition to its descriptive meaning, the word 'I'
has a prescriptive meaning: in using it of a person, I thereby express a
concern that his prescriptions, or the desires that they express, be
satisfied.[7] That yields an easy way of making sense of Plato's extended
'mine': we may say that it retains the prescriptive meaning of the
ordinary 'mine' while shedding its descriptive meaning. When one of
his citizens says of another's success, 'It is mine that is faring well', his
use of 'mine' simply expresses his identification with the other, that is
his pleasure in the other's pleasure. We might paraphrase what he is
saying, according to a parody of emotivism, as follows: 'He is faring
well—hurrah!' This is intelligible, but not really satisfactory for
Plato. The term 'mine' must then be taken not to generate, but simply
to express, a community in pleasure and pain (contrast 464a1–2). And
a variant of my objection to the extended sense of 'brother' is this:
even in Hare's terms, 'I' must derive its prescriptive from its descriptive meaning, its force from the inescapability of a special concern for
the person one knows oneself to be; once the word is applied to other
persons than the speaker, it can no longer express the same kind of
concern, so that its force either adapts to whatever concern he does
feel for them, or becomes an incoherent hangover. This is not an
objection to Hare, who does not allow one to apply the word 'I' to
other people in the actual world (only in other worlds in which one *is*
identical to them, cf. 'If I were you, . . .'), and it need not be any
objection to applying his semantic framework to Plato; but it shows
that Plato has still to be justified.

An early and shrewd critic was Aristotle (*Pol* 2.3.1261b16–32). He
complains that, in the sentence 'All say "mine" together', 'all' is
ambiguous between a distributive and a collective sense: it would be
fine if each individual separately could apply 'mine' to the same
things, but also impossible; if the citizen body taken collectively says
the same thing, that does nothing for unanimity (b30–2). Take a
political parallel: a cabinet may be 'agreed' on some proposal after
taking a vote, though its members are in disagreement. Similarly, a
community may welcome the success of one of its members as contributing to its own well-being (in the context of Plato's state if not our
own, we may imagine it declaring through some official mouthpiece

[7] *Moral Thinking* (Oxford, 1981), 96–7.

'It is mine that fares well'), even though that success is unwelcome to some others of its members. Since Plato is in pursuit of evaluative responses shared between individuals, he must rather intend 'all' distributively; but then how can 'mine' be used together? It might be that, under communism, individuals would agree in calling nothing 'mine', and everything 'not mine'; but that would rather convey alienation than solidarity. Of course, two individuals may lay claim to one and the same object by each calling it 'mine', but that is not what is meant either: as Aristotle notes elsewhere, 'The two parties must so desire the same thing that it is possible for both to get what they desire; for if they desire that which cannot belong to both, they will quarrel; but those in agreement will not quarrel' (*EE* 7.7.1241a27–30, cf. *NE* 9.6.1167a34–5).[8] It seems impossible to reconcile a distributive 'all' with a literal 'mine', and so hard to allow Plato even to be talking sense. One possibility is that 'mine' has taken on the meaning of 'ours'. W. L. Newman actually interprets Aristotle's criticism to something like that effect: 'When, for instance, all say of the same child "This is my child", they will only mean "This is my child in a collective sense", not "This is my own child."'[9] This thought seems at a distance from Aristotle's own wording: it is 'all', not 'mine', that he alleges to be ambiguous (1261b20). But is there any difference in substance? That depends on how we understand 'ours', or 'mine in a collective sense'. Newman's phrase suggests only a difference in context of utterance (which is no doubt why he takes himself to be interpreting Aristotle): whether we imagine a public spokesman speaking (which fits a collective 'all'), or all the citizens individually (which fits a collective 'mine'), what they are asserting in saying 'It is mine that fares well' is that the community is faring well; and that does nothing to prove a unanimity of response. But we might alternatively suppose that, in the mouth of an individual who is speaking for himself, 'mine' here expresses some sympathetic or vicarious interest; it will then, in Hare's terminology, be equivalent to an 'ours' that is at least partly prescriptive. To the extent that all the members of a community apply a prescriptive 'ours' together, that community is indeed unanimous in its interpersonal preferences. This, then, is a

---

[8] J. Solomon has a nice illustration (in a note to his translation of the *Eudemian Ethics*, ad 1241a27–8): 'Charles V and Francis I did not "agree"—as the former said—because both desired Milan.'

[9] *The Politics of Aristotle*, i. 161. T. J. Saunders similarly comments (ad 1261b30–2) that Aristotle is distinguishing 'the usual strong and private sense of "own"' from 'the weak sense of "own", as being possessed by many others also'.

different interpretation of Plato, one that saves him at once from Aristotle's criticism and from the charge of incoherence. However, it leaves the substantial issue untouched. In pursuit of a community in pleasure and pain, Plato wishes 'It is mine that fares well' to express on the wide reading ('mine' equivalent to 'ours') a concern like that which it expresses on the narrow reading ('mine' contrasting with 'yours'); but that speakers sincerely have such a concern for one another cannot be brought about simply by giving 'mine' a new sense and force. Civic solidarity cannot be achieved by mere verbal manipulation, as if a new way of talking would automatically yield a new way of thinking (cf. 464a1). It seems that Plato has been deflected into playing with words when he still needs to justify his substantial thought, which is that, so long as private property is abolished within a society (or some dominant section of it), citizens can take on a concern for one another that will preclude any dissension between them.

In itself, the institution of communism in respect of each individual's possessive concerns simply creates a vacuum; but it is one that demands to be filled. Plato's emphasis in the *Republic* upon what is only a negative precondition of a community in pleasure and pain is intelligible (given the radical nature of that condition), but also misleading. To fill in the positive side, we have to go by only occasional remarks, but also by a background already familiar to us. In part, the political theory of the *Republic* is an application of the erotic theory of the *Symposium*. That already mentioned the role of the legislator: through his laws, Lycurgus begot virtue of all kinds, and made the Spartans as it were his children (209d4–e4). Even the private lover 'finds much to say' to his boy 'about virtue and the qualities and actions which mark a good man' (209b8–9); though his prime concern is to educate *him* (c1–2), his words are also more generally 'such as will improve young men' (210c2–3). And yet there must be limits even to what a legislator can count as bringing about in a civic community that stops at the privacy of the house-door, and is partly *laissez-faire* even about relations in public. Among the guardians of Plato's utopia everything of importance is regulated (cf. 5.458d9–10), and the barrier between the private and the public dismantled. Education becomes public education, and its effect directive as much as enabling. Once each guardian has caught sight of the world of Forms, he will take on a responsibility towards the lives of others like that towards his own: 'If, then, some compulsion is laid upon him to practise stamping on the plastic matter of human nature in public and private the patterns that he sees there, and not merely to mould himself, do you think he will prove a poor craftsman of temperance and justice and all forms of civic virtue?' (6.500d4–8). Here the phrase 'in public and private' simply amounts to 'everywhere', for there is no surviving distinction between the two; and it is precisely the obligation of each guardian not to exploit the distinction between himself and his fellows by pursuing his own good independently of theirs. In a similar passage, philosopher-kings will use the Form of Good as a pattern for ordering 'the state and private persons and themselves' (7.540a8–b1), a listing which notably denies the phrase 'private persons' (*idiōtās*) its connotation of privacy, and allows no contrast between running one's own life and running other people's. Emeritus rulers will retire to the Islands of the Blest only after educating successors to resemble themselves (b5–7). It is not enough for Plato to abolish private life: he wishes to create a common life which flows equally within each individual life from earlier to later selves, and within the guardian class from one individual to another. Once the guardians have achieved such a common life, through a circuit of formative influences, primarily from older to younger, no doubt also reciprocally between contemporaries (whether 'brothers' and 'sisters' or not), they may be expected to identify readily with one another, so as to share the mutual concern properly expressed by a 'mine' that is equivalent to a prescriptive 'ours'.[10]

It must assist this process of the mingling of lives that the guardians are the representatives, in the state, of reason within the mind. A parallel for the fully unified state is the body which feels pain as a whole when only a finger is wounded (5.462c10–d7). Of course no such mechanism for the transference of pain can be invented to link individuals. Those who place most value on bodily sensations are most likely to emphasize the dividing-lines between persons that no relationship can erase. That, for Plato, must be a further reason against identifying oneself with one's body.[11]

[10] A humdrum parallel is the college tutor who says after Finals, 'I got two Firsts this year', purporting to describe a joint achievement.

[11] I owe this point to Martha Nussbaum, *The Fragility of Goodness*, 159–60. For an elegant expression of the same thought within fiction, cf. Vikram Seth, *The Golden Gate* (New York, 1986), 8.19–20. Charles Williams disagreed: according to his doctrine of 'substitution', even actual physical pain can be taken over by someone willing to substitute himself for the sufferer; cf. Humphrey Carpenter, *The Inklings* (London, 1978), 104–5. Others may object that making love can yield an impression of two becoming one as vividly, say, as any tutorial. Plato need not deny the phenomenology, but might claim that only Hephaestean welding (cf. *Symp* 192d2–e9) could make it

If communism among guardians prepares the way for a valuing and sharing of intellectual interests (and that life with and for others that manifests them in action), non-communism among artisans reflects the fact that creatures of appetite are set on goods (to which material possessions are only a means) which cannot be shared. To the network of reciprocal influences among the guardians could correspond only a policy of mutual back-scratching among the artisans, if the latter lived independently of the former. How are they to live? Apparently, the common application of 'mine' is to extend throughout the city.[12] Plato certainly starts inclusively: the best ordered city is that in which the greatest number of people apply 'mine' to the same things (5.462c7–8). Our city, like others, contains rulers and common people (463a1–2). The common people call the rulers saviours and helpers (b1), and are called in turn wage-givers and providers (b3). The guardians will view each other as relations, and treat one another accordingly (463c5–e2). So our citizens especially will have one and the same thing in common which they will call 'mine' (464a4–5); that is particularly due, within the constitution, to the community of women and children among the guardians (a8–9). The guardians will live at perfect peace with one another (465b5–6); if they don't quarrel, there will be no danger of rebellion or faction within the rest of the city (b8–10). The position turns out to be that, so long as the guardians are perfectly united as an extended family, even the artisans will identify with them and with one another. But how can that be when they are the possessors of private property and the representatives of appetite? That is hardly made clear within this passage (where 465b8–11 seem especially brisk). The best help we get comes much later, in Book 9, when Plato mentions the man whose own reason is too weak to control his appetites, so that he needs to depend on the reason of others:

Is it not in order that such a one may be under a similar rule as the best man that we say he ought to be the slave of the best man who has within himself the divine ruling principle . . . on the ground that it is better for everyone to be ruled by the divine and the intelligent, preferably his own and in himself, but, if not, set over him from outside, in order that we all so far as possible may be similar and friends because we share the same guidance (590c8–d6)?

more than an illusion; to which it might be replied that impressions and illusions can be shared, even if sensations cannot be. However, even if that is an exception, it is not one that could be extended to unite a society; 'the shared touch of conversation' (Seth, 8.20.12) is better able to escape *égoisme à deux*.

    [12] This may have been another reason for Aristotle's thinking it unclear whether communism extends even to the artisans.

This spells out what was only labelled earlier, that the guardians are to stand to the artisans as 'saviours and helpers' (5.463b1). Their relation to them is like that of teachers to children (590e1–591a3), with the great difference, which is what makes artisans metaphorical 'slaves', that artisans will never grow up into guardians. Because they represent appetite, and possess private property, the artisans would never come by themselves to use 'mine' together; it is as incomplete beings, as parts of a single tally, that they are capable of a wider view. Ruled by reason from outside, they will become mouthpieces of that reason, and apply 'mine' as it does. The proposition that even private owners can be so directed is the equivalent, within the city, of the proposition that, within the soul, appetites can be fully subordinated. If any of the artisans stayed obstinately with a personal or factional use of 'mine', that would be a kind of intemperance (cf. 4.442c10–d1). A city can be called brave as a whole not if merely some part of it is brave, but if that part fights on behalf of the whole city (4.429b1–3); similarly, a city can only be called wise as a whole if the wise element within it is ruling and in charge (428e7–9). The benevolent impartiality that the extended use of 'mine' expresses belongs primarily to the guardians alone; it belongs derivatively to the artisans, in virtue not of their own motivations and way of life, but of the mentality that they owe to their rulers. That they are still human beings, if incomplete ones, with a tripartite soul, is implicit in their capacity to understand that direction, and their willingness to obey it. So long as they have those traits, they may borrow civic unity from the guardians, and so make the whole city unified.

The individual who through temperance has become one instead of many may be called 'a friend to himself' (4.443d5). Justice also, whether internal or interpersonal, produces agreement and friendship (1.351d5–6). It is the effect of the communal 'mine' to make true of all the citizens one thing that Aristotle asserts of friends: 'Your friend is the sort of man who shares your pleasure in what is good and your pain in what is unpleasant, for your sake and for no other reason. This pleasure and pain of his will be the token of his good wishes for you', and so on (*Rhet* 2.4.1381a3 ff.). An earlier statement can now be placed in a richer context: 'One would especially love that whose interests one supposed to be the same as one's own, thinking that when it prospered one would also prosper oneself, and when not, the contrary' (3.412d4–7). Even there, it was clear that this could not be a mere vulgar coincidence of interest: that would be too vulnerable to chance, and could hardly motivate men 'to be jealous to do, through their entire lives, whatever they think is in the interest of the city' (d10–e2). The self-interest that must reflect the interest of the city must be not the individual's *proper* interest, but his *extended* interest.[13] The desirable thought is that whatever benefits the city *ipso facto* benefits oneself; it is precisely that which is expressed by greeting any good news within the city with the words 'It is mine that fares well.' The structure of education among the guardians, and of government among all the citizens, makes the thought more than an exercise in free identification. The guardians are not merely lavish in vicarious sympathy, but mindful of their debts to one another, and of their responsibilities to the whole city. Their sympathies pursue not any path, but the paths defined by the influence of others upon themselves, and of themselves upon others. The political application of the term 'family' often amounts to no more than a sentimental gesture (as in the modern phrase 'the family of nations'); Plato's citizens will form one family with the richer connotation of mutual interaction. The guardians will be linked at least by the language of biological relationships; all the citizens will be linked by the reality of psychological connections. Pregnant in soul as in body, the guardians turn out the most prolific of lovers, whose domain is not a narrow circle of family or friends, but the whole city.

It is questionable, of course, whether actuality could live up to this description. Aristotle's criticism of the extended use of terms like 'mine' and 'son' and 'father' is well-known. He predicts a dilution of responsibility: 'Everybody is more inclined to neglect something which he expects another to fulfil . . . Each citizen will have a thousand sons who will not be his individually, but anybody will be equally the son of anybody, and will therefore be neglected by all alike' (*Pol* 2.3.1261b35–40). (It makes little difference that Aristotle exaggerates what Plato envisages.) Also a dilution of sentiment:

In a state having women and children common, love will be diluted [literally, 'watery'] ; and the father will certainly not say 'my son', or the son 'my father'. As a little sweet wine mingled with a great deal of water is imperceptible in the mixture, so, in this sort of community, the idea of relationship which is based upon these names will be lost (4.1262b15–20).

---

[13] I borrow this way of speaking from Richard Kraut, 'Egoism, Love, and Political Office in Plato', § 2. Kraut has influenced my view of the relation of the *Republic* to the *Symposium*.

The thought is not (*pace* Bornemann, op. cit. 138) that civic friendship will be weaker in Plato's utopia than elsewhere, but that it will not
succeed in annexing even the titles, let alone the reality, of friendships
within the family. The linguistic claim may be doubted; the substantial one is cogent. I shall not try to answer it.

Plato's intention in devising his utopia is to model relations within it
on relations familiar to him between friends and within the family. A
further problem (which I mentioned earlier) arises if that model is not
familiar to its inhabitants; it then becomes obscure how terms bor-
rowed from that model (like 'father' and 'son') can have any force for
those who are to use them. The extension of 'mine' was safe from that
complaint, for the individual is not to be abolished; but one may
doubt whether a capacity to devote oneself to others, for instance by
taking to heart sufferings that one does not share as well as those that
one does, could ever be acquired by someone who had no opportunity
to practise it first on a few to whom he was naturally attached by ties of
affection or attraction. Are the guardians to be denied any personal
relationships that might school them in the interpersonal love that is
to be extended to all their fellow-citizens? Whether this is so is less
clear. It would be hard to reconcile any passionate sexual liaisons with
the institution of marriage festivals; certainly all that Plato mentions
is an undirected 'sexual necessity' (5.458d5). The only personal
relations considered, somewhat earlier in the *Republic*, are pederastic: lover and beloved may associate together as father and son, but
will be rebuked for want of culture if they go any further (3.403b1–
c2). For whatever reason, their love-life must be more inhibited and
intense than the elderly escapades of those who 'may mate as they
please' (5.461b9–c1). Once women have been admitted to equality
with men, the pederastic paradigm should extend to those relations
between the sexes to which sexual differences are immaterial.[14] Are
such personal partialities reconcilable with the intended civic solidarity? Implicit in that may be a conception incompatible with any
particular friendships. Martha Nussbaum gives a strong statement of
such a conception: 'These citizens will learn in every part of their
experience to treat all citizens as "alike and beloved friends", interchangeable exemplars of the same values' (*The Fragility of Goodness*,

---

[14] It will greatly help the extension that Plato's utopia knows no interesting mental
differences between the sexes (cf. what I say about loving women as boys in Appendix
3).

159). On my grounding of mutual identification upon social interaction, that cannot quite be right: however impartial a man may be between his fellow-citizens, he cannot act upon them, or co-operate with them, without making causal investments in individuals, say in the form of particular instances of influence or benefit, which cannot be interchanged as if by magic (though they may be passed on). Nor could everyone be equally a friend of everyone else, for not everyone can turn out equally dependent or influential upon everyone else. Yet it may be implicit that the pederastic affections of Book 3 are to be sacrificed to the impartial benevolence of Book 5; to me the evidence seems indecisive. There would seem to be two ways in which a community of pleasures and pains might be achieved: firstly, the guardians renounce interests in which others cannot directly share in favour of interests with communal objects, so that personal commitments are supplanted by public causes; secondly, they take each other's personal concerns vicariously to heart, so as to be pleased if they go well, sorry if they go badly. As I understand Plato, both ways have their place. Of course he holds that the second is psychologically hard to unite with many personal interests, those which, being possessive by nature, are liable to produce dissention and ill-will; consider the litigation to which men are prone when they 'possess' property, children, or relatives (5.464d7–e2). But other individual commitments may be innocuous, or even help to forward the understanding of values on which the community depends. Plato may well have thought that of the higher pederasty of the *Symposium*, which has nothing to do with property (however evident it may be to us that, on my interpretation, its high-mindedness does not rule out a metaphorical 'possessiveness' that may give rise to jealousy).[15] It is true that being in love with someone requires identifying more vividly with his concerns than with those of others; but it is already true that *being* someone involves a special closeness to his concerns. Plato's communism would be very radical in intention if it were meant to subvert even the individual's proprietary interest in his own well-being (cf. *Symp* 204e2–4). More credibly, just as that special concern was compatible with a personal devotion (perhaps even self-sacrificing) to another, so a devotion to one other person may be compatible with an active commitment to the rest of one's fellow-citizens. Whether things work out like that depends on the form that one's self-

---

[15] Plato would not see it as a coincidence that marketable property should both tend to cause dissention, and appeal to appetite.

concern, or personal affection, takes.[16] It is even coherent, if not very credible, that, just as a special concern for oneself need not be stronger than a concern for others, for all that it is peculiar in kind,[17] so a particular concern for another should stand out from wider concerns not by overriding them, but just in felt quality. Whether Plato demands even that degree of impartiality is unclear, I think. It may be enough if each citizen finds any other's success in itself a pleasure, without its being required that it be indifferent to him whose it is. Conflicts of preference could then arise, for instance if A's beloved is competing with B's beloved in a foot-race; but that will hardly give rise to dissension if A and B are just and sensible men who can enter into each other's feelings, even if their overriding desires cannot both be fulfilled. Whatever happens, each will be able to say 'It is mine that fares well', in the extended sense of 'mine', if with unequal enthusiasm. (They will then be subject to some internal conflict as well; but one that amounts merely to mixed feelings, and not to intemperance.) It is hard to make up one's own mind about these things, or to identify Plato's.

It is clear enough that one corollary of the abolition of personal friendships as well as kinships would be welcome to Plato: the rejection of lamentation, or (to put it more appealingly) the mitigation of bereavement. But as an argument on the side of reading that abolition into Plato it is two-edged, for he never argues from the desirability of one to that of the other. Evidence early or late in the *Republic* may have less weight. That the good man will not mourn his friend either on his own or the other's behalf is first argued before communism has been introduced (3.387d5–e5); that the good man who loses his son will bear his loss more easily than others is finally argued (as it would have to be) when communism has been forgotten (10.603e3–604d7). But the only thought soon after the discussion of communism that tells in the same direction is simply that the philosopher will not think that human life is of much importance (6.486a8–b2). It is never remarked that, once the citizens are properly devoted to their city, they will suffer no personal griefs. That would be implicit if they lacked sympathies: then those griefs would be excluded by the demand that they suffer together. But an empathetic sharing of

[16] One may think, for instance, of the Theban Sacred Band, a company of lovers destined, in Plato's lifetime, to die side by side for their city; Phaedrus makes what is clearly an anachronistic allusion to them in the *Symposium* (178e3–179a8).

[17] Cf. Richard Wollheim's distinction between self-concern and egoism (*The Thread of Life*, 243–4).

personal pleasure or pain is one way in which community can be achieved.

In the *Laws* such communism is given up except as an ideal, and a more practicable alternative worked over in detail. I shall not discuss that in its own right, but I shall document briefly how Plato retains many of the same aspirations even after relinquishing any adequately radical means of attaining them. Private property and family life are readmitted, with warning injunctions attached. Each man who receives a portion of land must regard it as the common property of the whole city (5.740a3–4); citizens and their property belong to their families, and those in turn even more to the city (11.923a6–b1). Even in selecting a spouse, partners must put the advantage of the state before their own likings (6.773b5–6). As if in place of an intelligible description of the creation of extended interests, the proper interests of all citizens are somewhat mystically asserted to coincide: each individual is a speck who exists for the sake of the universe, but what benefits the universe benefits the individual, thanks to their common origin (10.903c1–d3). The importance of friendship is repeatedly emphasized: it is one and the same aim that a city should be free and wise and 'friendly to itself' (3.693b3–4, c1–4, 701d7–9); a compromise between the equality which treats all the same, and that which respects merit, will produce friendship and prevent dissension (6.757a1–758a2); the object of our laws is to maximize happiness and friendship (5.743c5–6). Double honour is to be paid to those who not only do no wrong themselves but will not allow others to get away with doing it, and to those who not only display virtues themselves but can impart them to others; we must censure the man who will never share his advantages with another through friendship (5.730d1–731a1). That equation of the police informer and the inspiring friend is disconcerting. So also is the nonchalance of the legislator who excuses 'not totally fear-free' military exercises (8.830e4–5) with the thought that if a few people die, others just as good will be born in their place (831a5–7). Untypically, that does indeed treat individuals as interchangeable receptacles of virtue disposable after use. Plato does not state whether he expects them to agree; even on his own view of human relations (as I have interpreted it), they could not.[18]

[18] Plato's attitude here in theory is rather too close to Napoleon's in practice: 'Walking across the field of Eylau, . . . where 29,000 corpses then lay scattered, he was observed to turn over one or two with his boot, remarking merely, "Small change"' (Peter Quennell in the *Spectator*, 22 August 1987, 25).

At his best, Plato matches a boldness of ends with a boldness of means. The dominant class within the city is to become a band of comrades who hold all their possessions in common, and the whole city is to become an association of mutual sympathy and support. The civic unity and solidarity on which Plato is set is nothing but friendship at once intimate and open-armed.

2

Plato wishes, ideally, to abolish the private household among his rulers and replace it by a wider community not divided into any units defined by property. Aristotle, very differently, sees the household as the prototype of the state which will be taken up into it as it develops. Household becomes to city not stumbling-block, but building-brick; the city emerges out of a history which starts, and continues, with the household.[19]

Humans naturally form couples, not only to bring up children (like other animals), but for the various necessities of life (*NE* 8.12.1162a16–22). They supplement one another by playing distinctive roles in ways that yield utility and pleasure (a22–5). The household contains 'patterns' that anticipate the various kinds of constitution: the association of father and son is like a monarchy, that of master and slave like a tyranny, that of man and wife like an aristocracy, and that of brothers like a timocracy (8.10.1160b22–1161a6).[20] Unlike a city, which tends to equality (*Pol* 4.11.1295b25–6), the household tends to inequality, and so to preserve in microcosm the varieties of political inequality. Yet obedience is all the more willing for being to a relative and benefactor (*NE* 10.9.1180b5–6). Households multiply as it were through the sending out of colonies (when children and grandchildren set up house on their own); a union of such households is the most natural cause of the village, which

[19] It is no accident that the *Republic* traces the origin of the city back not to households, but to the interchange of produce (2.369b5–371e11); the *Laws*, which will reinstate the household in all classes, can derive the city from an agglomeration of households, which better explains the early forms of civic organization (3.680e6–681d5).

[20] More precisely, as I distinguished in Chapter 6, in the case of natural slaves it is to the slave *qua* slave that the master stands as a tyrant, while to the slave *qua* man he stands as a king.

supplies more than daily needs (*Pol* 1.2.1252b15–18). Finally, an association of several villages forms a city, which achieves self-sufficiency (b27–9).

What constitutes self-sufficiency must depend on the purpose of the association. A city serves three ends that correspond to the three kinds of friendship: living (a goal of utility), living together (a source of pleasure), and living well (the goal of goodness). Its initial purposes are living (*Pol* 1.2.1252b29–30), and living together (*EE* 7.10.1242a8–9, *Pol* 3.6.1278b20–1); yet, once established, it aims less at living and living together than at living well (*Pol* 1.2.1252b30, 3.9.1280a31–2, 1281a2–4). The self-sufficiency for which a city is needed is first material (*EE* 7.10.1242a6–8), and then moral (*Pol* 3.9.1280b33–5, b40–1281a2). If the good life were not its goal, there could be a city of slaves or animals (1280a32–3). As it is, a city properly so called emerges into existence together with a new conception of living well which only it can hope to realize. Instituted initially for living and living together, it makes possible at once a new ideal and a new reality, so transcending its own causes. It thereby answers perfectly to human nature, but a nature waiting to be created; for the nature of a thing is not its initial but its fully developed state (1.2.1252b30–3). In the famous slogan, man is by nature a civic animal (*politikon zō(i)on*, e.g. 1.2.1253a2–3). In the weakest sense, that merely means that he abhors solitude (e.g. *NE* 9.9.1169b16–19), and prefers to live with others even when he has no need of their assistance (*Pol* 3.6.1278b19–21). Somewhat more precisely, Aristotle differentiates among gregarious animals those who have a single common task (*ergon*): that classes men with bees, wasps, ants, and cranes (*Hist an* 1.1.488a7–10), whether or not they are subject to rule (ants and many others are not, a12–13), in contrast to animals who merely tend to graze in herds (*NE* 9.9.1170b12–14). But most precise is the sense of 'civic' (*politikos*) that goes with the city (*polis*), and cannot precede its invention. The man without a city is no better off than an isolated piece in draughts (*Pol* 1.2.1253a7). Man's peculiarly civic nature is revealed (since nature does nothing in vain) by his gift of speech; that enables him to communicate not only about the pleasant and painful (which animals can signify by making noises), but also the beneficial and harmful, and the just and unjust (a7–15). Understanding values needs a language; implementing them needs a city. Without linguistic and political structures man cannot achieve a distinctively human life.

The development of the city's goals from utility and pleasure to a
goodness that it alone makes conceivable and achievable is reflected in
the development of Aristotle's own conception of its goals from the
two *Ethics* to the *Politics*.[21] The *Eudemian Ethics* states baldly, 'Civic
friendship is according to utility' (7.10.1242b22–3); it even seems to
distinguish as 'civic' that pure friendship of utility that proceeds by
contract (b35), at once because it is defined by law (and so can also be
called 'legal'), and because it does not pretend to be 'moral' (first
contrasted with 'legal' at b32).[22] The mutual attitude of citizens is
explicitly assimilated to that of allies: the useless are forgotten (b23–
7). It is conceded (consistently or not) that, while the city came into
being mainly for utility, it would anyhow have come into being for the
sake of living together (b6–9). The *Nicomachean Ethics* states that
the civic association both came together and endures for the sake of
utility (8.9.1160a11–12). That does not exclude supplementary
goals, but serves the immediate context, which is a claim that more
restricted associations for utility are part of the civic association (a8–9,
14–15). When this claim is then extended to include associations for
pleasure as well, it most likely becomes implicit that the civic association is also for the sake of pleasure (or living together as well as
living).[23] It might be argued, in support of an exclusive reading of
a11–12, that associations for pleasure subserve the general utility that
is the goal of the civic association by providing the participants with
refreshment before they return to work.[24] That argument would not

[21] What makes civic friendship an elusive topic in Aristotle is that the *Politics*, which
alone spells out an adequately generous view of a city's goals, mentions it (at
4.11.1295b23–4) without ever attempting to characterize it; the interpreter has to
proceed, unsatisfactorily, by applying to the concept of the city in the *Politics* the
concepts of friendship in the *Ethics*. Hence my reconstruction of civic friendship now
will in part be more speculative than any of my earlier treatment of friendship in the
Ethics.

[22] The text of 1242b35 is disputed; I follow the reading adopted by Solomon.
Jonathan Barnes, adopting Susemihl's emendation, makes 'civic' there cover both
'legal' and 'moral'; that seems to me excluded by the contrast between 'civic' and 'moral'
at 1243a31–2.

[23] The text of 1160a19–25 is corrupt. W. D. Ross and Barnes follow John Cook
Wilson in supposing that 19–23 belong to an alternative version; that seems better at
home within Cook Wilson's general view (which he elaborated, unconvincingly, for
7.1–10) that the *Nicomachean Ethics* is built up from a conflation of parallel versions. I
would prefer to follow a proposal that D. J. Allan pencilled into his text: that we
bracket, presumably as a gloss, *thusiās* in 23 to *hēdonēs* in 25. However, all that I need
to resist is any suggestion that 19–20 be ignored.

[24] Thus the ancient paraphrast quoted by J. A. Stewart; *Notes on the Nicomachean
Ethics* (Oxford, 1892), ad a19.

imply that limited pleasure-associations fall under limited utility-associations, and so (contrary to Aristotle) that pleasure-friendship is just an aspect of utility-friendship: that may be true, say, of works-outings, but not where (as with sacrifices, and Aristotle's other examples here) people form different groups for business and for entertainment. However, that pleasure-associations fall within the civic association because they subserve utility is not argued explicitly by Aristotle, and need not be assumed for consistency (since a11–12 may not be stating the only goal of the civic association); it could only with ingenuity be reconciled with a later remark that 'we are busy in order that we may have leisure' (10.7.1177b4–5).[25] Thus it is true of both *Ethics* that they present the city as serving utility and pleasure, with an emphasis upon the former.[26]

However, there is already one indication of a different view, promissory in the context of the *Ethics*, and yet more explicit than anything in the *Politics*. It is said to be an aspect of man's being naturally civic that he cannot count fully as achieving *eudaimoniā* unless his fellow-citizens do so as well (*NE* 1.7.1097b8–11). This is quite different from the material dependency of *Eudemian Ethics* 7.10.1242a7–8: the thought has to be that the flourishing of others is necessary not as a means, but as a contribution, to one's own. That means that one makes their flourishing an end of one's own that one values for its own sake; in effect, that one's relation to them is one of goodwill in action. It will then be an implication of that (as I discussed in Chapter 4) that every citizen has an interest in the virtues of his fellows. Now it would not seem that the inference goes the other way: I might wish my fellows to think and live virtuously because only so can I depend upon them to treat me justly. (If my morals are poor, I will wish them to act justly though I am unwilling to do so myself; *NE* 9.6.1167b14–16.) Hence, in the *Politics*, we cannot infer goodwill (which it does not even mention, if 1.6.1255a17 be emended) from an interest in the virtue of others (which it does). However, considerations already mentioned do seem to exclude that citizens should wish one another to live well, for instance justly, simply as a means to their own *eudaimoniā*. That would make of each household a kind of city in

[25] The position would have to be that pleasure-associations fall within the civic association *qua* providers of pleasure as an instrumental good, but not *qua* providers of it as an intrinsic good.

[26] That emphasis is unsurprising in view of the fact that it was natural to state the goal of the city as the 'common advantage', even identifying that with justice (8.9.1160a11–14, cf. 5.1.1129b14–17).

itself, linked with others in an alliance that did not alter the nature of the ways in which individuals associate with one another (cf. 3.10.1280b25–9); but a city is not an alliance (b23). The man without a city might be at a practical disadvantage, but he would not be cut off from his own true character like an isolated piece in draughts (1.2.1253a7). That civic life not only facilitates an old *eudaimoniā*, but also makes possible a new one, must imply that the living well that each citizen pursues is not merely his own (which every man desires), but also the city's (which he desires *qua* citizen).

Thus the development of Aristotle's view of civic friendship from the *Ethics* into the *Politics* seems partly an explication, and partly a change of mind. We can speculate about why a less generous view of the city was bound to be insecure. A conception of the city as existing solely for utility (if we keep for simplicity to that) must require what Bernard Williams has called a 'Government House' morality;[27] for even if private citizens are solely self-interested *qua* citizens, too few of them will succeed to ensure political stability unless they enjoy rulers who pursue, where these are different, not their own advantage but the advantage of all (or at any rate of most).[28] But such a contrast between the motivation of the rulers and of the ruled is not sustainable: logic excludes it in a democracy (in which the mentality of the government simply is that of its subjects, at least in their role as legislators or electors); practicalities exclude it in an aristocracy (unless the government is powerful or cunning enough never to need the co-operation of those it is not immediately benefiting). It is therefore necessary if a city is to flourish that its members should value the general well-being for its own sake, in short that they should have goodwill towards one another; and goodwill presupposes a belief that the other has (or can develop) the virtues required for *eudaimoniā*. Thus the foundation of a flourishing city must be a kind of friendship on account of virtue.[29]

[27] e.g. *Ethics and the Limits of Philosophy* (London, 1985), 108–10.
[28] It is easy here to be confused (and even possible that Aristotle was not quite clear): an association for utility, as I understand his use of the phrase, is one whose members pursue utility together, but each solely for his own sake; the phrase does not apply to an association whose members value the general utility also for the sake of one another.
[29] Given Aristotle's belief in the role of laws, it is naturally to legislators that he especially prescribes a concern that the citizens live well (e.g. *Pol* 7.14.1333a14–16). But it should be to all citizens that he ascribes that concern when he writes, 'Those who care for good government (*eunomiā*) take into consideration civic virtue and vice' (3.9.1280b5–6), i.e. character (cf. b2); for *eunomiā* requires that the laws be not only good but obeyed (4.8.1294a3–4), which rests on every responsible citizen.

I do not claim that the argument that I have just rehearsed is irrefutable; some will think that it neglects the role in politics of enlightened self-interest, on the part both of the government and of its subjects. I do suggest that it is Aristotelian. That is already intimated in the *Ethics* by their treatment of 'unanimity' (*homonoia*), which they identify with civic friendship (*NE* 9.6.1167b2–3, *EE* 7.7.1241a32–3). This differs from mere 'identity in opinion' (*homodoxiā*) in involving mutual knowledge (1167a22–4), which in both *Ethics* was part of the initial definition of friendship (*NE* 8.2.1155b34–1156a4, *EE* 7.2.1236a15). The subject-matter of unanimity is, most broadly, practical matters (1167b4, 1241a17); within those, the emphasis falls on matters of utility (1167a27, b3, 8), perhaps subserving living together (1241a17–18). And yet it is asserted that unanimity can only be adequately achieved by the good (1167b4–5, 1241a21); in the *Nicomachean Ethics* that is argued for two reasons, of which one should apply to any association (only the good are constant in their intentions, 1167b6–7), but the other draws on the special conflicts that are bound to arise within cities when individuals are only pursuing their own interests (1167b10–16). If it is true in general that 'the friendship of utility is full of complaints' (*NE* 8.13.1162b16, cf. *EE* 7.10.1243a2–3), it must be a poor basis for unifying a city, for cities always contain deep divisions between classes, and often make demands that offer only remote rewards.[30]

Thus the friendship which best preserves cities from faction (*Pol* 2.4.1262b7–9, cf. *NE* 8.1.1155a22–6) is grounded on mutual knowledge and shared virtues; it must be a friendship in respect, and for the sake, of goodness of a kind. It may seem strange to us that a city could be so cemented, but we can extract, from the *Ethics* and the *Politics*, replies to the obvious objections. Within the modern state, mutual knowledge between different circles only links celebrities, but Aristotle wants his citizens not only to know of one another but to know one another's characters, in order to be able to distribute offices according to merit (*Pol* 7.4.1326b14–17). Even so, the kind of familiarity and of life in common possible between all citizens will hardly be intimate (which would be extraordinary, cf. 2.5.1263b17–18). The moral demands of comradeship are stricter than those of mere fellow-citizenship (*NE* 8.9.1160a3–5). Thinking of friendship

---

[30] What, in any case, of external conflict? Aristotle could not forget, though most of us can, that a country, unlike a business, may have to ask its members to sacrifice their lives for its sake (cf. *NE* 9.8.1169a18–20).

according to goodness on the model of comradeship (9.10.1171a14–15), Aristotle denies that it can link more than a few, and so distinguishes it from civic friendship, even that of the good (a15–20). Yet he may still conceive civic friendship as an extended variant of full virtue-friendship. Perhaps harder to determine are his hopes of moral education. On the one hand, the city properly so called must be concerned to make its citizens good and just; otherwise it is merely an alliance (*Pol* 3.9.1280b6–12). Even its prohibitions of vicious acts (cf. *NE* 5.1.1129b19–24) must serve to promote moral motivation in the educable through habituation in virtuous action.[31] This implies, if not that civic friendship is already unanimity, rather that unanimity is the state towards which it aspires. On the other hand, we meet some cynicism about the motivations of which most men are capable: 'The many obey necessity rather than argument, and punishments rather than the fine' (10.9.1180a4–5).[32] Yet even on this generally cynical supposition there is a kind of civic goodness that may be the ground and goal of civic friendship. This friendship holds between men *qua* citizens, and in that role men may take on qualities from one another in the course of the political process:

The many, of whom each individual is not a good man, when they meet together may be better than the few good, if regarded not individually but collectively, just as a feast to which many contribute is better than a dinner provided out of a single purse. For each individual among the many has a share of virtue and practical wisdom, and when they meet together, just as they become in a manner one man, who has many feet, and hands, and senses, so too with regard to their character and thought (*Pol* 3.11.1281a42–b7, cf. 4.4.1292a10–13).

In this way it is by reason of their very variability ('like the Euripus', *NE* 9.6.1167b7) that they are susceptible to collective influences that may generate in them a wisdom, and mutual goodwill, that they lacked individually. Political friendship with the transient and partial personas that result may indeed fail to be 'for virtue and for themselves' (9.8.1171a19): the virtue that grounds it is too limited in

31 This is suggested by Paul Moraux in discussion of Allan, 'Individual and State in the *Ethics* and *Politics*', 90.

32 It has been plausibly argued that Aristotle is here expressing the views of others (Allan, op. cit. 76); similar, however, are 8.13.1162b35–6, and *EE* 7.10.1243a38. The *Politics* is often, though not always, suggestive of a more generous view (as when it states that the civic association exists for the sake of fine actions, 3.9.1281a2–3); if on this point Aristotle did shift in attitude or emphasis, that will have contributed to developing his conception of civic friendship.

domain and duration, and too dependent upon others, to amount to 'themselves'. But goodness, of a kind, and not mere utility, is still its concern.

Aristotle speaks of the pooling of individual talents in a way reminiscent of a passage in the *Laws* in which Plato vividly conveys the transforming effect of ideal communism even as he is renouncing it as a practicable option:

The notion of the private will have been, by every possible stratagem, completely uprooted from every sphere of life. Everything possible will have been devised to make what is by nature private, such as eyes and ears and hands, common in some way, in the sense that they will seem to see and hear and act in common (5.739c5–d1, adapted from Nussbaum, *The Fragility of Goodness*, 160).

But Plato rests such solidarity upon the abolition of subordinate institutions (notably the family), Aristotle upon the unification of expanding circles of loyalty which mediate between the atomic individual and the molecular state. Though the city is in a way an aggregate of citizens (*Pol* 3.1.1274b41), it is also 'an association in perfect and self-sufficient life of families and villages' (3.9.1280b40–1281a1), not of otherwise isolated individuals. Lesser associations are needed to exercise men's social nature in preparation for full citizenship. The foundations of a city are connections by marriage, fraternities, common sacrifices, and activities that bring men together (3.9.1280b36–8). To take a view as it were from above, 'The legislator could not form a state at all without distributing and dividing its constituents into associations for common meals, and into phratries and tribes' (2.5.1264a6–8). Associations outside the family prepare individuals for citizenship by extending the intimacy of domestic, and the equality of fraternal, relations (cf. *EE* 7.10.1242a35–b1). Yet it is the household itself that becomes crucial in another way. Who are the 'citizens' who constitute the city? Strictly speaking, they are those who participate in judging and legislating (3.1.1275a22–3, cf. b18–21). In a qualified sense, they also include future and past participants (the young who have still to be registered, and the old who have been relieved of state duties), and even resident aliens who can only take part in litigation through a patron (a11–19). But further, even the subjects of kings and tyrants who have no role in legislating may count as citizens (3.14.1285a25–7). It suffices to be able either to rule, or to be ruled, 'with a view to the most eligible life' (3.17.1288a36–7). For Aristotle, that is equivalent to making the city an association of those who are 'free' (*eleutheros*, 3.6.1279a21), not in the limited political sense of ruling and being ruled in turn (6.2.1317b2–3), nor in the sense most familiar to us of living as one likes (b11–13), which Aristotle rejects as a false democratic conception (5.9.1310a25–36), but in that of being 'one's own and not another's' (*Met* 1.2.982b26). In this sense, any member of the community can count as a citizen who is or will be able, with whatever help, to form a conception of *eudaimoniā* and realize it in practice. Thus a distinction becomes clear between the city, which is an association of freemen, and the constitution (*politeia*), which is an association of citizens in the strict sense (cf. *Pol* 1.13.1260b20, 7.13.1332a33–5).[33] That is clearly still taken to exclude slaves from membership of the city, presumably because they are too dependent upon others (even if their value is not solely instrumental); but it lets in women and children, despite the 'civic' rule of husbands and 'royal' rule of fathers (*Pol* 1.12.1259a39–b1). Indeed, women form half of the free members of the city, so that their quality must affect its quality (1.13.1260b16–19). That threatens a problem: the city is not merely an aggregate of freemen, and women cannot count as part of it simply through being *there*; yet in Aristotle's own society they had no political role, indeed very little role at all outside the household. His solution is to count the household of which women are part as itself part of the city (1260b13–14); that is why they themselves constitute half the city (2.9.1269b14–19). The ground for that is not the physical location of the home, but the interactions between a household and its civic context. Women are to be educated with an eye to the constitution (1.13.1260b15–16), most clearly because of their influence upon husbands who are strictly citizens (especially in warlike societies not openly given to homosexuality, where they rule their rulers, 2.9.1269b22–34), and upon sons who will become so (1.13.1260b15–20). Indirectly, under whatever constitution, women too play a civic role, influencing even the political life of the city (let alone its wider social life) through the persons of their menfolk. Thus, whereas Plato prefers to make women into full members of the city through rescuing them from family ties, Aristotle is content that they should already be half members of the city precisely through their role within the family.

---

[33] Not that the verbal distinction is always respected: cf. 3.3.1276b1–2, in a chapter where Aristotle needs to connect 'city' and 'constitution' closely in order to argue that a new constitution creates a new city.

The family is the most important subsidiary institution within the city because it brings within the city half its members, but all associations are embraced within the city (1.1.1252a5–6) and seem like parts of it (*NE* 8.9.1160a9). At the start of the *Nicomachean Ethics* the subordination of the other sciences to political science is spelled out strongly and precisely: their ends subserve its end, and it regulates which should be pursued and up to what point; so its end is human good (1.1–2, especially 1.2.1094a28–b7). Yet that leaves unclear the kind of unity that subordinate institutions can achieve within a city. Do their ends simply form a heterogeneous collection, a social ragbag, with, at best, an obliteration of conflict? Or do they take on a single new end in place of many old ones within a civic context that allows only the good of the city to be a final end, that is to have any intrinsic value?[34] The second possibility is intelligible if we take it not to imply that the city is a kind of superperson (in which case it would need to possess a supermind), but to mean, say, that action has value of its own only under its civic aspect; but that is neither plausible, nor plausibly Aristotelian. The first possibility is implicit in a more common-sensical proposal by Stephen Clark: 'Strictly, no state can do more than provide the conditions and encouragement for its citizens' *eudaimoniā*, can only do what is *sumpheron*, advantageous: but this latter category is defined in terms of the good life, not merely of economic survival' (*Aristotle's Man*, 102, n. 3). However, once we guarantee sense by interpreting 'state' as equivalent, say, to 'citizens co-operating *qua* citizens', that badly underplays the civic nature of man emphasized in the *Politics*, and is anyway unpersuasive: essentially co-operative civic acts (such as electing the right person to office) may help constitute each agent's *eudaimoniā* just as well as acts which a city merely facilitates. I think that Aristotle could best justify an intermediate position: the various ends of subordinate institutions will be modified but not discarded, so that each contributes to civic life without relinquishing its own independent value. For instance, education within the family must also look beyond its confines to the constitution (*Pol* 1.13.1260b13–20). It is true that, under the best constitution, it is the same thing to be a good man and a good citizen (4.7.1293b5–7, 7.9.1328b37–9, cf. 3.4). But that does not mean that one could become a good man first, and later find oneself, as if by a happy coincidence, fitting in as a good citizen as well; rather, the ideal

---

[34] For a discussion of an analogous issue that arises within the life of each individual, cf. my 'Aristotle's Ethical Holism'.

of being a good citizen must modify, from early on, one's education into a good man. It is such education that unites the plurality that is a city into a single unity (2.5.1263b36–7). Even philosophy has a civic role, in helping people to enjoy leisure without becoming insolent (7.15.1334a23–8). What marks it off from practical studies must be not that no further good comes of it (*pace NE* 10.7.1177b2), but that it is out of place, if indeed it is possible, to let thought of that influence its content; it is in this sense that practical wisdom can prescribe for it, but not to it (*NE* 6.13.1145a9).[35]

The ascription of ends to individuals, sciences, and institutions threatens a confusing proliferation, as if every decision would involve consideration of a multitude of categories not only of values, but of locations of value, personal and impersonal, abstract and concrete. We should rather think of the ultimate possessors of value as persons: 'It is evident that that form of government is best in which every man, whoever he is, can act best and live happily' (*Pol* 7.2.1324a23–5). But the values that they possess may be individual (each man for himself), or communal (depending on his relations to other men). That the city is prior to each of us, like whole to part, since none of us is self-sufficient on his own (1.2.1253a25–7), means not, say, that government action alone has a value of its own (which would be strange when there is no collective mind for it to express), nor simply that the city provides the background conditions of individual achievement (which would make of it a mere public utility), but rather that co-operation with one's fellow citizens, ideally in the exercise of full citizen-rights, is a necessary constituent of a wholly satisfying human life. The thought is not that the city alone is the bearer of value; indeed, the qualities that it possesses, such as courage, justice, and wisdom, are also possessed by individuals (7.1.1323b33–6, cf. 7.15.1334a11–13). It is rather that many human values are essentially civic, and can be realized only in the context of a political community. To be part of that community is to take part in communal activities that help constitute the *eudaimoniā* of all the participants; however useful they may be, artisans cannot count as citizens and constituents of the city if they are not 'craftsmen of virtue' (7.9.1329a19–24), that is if they are merely accessory, and not party, to virtuous activities. A city is an 'association' (in the sense glossed towards the end of Chapter 5): its members are not its servants, and must share in the ends that

---

[35] Thus Aristotle's separation of theoretical from practical wisdom implies in effect a freedom of thought unwelcome to Plato; so Allan, op. cit. 80–2.

they help to achieve (cf. 7.8.1328a21–37). If we forget that requirement, we may read too much into statements like this: 'Neither must
we suppose that anyone of the citizens belongs to himself, for they all
belong to the state, and are each of them a part of the state, and the
care of each part is inseparable from the care of the whole'
(7.8.1337a27–30). That is true to the extent that individuals pursue
communal goals, so that the success of each cannot be judged by a
blinkered scrutiny of his or her 'own' life. The fact that utility-
friendships do not extend the range of goals that a man can value for
their own sake makes the city, and civic friendship, essential to the
well-being of a man as a social animal. Goodwill towards one's fellow-
men is in itself idle, while co-operation with partners in limited
associations for pleasure or utility is in itself egoistic. I have already
suggested (in Chapter 5) that we may be misled by Aristotle's conception of such associations unless we place it as a product of abstraction. We can now see that there are two ways in which, in practice,
they take on an aspect of goodwill: as if from below, they are tempered
by an underlying humanity that links men *qua* fellow-men; as if from
above, they are coloured by a mutual identification with a city (which
we call patriotism) that links men *qua* fellow-citizens (cf.
3.9.1280b36–40). Yet the goals of a city are precisely the goals of
individuals who are citizens as well as men. It is a wide view of
personal achievement, not a denial of it, that is being taken in this
passage:

Even if the end is the same for a single man and for a city, that of the city seems
at all events something greater and more complete both to attain and to
preserve; for though it is worth while to attain the end merely for one man, it
is finer and more godlike to attain it for a people or for cities (*NE* 1.4.1094b7–
10).

Even if a man could be assessed as *eudaimōn* in isolation, it would still
be by contributing towards the *eudaimoniā* of his fellow-citizens (or
even fellow-nationals), and thereby appropriating it so that he can
value it for itself, that he would achieve the greatest and finest part of
his own *eudaimoniā*.

Conceptually this is already familiar. In its newly wider application
it confirms that civic friendship is indeed an extended variety of the
friendship of the good: within both, choices and activities are shared
in such a way that individuals become as it were centres of overlapping
circles of *eudaimoniā*; achievement really can, to an extent, be

shared. What valuably becomes salient in the civic context is that the unity must not be overdone. A city is by nature a plurality; to achieve perfect unity it would have to undergo metamorphosis from a city into a household, and from a household into a man, that is, to be destroyed (*Pol* 2.2.1261a18–22). It is by the opposite transition, from individual to household and so to city, that self-sufficiency is achieved (b10–15). Too much unity would change a city into a worse city or no city at all, like harmony turning into unison, or a rhythm into a single foot (2.5.1263b31–5); a city is not a blend whose elements are confounded, as Aristophanes' lovers in the *Symposium* would wish to become (2.4.1262b11–14). Justice can only hold between individuals who are separate, and not parts of one another (*NE* 5.6.1134b9–13), and civic friendship extends as widely as justice (8.11.1161a10–11). Moreover, a city must preserve not only the multiplicity of its elements, but their diversity: 'A city is not made up only of so many men, but of different kinds of men; for similars do not constitute a city' (*Pol* 2.1.1261a22–4). In all wholes made up of discernible parts there is a ruling element, and a subject element (1.5.1254b28–31). Political equality is achieved by an alternation of roles, and not an abolition of them (1.12.1259b4–6). Thus in a shared communal life it is variety, not uniformity, that citizens can offer one another; for them to co-operate in choice and action is not for them all to do the same, but for each of them to make his own contribution towards some common end. *Eudaimoniā* is shared through mutual indebtedness, so that, ideally, the idiosyncrasy of each citizen would leave its imprint on the lives of all the others. Moral ends and conceptions must be held in common for interaction to amount to full co-operation; but individual capacities and social roles will, and must, be multifarious.[36]

[36] In revising and (I hope) clarifying this section, I was helped by hearing a paper on civic friendship by John Cooper, and discussion of it, at a meeting of the Southern Association for Ancient Philosophy in Oxford in September 1987. Although Cooper and I have to attach different labels to civic friendship (he of 'utility', I of 'virtue'), we are trying to make sense, in overlapping ways, of what is in substance the same conception.

EPILOGUE

M. Guyau, *Esquisse d'une morale sans obligation ni sanction*, 246–7:

The character of life that has permitted us to unite egoism and altruism *to a certain degree*—a union which is the moralists' philosophical stone—is that which we have called *moral fecundity*. It is necessary that individual life should diffuse itself for another, in another, and, if need be, give itself. Well, this diffusion is not contrary to nature: it is, on the contrary, according to nature; furthermore, it is the very condition of true life. The utilitarian school has been forced to halt, more or less hesitantly, before this perpetual antithesis of 'I' and 'thou', of mine and thine, of the personal interest of each and the general interest of both; but living nature does not halt at this cut-and-dried, and logically inflexible, division: intellectual life is diffusive for another because it is *fecund*, and it is fecund for the very reason that it is life. From the physical point of view, as we have seen, the individual needs to *procreate* another individual, so that this *other* becomes virtually a condition of *ourselves*. Life, like fire, only conserves itself in communicating itself. And that is true of our intelligence no less than of the body: it is as impossible to confine intelligence within itself as flame—it is made to radiate. There is the same diffusive force in our sensibility: we have to share our joy, we have to share our grief. It is our whole nature that is *sociable*: life does not know the absolute classifications and divisions of the logicians and metaphysicians; it cannot be completely *egoistic* even if it wished to be. We are everywhere open, everywhere invading and invaded. That is a corollary of the fundamental law with which biology has supplied us: *Life is not only nutrition*, it is *production* and *fecundity*. To live is to *spend* as well to *acquire*.

APPENDIX 1

Homogeneity and Beauty in the *Symposium*

In distinguishing horizontal from vertical steps within the ascent-passage of the *Symposium*, I intended to convey a clear contrast between pursuing *more* of some kind of beauty, and conceiving a *new* kind: one could say that the horizontal moves are quantitative, and the vertical qualitative. That contrast is denied in an interesting recent interpretation by Martha Nussbaum. In her view, indeed, denying that contrast is precisely the lesson of the ascent: 'At each subsequent stage, the aspiring lover learns to consider apparently heterogeneous values to be comparable and intersubstitutable, differing only in quantity' ('Plato on Commensurability and Desire', 67). He is to move not along a rocky path, but within 'a flat uniform landscape of value, with no jagged promontories or deep valleys' (*The Fragility of Goodness*, 181).[1] Seeing the world of value (or at least of beauty) in this new way is justifiable in two ways. Firstly, there is the call of truth, but on an uncertain note. The lover comes 'to see a truth that he had not previously seen' (179), but a truth that 'requires us to sacrifice "truths" that we deeply know' (182). 'In fact, questions of truth seem muted', for 'the ascent may be playing fast and loose with the truth, at least as human beings experience it' (180). Secondly, there is the call of prudence. Our current emotional lives are full of tension and vulnerability; 'considerations of "senselessness" and good sense' prompt us to *decide* (179) that we must view beauties with a contemplative indifference (181). Practical good sense combines with a kind of truth to demand a radical change of evaluative vision.

Nussbaum's Diotima appears ambivalent about truth. Nussbaum finds an open disregard for logic in a shift from realizing that 'the beauty of any one body is closely akin (*adelphon*, literally "a sibling") to that of any other' (210a8–b1) to realizing that 'it is great folly (*anoia*) not to consider the beauty of all bodies one and the same' (b2–3). *Anoia* is a lack of practical sense; here respect for truth, or perhaps for human truth, goes into eclipse (179–80). I find this evidence ambiguous. The term *anoia* is too indeterminate to imply a *decision* to believe: it does often signify practical folly (as in *Meno* 90e1); but

---

[1] My references to Nussbaum are now all to this last work.

it probably means 'ignorance' in *Phaedo* 91b5,[2] and Plato most frequently opposes it to 'sense' or 'reason' (*nous*) in general.[3] There is more to the point that 'one and same' is a *non sequitur* from 'closely akin'; but, if we look more closely, we find that it appears to be *instances* of physical beauty that are akin ('the beauty of any one body' in relation to 'that of any other'), and physical beauty as a *kind* that is the same ('the beauty of all bodies'). What is truth? The ascent-passage does not distinguish kinds of truth, and it cannot be (cf. 212a5) that the ascent is based on a lie.[4] However, it emerges that Nussbaum's thought is not that truth is to be sacrificed to prudence. Firstly, she tells me what tells in favour of prudence is not that it is preferable to truth, but that it is more evident to an interlocutor (say, the young Socrates) who has yet to see the truth. Secondly, as we read further in the *Symposium*, and Diotima's teaching is followed by Alcibiades' narrative, we find, on Nussbaum's reading, that what has to be sacrificed is not truth to falsehood, but one truth to another: we have to opt between 'two mutually exclusive varieties of vision' (198), one valuing the individual and irreplaceable, the other the uniform and universal; as she nicely puts it, 'We cannot simply add the love of Alcibiades to the ascent of Diotima' (197–8). The evidence remains uncertain, and the conclusion perhaps alien to Plato; I shall not attempt to resolve the issue here.[5]

Whether or not Diotima presents the thesis of the homogeneity of beauty as true, what is the evidence in the ascent-passage that she is presenting it? Nussbaum cites the language of quantitative comparison,

[2] Cf. David Gallop, *Plato: Phaedo* (Oxford, 1975), 232, n. 47.

[3] Cf. *Pdo* 93b8–9, *Phdr* 270a5, *Tim* 92c2, *Laws* 10.897b1–3.

[4] On Plato's attitude to the truth, cf. W. K. C. Guthrie, *A History of Greek Philosophy*, iv. 457–9, v. 327. It is notorious that he advises rulers to lie to their subjects (e.g. *Rep* 5.459c8–d5, *Laws* 2.663d6–e2); but one is never to lie to oneself, for living well requires a grasp of truth (e.g. *Rep* 6.490b5–7, *Laws* 5.730c1–4, 10.888b3–4). Plato is at the opposite pole from Nietzsche's paradox, 'Truth is the kind of error without which a certain species could not live'; *The Will to Power* (New York, 1968), 3.493.

[5] I am persuaded by points made in Christopher Gill's judicious and illuminating rejoinder to Nussbaum's whole approach: 'Platonic Love and Individuality', in Harry Lesser and Andreas Loizon (eds.), *The Good of Community* (Gower, forthcoming). My interpretation of the ascent was intended to reconcile recognition of the universal with a kind of respect for the particular: the person one loves becomes a drop in the ocean *qua* object of contemplation, but a major investment *qua* recipient of a mentality. The modern idea that one might cherish the singularity of another person in a way that is independent, and indeed preclusive, of making an investment of him (cf. Richard Wollheim, *The Thread of Life*, 275–6) seems to me alien to Plato (and to Aristotle).

'We hear talk about comparisons of *size* between one value and another (210b6, 210c5), of a "vast amount" of value (210d1)' (180); and she infers from 210c7–d6 that the lover is 'to conceive of the whole of beauty as a vast ocean, whose components are, like droplets, qualitatively indistinguishable' (ibid.). These are nice points, but not compelling. 'Vast' or 'wide' (*polu*, d1, 4) does not entail, and need not convey, uniformity; no doubt the waters of an ocean have a certain monotony, but Diotima's explicit use of the metaphor is to contrast universality with particularity, not homogeneity with heterogeneity. The phrases 'thinking little of' (b6) and 'thinking to be a little thing' (c5) need not imply different quantities of beauty: one may think little of particular or universal physical beauty not because it does not add up to much beauty, but because one credits that kind of beauty with little importance. Moreover, even if physical and mental beauties are comparable in terms of instancing 'more' or 'less' beauty, it is not a self-evident inference that they must be identical in kind.[6] Other indications tell, perhaps more strongly, against the homogeneity of all beauty. It is the beauty of bodies that is called 'one and the same' (b3), and beauty of character that is called 'all akin itself to itself' (c4–5); Diotima nowhere applies such phrases to the beauties of different levels. Instead, she calls the second kind of beauty 'more honourable' than the first (b6–7); while that is not decisive (Nussbaum comments, 'It is just what is at issue whether differences in honorableness are qualitative or only quantitative', 467, n. 32), it is indicative, both in itself (more is rather to be *preferred* to less than *honoured* above it), and in context, where it is not easy to deny a contrast between the uniformity of physical beauty and the diversity of physical and mental beauty. When Diotima calls all bodily beauty 'one and the same' she cannot mean that all bodies are equally beautiful; in her sense, if Nussbaum is right, she ought to call physical and mental beauty 'one and the same' also, but that she shows no sign of doing. Nussbaum also resists appeal to a later passage where Alcibiades has Socrates compare getting true beauty in return for sham (literally, the 'truth' for an 'opinion' of beauty) to exchanging bronze for gold (218e6–7). She remarks that 'gold is worth *more* on a single scale of financial

---

[6] Aristotle himself vacillates about this inference: for it, *Cat* 8.11a12–13, *Phys* 7.4.249a3–8, *Pol* 1.13.1259b36–8; against it, *NE* 8.1.1155b14–15. Although he ascribes to friendship no single nature, he now and then finds in its varieties different degrees of friendship (*NE* 8.3.1156b10, 8.4.1157a13, 9.8.1168b2). On the complexities of measuring values, cf. James Griffin, *Well-Being* (Oxford, 1986), pt. 2.

measure' (ibid.). That is only relevant if it can be presumed that comparability entails homogeneity; in any case, it cannot be an implication of the homogeneity thesis that true and sham beauty are one in kind. Possibly more damaging is something that Alcibiades recalls Socrates saying to him a little earlier: 'You must be seeing, I think, an extraordinary beauty in me and one utterly different from your beauty of form' (218e2–3). In what manner the two speeches are to be set together is a question that Nussbaum herself has turned into an issue; but it is still Socrates speaking (unless Alcibiades is mis-remembering him), and the contrast between bodily beauty that is 'one and the same' (210b3), and bodily and intellectual beauty that are 'utterly different', is striking.

And yet, while the text of the *Symposium* turns out to tell rather against Nussbaum than in her favour, I believe that it actually leaves the issue of homogeneity open. She might better have argued not from the text of the ascent-passage, but in a way that undercuts it: it is only within the perspective of the Form of Beauty that all beauty shows up as uniform; so the homogeneity of physical and mental beauty cannot be intelligibly, let alone persuasively, assertible until the ascent is complete. I would not wish to cite Diotima against the presumably Platonic proposition that participating in Beauty is a single relational property. What now becomes crucial is to scrutinize what the ascription of homogeneity really signifies.

Nussbaum is eloquent on its 'startling' quality, as here:

What would it be like to look at a body and to see in it exactly the same shade and tone of goodness and beauty as in a mathematical proof—*exactly* the same, differing only in amount and in location, so that the choice between making love with that person and contemplating that proof presented itself as a choice between having n measures of water and having $n + 100$ (180)?

It is not surprising that she finds such proposals 'so bold as to be pretty well incomprehensible from the ordinary point of view' (181). Possibly a philosopher could be sufficiently self-confident not to find that an objection. But before we hold up our hands in surprise, we need to have a firmer grasp of the homogeneity thesis: ways of explicating it familiar to us render it too clearly true, or too clearly false. On the one hand, there is a single Form of Beauty in which all other beauties partake (211b1–2); so what they partake of is one and the same. To put it semantically, everything else (at least) is 'beauti-ful' in the same sense. What should one say to put it materially? That everything (else) possesses one and the same beauty? I have suggested that Diotima avoids saying that; but if she did say it, it might be no more than the material correlate of the semantic thesis. On the other hand, what a thing must be like to partake of the Form of Beauty varies in detail in almost each case, and in category between kinds of case. The *Phaedo* tells us not to cite a thing's 'blooming colour, or shape, or anything of that kind' as the reason why it is beautiful (100c10–d2); but that should not be to deny that its beauty is supervenient, as we would put it (meaning that it could not change in beauty without changing in any of these other ways). Supervenience remains a source of puzzlement: it is a peculiarly close relation that none the less falls short of entailment in either direction.[7] In the *Symposium*, Plato expresses the closeness of the relation, predictably enough, in a metaphor: bodily beauty is 'full of' (or 'suffused in') flesh and hues and the rest (211e2–3). If, as I understand her, Diotima counts all bodily beauty, but not all beauty, as 'one and the same' (210b3), this is presumably because its subjacent properties, however much they vary (Cleopatra's nose might have looked absurd on Caesar), are of one broad kind or category (that of the 'bodily'). We might say that any concrete instance of beauty (say that of Alcibiades) is constituted by a set of subjacent properties, and that each kind of beauty, discriminated more or less finely, is determined by a category of such properties. This is very approximate (and its elaboration would require a theory of categories), but the homogeneity thesis had better not be denying it. What, then, is it asserting? Presumably it is intended to fall between an uncontentious assertion of semantic sameness and an impossible denial of subjacent differences. Now it is unlikely that Plato would, or could, have separated off the semantic point as a truism: meaning and metaphysics were for him one subject, not two. But that he intended to tread what *we* can see as a middle path is evidenced elsewhere (as Nussbaum has pointed out to me): when it is agreed in the *Meno* that there are different kinds of bee, and yet that bees do not differ from one another in so far as they are bees (72b1–9), it is not plausible to reduce the second proposition to a simple denial that 'bee' is ambiguous; and the lovers of sights and sounds in *Republic* 5 who can believe in beautiful things but not in Beauty itself, because beauty appears to them to be not one thing but

---

[7] The denial of any entailment between justice and any descriptive criteria seems, if the modern jargon be allowed, to be a lesson of *Republic* 1 (331e1–332c1); in general, supervenience was one stimulus towards a theory of Forms.

many (475e9–476c4), are surely not denying 'beautiful' a single meaning (in our sense), but beauty a single nature. Our problem is to clarify that distinction.

We should understand the issue better, and in more Platonic terms, if we could identify the Platonist view about goodness twice attacked by Aristotle (in *NE* 1.6 and *EE* 1.8).[8] It appears that certain Platonists held a view about the nature of goodness which Aristotle wished to reject not simply on the ground of his disbelief in the existence of transcendent Forms. If they alleged 'synonymy' where he alleged 'homonymy', it is best to understand these terms as expressing a disagreement not about semantics (as we might di tinguish it), but about reality.[9] Aristotle is happy to offer a wide paraphrase of 'good', as that for whose sake things are done (cf. *NE* 1.7.1097a18–19); what he denies is that there is a single real nature of which 'good' is the name. By contrast, the Platonists held that there is a single Form of Goodness (as of Beauty) in which good things participate, for all the multiplicity of their subjacent properties. Apparently a distinction was made between intrinsic and instrumental goods, to the effect that it is only the former that participate directly in the Form (*NE* 1.6.1096b8–14). That is not enough to satisfy Aristotle:

The good will have to appear as something identical in them all, as that of whiteness is identical in snow and in white lead. But of honour, wisdom, and pleasure, just in respect of their goodness, the accounts are distinct and diverse. The good, therefore, is not something common answering to one Idea (b21–6).

It is unclear quite what is going on. It would suit Nussbaum to suppose that the Platonists held that a human body and a mathematical proof do indeed possess 'exactly the same shade and tone of goodness' (180), just as snow and white lead may be white in exactly the same way. That is one possibility, and it is not elementary to formulate another. However, it seems to me that that would leave Aristotle with a bare denial in place of an argument: if the Platonists really embraced Nussbaum's paradox, he is merely contradicting them (however plausibly). I prefer to suppose that it is Aristotle who infers from their position that goodness would become a single and simple intrinsic quality, like whiteness, and that they would have agreed that this cannot be right. How to reconstruct their position is

---

[8] A remark by Lindsay Judson saved me from overlooking this.
[9] Cf. Terence Irwin, 'Homonymy in Aristotle', §§ 6–9.

then a problem to which we lack the evidence to identify the correct solution. It is even unclear in what way they would have disagreed with Aristotle's own proposal: 'Are goods one . . . by analogy? Certainly as sight is in the body, so is reason in the soul, and so on in other cases' (b27–9). But I speculate as follows. Aristotle holds that there is nothing more in reality to the goodness of a body than the presence of sight (and the like); the Platonists claim that its goodness is a further and real, though supervenient, property. However, they agree that there is no single quality of goodness present even in all non-instrumental goods (there would be no need for a Form if there were); rather, what good things have in common is a real relation, direct or indirect, to something independent of them, the Form of Goodness. The Platonists concede that what grounds the relation of participation in the Form varies in category in different kinds of case, but they contend that the Form itself retains a single nature by virtue of its separation from any grounding properties (cf. *Symp* 211d8–e4, *Rep* 5.476a4–7). Aristotle's criticism is apt, but too Aristotelian: rewriting the relational property of participation in a uniform Form as a uniform non-relational intrinsic property, he generates the absurdity that goodness comes out as a single qualitative aspect of things, rather like whiteness. The Platonists resisted the inference, and rightly.

Slippery here is what best to say on behalf of the Platonists not about the Form, but about the one-place relational property of participation in it, and particular instantiations of that property.[10] Both these seem Janus-faced, appearing uniform when viewed in relation to the Form itself, but various when viewed in relation to the subjacent properties of the many things that participate in it. However, it seems plausible to say that the relational property takes on a derivative uniformity from the Form, despite the diversity of the subjacent properties; if (like Aristotle) we cease to view the property relationally, we shall become blind to its uniformity. If that is right, the particular instantiations of that property, taken precisely as such, must be uniform in kind; that seems acceptable so long as we conceive them Platonically as reflections of a Form in its participants, and not in Aristotelian fashion as intrinsic to their possessors, for then their homogeneity itself will be derivative and not original. Does this give

---

[10] Cf. *Phaedo* 102b8–d2 on the instances of largeness in Phaedo, or Simmias; but it seems to be supposed that those instances are themselves large (d7–8), which would make them more like particularized Forms, since (if either) it is Largeness which is large, not participating in Largeness.

Nussbaum what she wants? I am happy if it does. However, if what I have now granted amounts to a restatement of the homogeneity thesis, it also qualifies it in a way that possibly removes its 'startling' quality: within the perspective of a theory of Forms, particular beauties will count as uniform in kind only if taken, in severe abstraction, purely as instances of the property of participating in Beauty itself; taken in their concrete reality, they rather resemble 'the sea-god Glaucus whose first nature can hardly be made out by those who catch glimpses of him, because . . . other parts have attached themselves to him, accretions of shells and sea-weed and rocks' (*Rep* 10.611c7–d5). It is perhaps only if we assert homogeneity without abstracting from all that that we say anything contradictory of common sense; if the instances are taken concretely (which is the only way in which they offer themselves to experience), they indeed show up as often 'utterly different' (*Symp* 218e3).[11] Unique about the Form is not merely that it is eternal (*pace NE* 1.6.1096a34–b5), but that it is 'single in form' not abstractly and derivatively, but simply 'in itself' (*Symp* 211b1).

I conclude that Nussbaum's highly original mooting of a thesis that beauty is homogeneous is insufficiently supported as an interpretation of the ascent-passage in the *Symposium*, but revives a genuine issue for the Platonist.

[11] On the other hand, the later claim that Beauty is perceptible (*Phdr* 250c8–e1) may imply that it can impinge upon experience even in its purity: the extraordinary vividness of the erotic vision seems to be explained by the absence of any perceived intermediary between the subjacent properties and the Form, so that the beauty seen is nothing short of Beauty itself. And yet, as I noted, the context restricts this thought narrowly to the beauty of boys. However Plato would now explain it, he implicitly still accepts that scrutinizing a beautiful face and contemplating a mathematical proof are quite different experiences of beauty; what are similar, or at least comparable, in their effects are looking at the beloved and gazing directly upon Beauty itself (*Symp* 211d3–e4).

APPENDIX 2

Psychoanalysis Looks at the *Phaedrus*

Freud distinguishes within erotic object-choice a '*narcissistic type*, where the subject's own ego is replaced by another one that is as similar as possible' (i. 477, cf. xi. 81). Narcissistic libido was originally 'lodged in the ego' (xi. 325), and 'then passes over on to objects, which have been incorporated into the extended ego' (xi. 136). Such incorporation, trading on similarity, tends to blur the boundary between ego and object (cf. xii. 253), even so as to form a 'double individual' (xii. 298). Similar language recurs in Melanie Klein: the ego makes an external object 'into an extension of the self', so that 'the object becomes to some extent a representative of the ego'.[1] We can at once hear pre-echoes of such talk in the *Phaedrus*: its lovers select an object of love with a character that each can model upon his own (252c3–253c2), so that, in due course, they will win the same plumage (*homopterous*, 256e1, signifying more than simultaneity). It fits also that narcissistic object-choice is characteristic of homosexuality in general (i. 476–7, xi. 81), and of pederasty in particular (xiv. 191–2). To trace more detailed parallels and contrasts, we need first to articulate the Freudian account.

There is a usefully ordered presentation by Thomas Ogden.[2] He articulates a four-phase process:

1. One person (the projector) projects in phantasy some aspect of himself, say for safe-keeping, into another (the recipient).
2. He then acts on the other to make him conform to the projection, say by inducing in him through personal interaction feelings similar, or answering, to his own.

---

[1] 'Some Theoretical Conclusions Regarding the Emotional Life of the Infant', in *Envy and Gratitude* (London, 1975), 68.

[2] 'On Projective Identification', *International Journal of Psycho-analysis* 60 (1979), § 2. Certain features of Ogden's description (derived from Klein) are far from Plato: he takes what is projected to be perceived as a danger to the self, or in danger from other aspects of the self (by which he does not merely have in mind the self's mortality); and he stresses the role of personal differences between projector and recipient. What I am taking over, and applying to the *Phaedrus*, is a structure.

3. The other experiences himself in a way that assimilates or reflects the projective phantasy.

4. The projector re-internalizes a modified version of what he had projected.

(2) and (3) are not discrete phases: rather, (3) is the state of the recipient that is the result of the projector's activity within (2). Yet the recipient's role is not to be understood as purely passive: he processes the projection in such a way that there is something partly new for the projector to re-internalize. Despite the inequality in role, the upshot is a joint creation. We may now put both Plato and Freud to use in order to clarify the phases.

Freud was much struck by what he calls 'sexual overvaluation' (e.g. xii. 142). He sees it arising in two ways (though he fails to keep them apart), which we might label 'revaluation' and 'idealization': to put it too briefly, the first distorts the lover's perception of values, the second his perception of facts. In the first way, the 'sensual charm' of the object lends to its other qualities the status of 'spiritual merits':

The loved object enjoys a certain amount of freedom from criticism, and . . . all its characteristics are valued more highly than those of people who are not loved, or than its own were at a time when it itself was not loved. If the sensual impulses are more or less effectively repressed or set aside, the illusion is produced that the object has come to be sensually loved on account of its spiritual merits, whereas on the contrary these merits may really only have been lent to it by its sensual charm (xii. 142–3).

Here there need be no deception about the factual qualities of the object: the deception is that the lover supposes that he loves the object because of its mental merits, whereas in fact he loves it because of its sensual appeal, and sees its mental qualities as merits because he loves it. The error is about causes, and thence about values: 'The functions allotted to the ego ideal entirely cease to operate. The criticism exercised by that agency is silent; everything that the object does and asks for is right and blameless . . . *The object has been put in the place of the ego ideal*' (xii. 143–4). However, this very common (and, we may think, rather amiable) form of overvaluation catches the attention of Plato and Freud less than a different one.[3] It is this other form that involves projection. Here, 'The object serves as a substitute for some unattained ego ideal of our own. We love it on account of the

---

[3] Not that even Plato wholly omits it: cf., in Lysias's speech, *Phdr* 233a5–b1, whether that speech was written by Lysias or by Plato himself.

perfections which we have striven to reach for our ego, and which we should now like to procure in this roundabout way as a means of satisfying our narcissism' (xii. 143). How this process involves at once narcissism and projection is stated clearly elsewhere: 'What he projects before him as his ideal is the substitute for the lost narcissism of his childhood in which he was his own ideal' (xi. 88). Projection is 'an externalization of an internal process' (xi. 231). More precisely: 'An internal perception is suppressed, and, instead, its content, after undergoing a certain kind of distortion, enters consciousness in the form of an external perception' (ix. 204). Thus the lover comes to see his ego ideal, his ideal of how he should be, as actually realized in the person of the beloved, and through not some finer perception but an illusion of the imagination. He now loves the other as he loves his ego ideal, which is as he used to love himself *sans phrase* before he became self-critical.

Plato is sharing the concept of sexual overvaluation when he describes the lover as viewing the beloved as a god (251a6–7, 252a7, d6). Such talk is itself indeterminate between the two varieties of overvaluation; in context, the second is clearly meant. However, it is characteristic of Plato's mentality that, without of course supposing that the beloved can really be divine (which, I suggested, betrays even in the lover only an initial state of confusion), yet he concedes enough to the idealization to cast it as a kind of recognition: the beloved is chosen according to his actual, if also prehistorical, disposition (e.g. 252e1–3). Perhaps Plato comes closest to the notion of projection when he describes lovers as holding the beloved responsible for their participation in the divine: remembering their god becomes displaced into perceiving the beloved (252e7–253a6), so that an internal process is externalized.

In another respect, it is the lover who is seen by the beloved as 'possessed by a god' (255b6–7), that is in his generosity. Talk of an undifferentiated extended self fails to explain why the lover is more than impartial between the beloved and himself. In Plato, the lover has a selective perception of the beloved as a follower of their god, while his own self-perception is both less selective and less explicit: he does not dwell upon himself idealizingly in thought. Freud, no doubt, allows a more elaborate explanation. Projecting my ego ideal upon another I take on a concern for him that matches not my adult self-love and self-concern, but my infantile narcissism, transferred upon my ego ideal; my present self-concern may then come to weigh for little in the balance compared with the other-concern that is the inheritor of my original self-love.[4]

In Ogden's second phase, the lover acts on the other so as to make him conform to the projection. There is an element of paradox inherent in this activity: who is the projector himself to see it as necessary? But then projection is an operation in phantasy by creatures who are no longer confidently phantastical. Both this phase, and the paradox, are emphasized by Plato. The lover not only sees the god in the boy, but strives to make them as similar as possible (252e7–253c2). The paradox is particularly alive in a sentence of apparent confusion: 'Treating the beloved as if he were himself a god, he fashions and adorns him like an image for himself, in order to honour and worship it' (252d6–e1). But the confusion is the lover's, not the writer's. The lover resolves it by reinterpreting his idolizing perception of the beloved as a recognition of his real potentialities.

In the third phase, the beloved experiences himself in a new way that adopts the projective phantasy. This is an instance of 'identification', which Freud defines as 'the assimilation of one ego to another one . . . as a result of which the first ego behaves like the second in certain respects, imitates it and in a sense takes it up into itself' (ii. 94–5). Where the other ego was a libidinal object, identification either follows (vii. 319), or generates (xi. 369)—Freud seems to vacillate—a desexualization or sublimation in which the first ego, through incorporating the other, becomes its own object. In terms of 'ego' and 'id', 'When the ego assumes the features of the object, it is forcing itself, so to speak, upon the id as a love-object and is trying to make good the id's loss by saying: "Look, you can love me too—I am so like the object"' (ibid.). The ego may go so far as to discard the other as object: 'It is by no means rare for a love-relation to be broken off through a process of identification on the part of the lover with the beloved object, a process equivalent to a kind of regression to narcissism' (ix. 364, n. 1). However, there are also 'cases of simultaneous object-cathexis and identification' (xi. 369), in which the lover wishes

---

[4] The obstacle to such narcissistic altruism is a sense of insecurity that gives the lover to suppose that what he gives he loses. Cf. Klein: 'The feeling of having dispersed goodness and good parts of the self into the external world adds to the sense of grievance and envy of others who are felt to contain the lost goodness' ('On Identification', in *Envy and Gratitude*, 172, n. 1). The generosity and freedom from envy of Plato's lover (253b7–8) is aided by his illusion of receiving from his beloved what in reality he is projecting into him (cf. a2–6).

at once to *be* and to *have* the other (cf. ii. 95, xii. 135). And if the object is discarded, the consequence may be not exclusive narcissism, but a new range of external objects. Thus, in cases of pederasty such as Leonardo's, 'The young man does not abandon his mother, but identifies himself with her; he transforms himself into her, and now looks about for objects which can replace his ego for him, and on which he can bestow such love and care as he has experienced from his mother' (xii. 138, cf. x. 205, xiv. 191).[5]

The process that Freud is capturing, or enriching, with a wealth of new concepts is crucial, though less densely conceptualized, in Plato. Within his mythology, lover and beloved identify with their common god, that is, in effect, with the best of each other as each perceives the other. The beloved is identifying at once with the lover's ideal self, and with an idealized perception of himself. In loving the other as a mirror of himself (cf. 255d6), he is loving himself through the eyes of the other; the mirror reflects what is visible to the lover, not to anyone, in respect of what he *is* like as well as what he *looks* like.[6] But Ganymede (cf. 255c2) is not Narcissus: he loves Zeus (who has the privilege of being to the boy at once god and lover), and will love others as Zeus loved him. The beloved too will see his god in the lover. Plato would apply to erotic love what Freud (much against Christ) asserts only of loving one's neighbour: 'If I love someone, he must deserve it in some way . . . He deserves it if he is so like me in important ways that I can love myself in him; and he deserves it if he is so much more perfect than myself than I can love my ideal of my own self in him' (xii. 299–300). This holds, in Plato, of the mutual relations of lover and beloved (without any elaborated distinction between the processes of projection and identification). In accepting the lover's attempt to put into effect his idealizing conception of the true nature of them both, in welcoming the pervasion through his own life of the lover's ideals, the beloved seconds the lover's creative devotion. When he is a few years older, and it is time for him to love

---

5 In so acting the pederast is displaying, in his own way, one of the major patterns of mental health: 'Gratitude is closely bound up with generosity. Inner wealth derives from having assimilated the good object so that the individual becomes able to share its gifts with others . . . Even the fact that generosity is often insufficiently appreciated does not necessarily undermine the ability to give' (Klein, 'Envy and Gratitude', in *Envy and Gratitude*, 189).

6 In reading Plato so, I am now interpreting the beauty that is reflected from the lover's eyes into those of the beloved as mental in addition to physical; that seems permissible, though it transcends the narrower interests of the *Phaedrus* context.

someone younger (as he must if the erotic succession is to be handed down), he will replicate that devotion through modelling himself on the lover, so transforming himself into him when he is no longer dependent upon him; it is by such unfaithfulness that he will prove himself faithful.[7]

In Ogden's final phase, the process of projective identification comes full circle: the projector re-internalizes what he had projected in a form modified by the recipient. No parallel to this is explicit in Plato, but we can see that it must have its parallel in Platonic love. The lover was inspired, in Freudian terms, to live up to his ego ideal through his projection of it upon the sexual object (cf. 252e7–253a6); if Ogden's second and third phases go through, he should be heartened through his perception of the object's acceptance of it. In terms less distant from Plato, the lover is inspired to imitate his god through seeing him in the beloved; the perception should become clearer, and more inspiring, if it becomes of actuality, not potentiality. And through perceiving what the realization of the divine comes to in another person, the lover will understand its nature more fully; his ideal will be developed and refined. Thus we can draw on Ogden to fill out Plato, as well as Freud.

Among the threats to the narcissism of the ego is the apprehension of death. One solution is the creation of offspring who, incorporated within an extended self, may be loved according to a narcissistic object-choice: 'At the touchy point in the narcissistic system, the immortality of the ego, which is so hard pressed by reality, security is achieved by taking refuge in the child' (xi. 85). Thus the child becomes, especially to the mother, a physical *alter ego*: 'In the child which they [sc. narcissistic women] bear, a part of their own body confronts them like an extraneous object, to which, starting out from their narcissism, they can then give complete object-love' (xi. 83). Plato expresses the same thought in different language in the *Symposium* when Diotima confirms that part of love's object is immortality (207a3–4) by citing the willingness of animals even to die for their young if need be (a6–b6). She explains that the child's body stands to those of its parents rather as it stands at one time to itself at a previous time (d3–e1), so that its body may be viewed as an extension of their bodies; thus if narcissism can stretch over time, it should also

---

[7] Cf. Proust: 'At most she whom we have loved so much has added a particular form to our loving, which will make us be faithful to her even in our infidelity' (*A la recherche du temps perdu*, iii. 908).

be able to extend between bodies. Of course such a view transcends
common sense. We may think that it distorts what is true, and is stated
by Freud elsewhere: 'Love strives after objects, and its chief function,
favoured in every way by nature, is the preservation of the species'
(xii. 308). Viewed common-sensibly, nature is not so benign to the
species-member:

The individual organism, which regards itself as the main thing and its
sexuality as a means, like any other, for its own satisfaction, is from the point
of view of biology only an episode in a succession of generations, a short-lived
appendage to a germ-plasm endowed with virtual immortality—like the
temporary holder of an entail which will outlast him (i. 463, cf. xi. 70–1, 316–
35).

Though distant from the *Symposium*, this sentence is close to a
passage in the *Phaedrus* which allows the mind an ersatz immortality:

A man makes use of the science of dialectic, and taking a fitting soul plants and
sows in it words accompanied by knowledge, which are able to help themselves and the man who planted them, and are not without fruit but contain a
seed, from which others grow in other souls, capable of rendering it for ever
immortal, and making the one who has it as happy as it is possible for a man to
be (276d5–277a4).

Plato's 'seed', taken literally, is the same as Freud's 'germ-plasm'; it,
and not the individual plant or animal, is the real beneficiary of
biology.

May one complain that both Plato and Freud vacillate inconsistently between different candidates for a kind of immortality? Only
unfairly, I think. In Plato seed keeps alive not the individual body
(inhabited by a single soul), but a sequence of bodily states that
outlives individual bodies. The individual body is not immortal; the
seed and the sequence are (or can be), in a way that constitutes a
physical after-effect of the activities of the soul within a body. In
Freud we must distinguish between the survival of the species, which
is offered by biology, and a quasi-survival of the individual, contingent upon his identifying with another individual who survives
him (like a mother with her child). It is less explicit in Plato that the
extended self is created not just through causality (passing on one's
own life, mental or physical), but through attitude (identifying with
one's inheritor); but of course this is implicit, in his descriptions of
the devotion of animals to their young, and of philosophers to their

favourites. In such a way love of self carries over into love of others, through psychological mechanisms that Plato and Freud perceive in common, but conceive rather differently.[8]

---

[8] In this appendix I have largely been concerned to redescribe the love recommended in the *Phaedrus* in psychoanalytical terms. It is really a distinct project to trace similarities between Plato's and Freud's theories; I attempt that, in discussion of the sublimation of desire, and the tripartite soul, in my essay 'Plato and Freud', in Christopher Gill (ed.) *The Person and the Human Mind: Issues in Ancient and Modern Philosophy* (Oxford, 1990), 247–70.

APPENDIX 3

Plato's Sexual Morality

We might expect of Plato the attitude that to be a philosopher is to disdain the pleasures of sex. That is duly stated in the *Phaedo*: the genuine philosopher is 'not at all' keen on them (64d6–7); he views all bodily perceptions and sensations as distractions to his soul, which strives to become 'alone by itself as far as possible' in order to grasp reality (c7–9). This skeleton takes on life in the depiction of Socrates. The force of his example depends on the fact that he is more, not less, susceptible than most of us. Alcibiades describes him as always out of his mind with hanging around young men (*Symp* 216d2–3). We might take that as ironical exaggeration, but for what Socrates himself tells us elsewhere. Most vivid is when, catching sight of Charmides' torso inside his cloak, he feels on fire, and absolutely beside himself (*Charm* 155d3–4). He then takes part in a discussion of temperance; Alcibiades proceeds to tell a story of his immunity to seduction. Socrates' appeal to Alcibiades, Charmides, Euthydemus, and many others, which makes them more lovers of him than he ever was of them (*Symp* 222b1–4), is precisely that he is so very susceptible, and so little seducible.[1] If Socrates is safe this is not because, by some personal quirk, he is endowed with that 'insensibility' which Aristotle denies to be human (*NE* 3.11.1119a6–7), but because he inhabits an evaluative perspective within which what he offers truly compares to what Alcibiades offers as gold to brass (*Symp* 218e3–219a1). What marks off the philosopher is not that he is incapable of the pleasures of other men, but that he is capable of his own.

And yet when he comes to make proposals for a community, Plato is less dismissive. This may be simply because he recognizes that someone has got to breed (escape from incarnation is not to be encompassed through a euthanasia of the species), and believes that the best

---

[1] Michel Foucault has an illuminating remark: 'What they do not know, and what Alcibiades discovers in the course of the famous "test", is that they only love Socrates to the extent that he is capable of resisting their seduction' (*L'Usage des plaisirs*, 265). The context of the *Charmides* passage (a narration by Socrates to the reader) does not suit an ingenious suggestion by Christopher Gill that, with an irony parallel to that of the Socratic elenchus, Socrates' susceptibility is a deliberate pretence, to be followed by an unexpected display of sexual indifference (in 'Platonic Love and Individuality').

parents produce the best children; perhaps also because he sees a difference between setting up an example and laying down laws; maybe further because, once he has divided the soul into three parts each with its own goals, he cannot hope for temperance (now defined as agreement about which should rule, *Rep* 4.432a6–9) without some mutual accommodation. It is still striking that the 'innate necessity' which he concedes is one not to procreate, but to have intercourse (5.458d2–5). This is accompanied by a habitual denigratory allusion to 'the common people' (d7); since the topic is the treatment of women among the guardians, the habit is out of place. Though innate, the necessity is not unconditioned: it is activated by eating and exercising together (d1–2). At least, since those are to involve both sexes, they will give rise to heterosexual necessity and not to the homosexual corruption of Crete and Sparta (*Laws* 1.636b1–c1). Of sexual desires some are necessary, others unnecessary (*Rep* 8.559c6). Necessary appetites are those which we cannot divert (they are immune to the sublimation described at 6.485d6–12), or whose satisfaction benefits us; nature compels us to seek to satisfy both (8.558d11–e3). The letter of this is quite close to the *Phaedo*: it too allowed that there are services to the body in which even the philosopher is compelled to share (64e1); and the philosopher's attitude to necessary pleasures is still that he would have no use for them if he were not compelled (*Rep* 9.581e3–4). But the spirit is more permissive, most surprisingly in allowing guardians beyond the permitted age for procreation to have intercourse with whomever they wish (5.461b9–c1).[2] In general, reason is to treat the appetites like a farmer who cultivates crops while inhibiting weeds (9.589b1–3); paternalism has replaced hostility.

About homosexual relations, however, Plato remains restrictive. No talk of 'erotic necessity' (5.458d5) is applied to them. The distinction between the sexes, otherwise minimized, remains alive here. Plato concedes to pederastic relations a restrained tenderness absent from the regulated or casual copulations of mixed couples. Lover and beloved are to be fully educated, away from madness and self-indulgence, towards temperance and culture (3.403a7–12). The lover

---

[2] This is the one positive piece of evidence offered by Terence Irwin for denying that Plato would have the guardians rid themselves of all unnecessary desires (*Plato's Moral Theory*, 340). I would rather suppose that Plato is conceding, still quite generously, that even those beyond the best age for breeding can have irradicable sexual desires which are distracting unless gratified.

may kiss and touch the beloved, with his consent, just like a son (b4–6).³ The tone is closer to that of Socrates' affectionate toying with Phaedo's hair as Phaedo sits beneath him by his prison bed (*Pdo* 89b2–4) than it is to his stony inattention to Alcibiades as he lies the night on a couch in Alcibiades' arms (behaving like 'a father or elder brother', *Symp* 219d1–2). Aristotle was rather shocked (*Pol* 2.4.1262a32–7). Tenderness towards the other sex is later introduced on the pederastic model: during a campaign the winner of the prize for valour will be permitted to kiss whom he likes, male or female, so that those in love with a man or woman may be all the keener to win the prize; here civic utility overrides the requirement of consent (5.468c1–4).

We may be puzzled that Plato should be so much stricter about erotic relations within the sexes than between them. Less alien to us is Aristophanes' picture of men innately attracted to other men, and women to women (*Symp* 191e2–192a1), divinely intended to be able to make love so that they may achieve satiation and turn their minds to other things (191b5–c8). Indeed, if one has the notion of an exclusive homosexual orientation determined from birth (or even from early childhood), it is reasonable to concede that it too should be gratified. However, it may be a mistake to interpret this aspect of the speech as more than a comic curiosity, for its appeal is anachronistic. One way in which it is more modern than Greek is in escaping the paradigm of one-sided pederasty (no doubt varied in practice) by a depiction of homosexual mutuality.⁴ Also modern is its conception of sexual orientation as a deep fact about individuals that must be almost as central to their own sense of identity as their gender.⁵ More Greek than modern, on the other hand, is its assumption that sexual orientation is a matter always of preference, never of exclusivity. Even adulterers are only said 'mostly' to derive from androgynes (191d8); it 'suffices' those deriving from doubles of the same sex to live together and not to marry (192b3). In this respect Aristophanes is not so distant from

---

³ James Adam has a good note (*The Republic of Plato*, ad loc.) preferring the MSS 'like a son' to Herwenden's 'like ⟨a father⟩ his son': 'Plato's text is better and more expressive, because it represents the object of affection almost as the lover's very son.'

⁴ This is pointed out by Foucault (op. cit. 255); he notes how reciprocity is emphasized by the repeated *sun*-compounds of 191e8, and *phil*-compounds of 192b4.

⁵ Foucault, again, rightly distinguishes the Greek view of a preference for boys or girls as 'a matter of taste which could lend itself to pleasantries' from its modern role as 'a matter of typology involving the very nature of the individual' (ibid. 210).

Pausanias, whose distinction between Uranian and Pandemian Aphrodite is more clearly alien to us. Uranian Aphrodite is exclusively pederastic in a high-minded way (and far from generally homosexual), while Pandemian is indiscriminate (*Symp* 180d–181d). The determinant of one's choice between them is whether one puts soul or body first (181b3–4, 183e1), for the male mind has more sense (181c5–6). We may talk here of 'bisexuality', but even that may mislead, if it implies not just a freedom of choice within the two sexes, but what Michel Foucault calls 'a double, ambivalent, and "bisexual" structure of desire' (op. cit. 208–9). Of course the Greeks were prone to their own categorizations and simplifications, but it was not their way to classify choices of sexual objects simply according to the genders of the two parties. Hence Plato had no concept of homosexuality, with its modern connotations, to guide him towards the thought that homosexual and heterosexual relations should be treated on a par.

At the heart of Plato's attitude is, I suggest, his very theory of love. According to the *Symposium*, love is the desire to beget in beauty (206e5). It might seem a simple counter-example to that that homosexual love is physically sterile. Plato's rejoinder, that offspring can be mental instead of physical, is not high-minded evasion: he clearly believes that there is a natural connection between pederasty and pregnancy in soul. Which way does the connection go, from mental pregnancy to pederasty, or from pederasty to mental pregnancy? I shall argue first that Plato is right to suppose that the lover set on mental procreation must either be a pederast, or treat women like boys.

A goal of Plato's preferred lovers is mental union in a shared life. What might constitute that? One would think that there were at least two possibilities:

1. Two souls of similar nature come together in a communion of shared attitude and incident, so that the experiences which constitute the life of each come to differ, and to differentiate them, only insignificantly. They come to share the same point of view upon the same events and activities, so that we might talk either of each life becoming two, or of their two lives becoming one.

2. Two souls of a dissimilar nature come together in a partnership
which, giving each a role complementary to that of the other,
achieves a mutual interplay, without conflict or hiatus, that
makes for differentiation not assimilation, harmony not unison.
Each responds to the other immediately and intuitively as if
there were no obstacles of egoism or ignorance. Their lives
become not the same, but at one.[6]

Of these two loves we may call (1) homoerotic, (2) heteroerotic. That
fits minimal etymology: (1) is the love of like for like, (2) the love of
unlikes. Moreover, (1) must operate between souls that are either
incarnate within the same sex, or mentally detached from a difference
of sex. What we may regret is that Plato ignores the possibility of
unification of kind (2) in assuming that souls seek out similar souls
(e.g. *Phdr* 252e1–253c2). Is there a rational explanation of his silence?
I think that there is: recognition of love of type (2) between souls
would subvert the foundation of love unearthed by Diotima (and still
present, if not as a starting-point, at *Phdr* 276e4–277a4). On her
account, 'Love is for the good to belong to oneself always' (*Symp*
206a11–12). Consequently, it aims at immortality, to be achieved
through generation and birth in beauty (206e8–207a4). The two
interesting possibilities are analogous: I may hope to live on in
another physical organism, or in another's thoughts and projects,
deriving from my own rather as my future life will derive from my
present one. I may be pregnant in body, or in soul, but all love is a
kind of pregnancy, whose goal is the creation of another life that will
be an extension of the lover's. That clarifies for Plato the point of (1):
loving someone who comes to be mentally the same as oneself dupli-
cates one's mind, and achieves a double mental life. There will be
further point if one is given not only to homoerotic but to pederastic
love: that alone makes likely an erotic succession whereby *A*'s way of
life is transmitted through the *B* he loves to a *C B* loves, to a *D C* loves,
and so on. But (2) can offer nothing like this: to love someone unlike
oneself is not to love a second self, and promises no continuation of
one's life in and through the other person. If one's spouse dies, one
may have lost one's 'better half'; there is no question that he or she is

[6] For a perfect illustration of the charm and realism of (2), cf. Goethe on a husband
and wife playing duets, quoted in W. H. Auden, *A Certain World* (London, 1971),
250–1. In Chapter 7, § 3 I mentioned a third possibility, that these souls take on one
another's complementary qualities; in the present context that may be set aside as
passing on, and keeping up, the life of each only in dilution.

more than minimally alive in oneself. (1) offers victory over death; (2) makes death intolerable. Within (1), I may hope that I and the other will be immortal, in a way; within (2), I can only wish that we were. Consequently, the Platonic love that is not satisfied by physical procreation is indeed fundamentally, and essentially, homoerotic. That is not to say that it could never unite, say, a man and a younger woman, but only if they can disregard the fact that they are not a man and a boy.[7]

Thus if mental union is conceived on the model of mental pregnancy, it does indeed point to pederasty. Let us now consider the reverse connection: had Plato any reason to suppose that a preference for pederasty that goes deep, and is not accidental or gratuitous, manifests pregnancy in soul even before it achieves sublimation? If he had, that would go towards explaining his refusal, given that Greek homosexuality was largely pederastic, to allow the phrase 'erotic necessity' (*Rep* 5.458d5) any homosexual application as an excuse for unsublimated indulgence. If pederastic desire is particularly susceptible to sublimation, then it is natural that those particularly capable of sublimation should incline towards pederasty; by contrast, those content with physical pleasure should be relatively indifferent about what form it takes. Accordingly, in the *Phaedrus*, men whose memory of the Platonic heaven is dimmed turn indifferently to sexual indulgence with either sex (250e1–251a1), whereas those whose response to human beauty is a kind of perception, blurred at first, of Beauty itself are only described as falling for boys (253e5 ff.).[8] Indeed, love between the sexes is never given as a possible starting-point for spiritual ascent. No doubt it can yield to a general programme of the sublimation of appetite (cf. *Rep* 6.485d6–12); it will never provide an impetus towards such a programme. Plato is likely to have had two grounds for supposing that a rational, and therefore (in his book) profound, preference for pederasty contains the seeds of spiritual growth. Firstly, we may take it that he would not have

---

[7] Baudelaire was not merely being mischievous when he wrote: 'The more alien women are to us the more we love them. Loving intelligent women is a pederastic pleasure' (*Journaux Intimes*, 'Fusées', § 5); *Œuvres complètes*, i. 653.

[8] There is some dispute about how to interpret *Phaedrus* 250e. Gregory Vlastos ('The Individual as Object of Love in Plato', 25, n. 76) takes both the clauses of 250e4–251a1 as homosexual in application; he is answered by K. J. Dover (*GH*, 163, n. 15). Vlastos's reading runs against Plato's assumption in the *Laws* that animals are models of exclusive heterosexuality (1.636b4–6, 8.836c3–6). I prefer to take 250e4–5 as heterosexual (or more precisely reproductive), e5–251a1 as homosexual (or more generally

disagreed with Goethe as he is reported speaking about pederasty two years before his death: 'He explained the true origin of that aberration by the fact that, judged by the purely aesthetic standard, man is far more beautiful, more excellent, nearer to perfection than woman.'⁹ In Platonic terms, the beauty of male adolescents (who have a visual bloom, but no pronounced sexual characteristics) is more evocative than woman's of a beauty of another order. (There results the paradox that it is the most transient beauty that is best reminiscent of timelessness.) Secondly, and more distinctively, the very physical sterility of a homosexual attachment must motivate it towards sublimation precisely in order to achieve the goal of love, which is procreation in beauty; until then, pederasty evinces a desire in want of a proper end. Consequently, after incarnation as a man, a soul that had initially to choose an object of sexual attraction without wishing to remain a subject of sexual desire would naturally, on Platonic grounds, choose a boy rather than a woman. The pederast by preference and vocation who pursues sexual indulgence is more culpable in so doing than the occasional or accidental pederast: he is seeking freely to discard the very privileges of pederasty, in disregard of his finer potentialities and of love's true nature. The option is his, but Plato does not permit him to plead 'erotic necessity'.¹⁰

The notion of what is according, or contrary, to nature is recurrent in Plato. According to nature is that soul rule over body (*Pdo* 79e8–80a2), that the right elements be dominant within body or soul (*Rep* 4.444d3–11), that men and women share the same education (5.456b8–c2), that the stronger rule over the weaker (*Laws* 3.690b4–8), that the ignorant be willing to be ruled by the wise (690b9–c3), that the homicide be done by as he did (9.870e1–3), that the gods listen to the complaints of wronged parents (11.931c3–5), that the

non-reproductive); the second *kai* in e5 will then be introducing a climactic alternative ('or even'), here something even less paradisal; cf. J. D. Denniston, *The Greek Particles* (Oxford, 1954), 291–2.

⁹ I quote from Theodor Gomperz, *Greek Thinkers* (London, 1901–12), ii. 379.

¹⁰ It is interesting to compare Freud. He held of homosexuality in general that it particularly lends itself to sublimation (ix. 199, x. 208, xii. 42); for he associated it with the 'sexual component instincts' whose sublimation is the origin of civilization (x. 111, cf. xii. 40–1). However, he came closer to Plato's (and perhaps perennial) experience in identifying a special reason why pederasty tends to be Platonic: as I quoted in Appendix 2, the pederast identifies himself with his mother, and looks for boys whom he may love *just as* his mother loved him (x. 205, xii. 138, xiv. 191); that is, chastely (cf. Richard Wollheim, *The Thread of Life*, 124).

man who abandons his weapons in battle be barred from military service (12.945a5–7), and that the founders' laws be irreversible (12.960d5–6). Clearly the term 'natural' (or the phrase *kata phusin*) is coming to signify just the right or fitting, as opposed to the purely conventional. That contrast is occasionally backed by what we would see as another, between the natural and artificial: the dominance of the stronger is confirmed as natural by its universality among the animals (3.690b7–8).[11] At the same time, Plato is quite willing to dismiss any popular appeal to animals when it suits him: pleasure is not the greatest good, though oxen and horses and all other beasts tell us that it is by pursuing it (*Phil* 67b1–4). Clearly the Greek concept of the natural cannot in itself explain Plato's variable application of it. We can surmise that he may have associated it with a teleological conception of the universe and the individual's place therein (cf. *Laws* 10.903b4–d3); but, instead of starting abstractly, we are wiser to to look directly for a specific criterion of the sexually natural. None is explicit in the *Phaedrus* when Plato first (to my knowledge) invokes 'nature' prescriptively in a sexual context: there is a kind of man who 'keeping close company with excess has no fear or shame in pursuing pleasure contrary to nature' (250e5–251a1). The mention of 'excess', or perhaps 'insolence' (*hubris*), is too slippery to be helpful;[12] it may be merited simply because its subject, unlike the second-best male lovers of 256b7–e2 (cf. c6–7), is in no two minds about indulging himself. Just what is contrary to nature, and why, is not stated. The most likely gloss is that, while there is a reproductive kind of sexual activity, common to men and animals (250e3–5), that falls outside our spiritual nature, there is another kind that falls outside our animal nature as well (and so is, simply, 'contrary to nature'). Presumably Plato is here thinking primarily of homosexual intercourse; but he should also mean any intercourse not of a reproductive kind (which would include what *Rep* 5.461b9–c1 permitted). This becomes explicit in the *Laws*. An early passage there contrasts a kind of heterosexuality with homosexuality: 'When male and female come together to share in procreation, the pleasure they experience seems to have been granted according to nature; but homosexual intercourse, between males or females, seems to be an unnatural crime of the first

---

[11] None of this was peculiar to Plato, or restricted to philosophers: cf. Dover, *GPM*, 75, 268–9.
[12] Cf. C. J. Rowe, *Plato: Phaedrus*, ad 238a2; Dover, *GH*, 34–6.

rank' (1.636c3–6).[13] What we are to think of men and women who come together not for procreation is not said.[14] That is made explicit in a later and more graphic passage: we need a device for reinforcing

the law about the natural use of the intercourse which procreates children, (1) abstaining from the male, not (a) deliberately killing human progeny or (b) 'sowing in rocks and stones', where it [sc. the seed] will never take root and be endowed with growth, (2) abstaining too from all female soil in which you would not want what you have sown to grow (8.838e6–839a3, tr. K. J. Dover, GH, 188).[15]

This passage denies men all homosexual intercourse, and all intercourse with women whom they would not wish to make mothers; its rejection of homosexuality must carry over to any recourse to contraception. Yet in one way it is significantly permissive: required of heterosexual intercourse is a willingness, but not an intention, to produce a child. The intention might be to preserve health (cf. 11.930c2–6, Tim 91b4–d5). A couple only beyond the *proper* age of child-bearing are denied intercourse, but not so clearly a couple beyond the *possible* age of child-bearing (or infertile for some other reason, transient or lasting). The Laws is less explicit than the Republic about sexually indulging senior citizens; but perhaps the 'mutual care' expected of people who remarry when they already have enough children (11.930b1–3) includes intercourse that has no chance of being procreative. An exact definition of the sexually natural is not going to be easy: it is not to be enough, for instance, to justify a homosexual act that the parties may be *willing* that it lead,

[13] The perfect tense of *apodedosthai* (c4) supports A. E. Taylor's 'to have been granted' over T. J. Saunders's 'to arise'; if so, it indicates an in-built teleology, natural or divine.

[14] Vlastos claims that the 'unnatural' is always specifically homosexual (*Platonic Studies*, 425); that fits 8.836b8–c7, but ignores that it is only procreative intercourse that is here called 'according to nature', while 8.841d3–5 oppose not homosexuality to heterosexuality as such, but homosexuality, unnatural because sterile, to harlotry, apparently reproductive, whose seed is 'unhallowed and bastard'.

[15] I have added numbers and letters to make perspicuous that (a) and (b) both fall within (1), as best fits the syntax. I read (a) and (b) as expressing different objections to homosexual intercourse: (a) presents sterile sex as a kind of murder (within a primitive biology ignorant of the role of the female ovum); (b) presents it as a neglect of natural teleology (as I shall be discussing). It is strange to find the phrase 'the intercourse which procreates children' used generically even of homosexual intercourse; but this spares Plato the clumsiness of writing more fully, 'the law about the natural use of the intercourse which used naturally procreates children', that is of sexual intercourse. If so, Vlastos was right not to cite this passage in support of his reading of *Phaedrus* 250e4–5, mentioned earlier.

miraculously, to a conception.[16] Plato is clearly feeling his way towards the notion of an act of an intrinsically reproductive kind, that is of an act itself broadly of a kind to lead to reproduction that is not performed either with the knowledge of having prevented that outcome, or with the intention of preventing it.[17] However, it is now explicit that what is unnatural is not the specifically homosexual, but the generally non-reproductive (in the desired sense). Whether the example of animals can plausibly be cited to justify precisely that criterion (cf. 1.636b4–6, 8.836c3–6) is questionable; the thought is doubtless (as I suggested in Chapter 2 about *Symp* 207a6 ff.) that they display a natural teleology, untainted by deliberation. It is evident that Plato is far from the more recent attitude which finds homosexual activity 'unnatural' to the extent that it manifests a disposition of homosexual desire; he lacks the conception to make that objection.

No doubt Plato is playing a slippery game. What look like counter-examples that fault his theory that the goal of love is procreation are being faulted themselves as 'contrary to nature', that is, in effect, as contrary to the theory. What began in the *Symposium* as a description of love has become by the time of the *Phaedrus* a prescription for love. That transition may be familiar to us under the heading of 'persuasive definitions'. Perhaps more surprising is that the theory is being applied not just to total loving relationships, but to every single act of making love. To that there were two more permissive alternatives. The more extreme would make no objection on grounds of 'unnaturalness' to a couple, say of the same sex, who are engaged in spiritual pregnancy, but allow themselves a sterile kind of sexual pleasure. The line could be that, while the final goal of love is to possess the good for ever (*Symp* 206a11–12), love may also manifest itself in ways that pursue the present good without themselves contributing to immortality. Such, in fact, could be the defence of the second-best lovers in the *Phaedrus* (if they wished to defend themselves) who are set on regaining their plumage but lapse occasionally

---

[16] Cf. an anecdote about Periander, Aristotle *Pol* 5.10.1311a39–b1.

[17] Cf. G. E. M. Anscombe, 'You Can have Sex without Children: Christianity and the New Offer', in *Ethics, Religion and Politics* (Oxford, 1981), 85–7. Perhaps more problematic than identifying the requisite degree of generality in describing the kind of act, or of restrictiveness in isolating the intrinsic nature of the act, is establishing the moral irrelevance of more specific descriptions making reference, say, to the fertility of the couple. (Why should it be morally relevant that *no* homosexual couple can reproduce, but not that *this* heterosexual couple cannot?)

(256b7–e2). However, Plato would probably object that this denies the in-built teleology of the sexual act: to permit a sterile kind of love-making within a theory of love as inherently reproductive would devalue making love, detaching it from the goal of love and leaving it as a minor indulgence on the side, like kissing. More acceptable to Plato should be to permit particular sexual acts of a sterile kind so long as they fall within a sexual relationship that as a whole is reproductive in kind. That modification was adopted by the commission whose majority report recommended to Pope Paul VI that particular acts of contraception should be permitted within a marriage so long as its overall purpose remains non-contraceptive; Plato's position is like that to which Paul adhered.[18] Here Plato may be more vulnerable than the Pope: proscriptions on individual acts seem more alien to a teleological morality than to one based on natural law, less subsumable under a good for the agent to achieve than under obligations that his nature requires him to respect.[19] What is the teleological objection to failing to achieve some goal by one act so long as it is achieved by another? It may be in our nature to seek immortality in every possible form (*Laws* 4.721b8–9), and that may even oblige everyone 'not maimed in his capacity for virtue' (Aristotle's words, *NE* 1.9.1099b19) to get married at the appropriate age, as Plato asserts (721c6–8); but why should nature require us to remain open to immortality in every act of sexual consummation? Plato's answer remains elusive.

Though Plato does not expect his prohibitions to be popular among the young (cf. *Laws* 8.839b3–6), he must intend his way of justifying them to preclude their being imposed from outside on agents who have no reason of their own to respect them. But then why should they be needed? As the notion of the 'natural' is intended to be at once prescriptive and descriptive, grounded on ends both desirable and desired, it should appeal without being imposed. Plato has to explain why the natural is too seldom the actual. It fits what I have been saying that he does not invoke any specifically homosexual disposition. Instead, he accuses the lover who gets his way of intemperance (836d7), of giving in to pleasure that he is too soft to resist (d9–e1, cf. 1.636c6–7), and the beloved who consents of effeminacy (836d5–7,

---

[18] For a brief account, cf. Charles Napier, 'The Design of the Creator: A Guide to Humanae Vitae' (London, 1969).

[19] There is a general problem here about the demands of justice; e.g. about how teleologically to ground the principle that one should *never* tell a lie.

e1–3).[20] In effect both fail, in a phrase familiar in Plato, to be 'masters of themselves' (cf. *Rep* 4.430e7, *Phdr* 232a4–5, *Laws* 1.626e7); in Platonic theory, their better part is dominated by their worse (*Rep* 4.431a3–b2). Lover as well as beloved may be accused of a lack of internal virility.[21] In this way Plato extends to both parties the shameful charge of submitting to sexual domination. If they succumb, that is evidence of 'madness' (8.839a7, cf. *Rep* 3.403a10, *Phdr* 241a4), and of 'slavery' (*Laws* 8.838d5, cf. *Rep* 9.577d2, 579d10, *Phdr* 238e3; Dover, *GPM*, 208), that is of a state in which the soul is overwhelmed by mastering appetites. Happiness is to be achieved by the conquest of pleasure (840c5–6, cf. 1.636d5–e1). Since it is out of weakness that men act contrary to nature, respecting nature serves a double goal: its own specific goal of serving love and achieving the good for ever, and an associated goal of preserving mastery and achieving the good here and now. Yet, because of human weakness, it is not enough to leave nature to rely upon its own appeal, or even that of an authoritative exposition (as at 4.721b7–c8). Plato as legislator envisages various aids, wisely (we may think) putting no particular trust in any one of them: the magic of early stories and songs (8.840c1–3); the salutary example of birds and other animals (d2–e2); the distraction of physical exercise (841a6–8); a schooled demand for privacy (b2–4); respect for religion, love of honour, and a mature passion for beauties of mind rather than of body (c4–6). Even so, he distinguishes an ideal law, forbidding any sexual relations outside marriage, from a second-best law requiring such relations to be secret and reproductive in kind (c8–e4). Since no one is expected to be wholly abstinent (b4–5), it is implied that this offers something to everyone; homosexuality is always excess, never necessity.

Thus Plato's evolving attitude towards sexuality soon takes on nuances beyond an undiscriminating philosophical distaste for physical indulgence. It is likely that in his eventual estimation and even imposition of parenthood he frees himself, without hypocrisy, from his own involuntary repugnance (which *Phaedrus* 250e3–5 fleetingly

[20] It was the presumed sexual passivity of the younger partner at which the Greeks looked askance in a citizen-to-be (e.g. Aristotle *Rhet* 2.6.1384a15–20; cf. Dover, *GPM*, 215, Foucault, op. cit. 243). That could provoke a popular complaint of 'unnaturalness' (as in Aeschines 1.185; cf. Dover, *GH*, 67–8); but Plato's ground for *that* complaint is the more idiosyncratic one that I have expounded (here in disagreement with Foucault, op. cit. 244).

[21] As Foucault puts it, 'In one's use of the pleasures of the male, one must be virile in respect of oneself' (op. cit. 96); cf. Dover, *GPM*, 101.

betray); if so, he has achieved the best of victories, that over oneself (*Laws* 1.626e2–3). However, to the extent that Plato is linked to John Paul II by a chain of influence, his heroism has cost others dear. Most of us must wish that his sexual prohibitions had never escaped from utopia; and yet, however questionable his grounding of them may be, in detail or in general, its integrity and originality invite from us all a detached curiosity and respect.

APPENDIX 4

Aristotle on Erotic Love

Aristotle and eros may seem to us an inapposite pairing of person and topic; yet the appearance may be deceptive. We must not be too influenced by what chances to survive: Diogenes Laertius lists an 'Eroticus, 1 book', and even a 'Theses on love, 4 books' (5.22–7).[1] Further, we must not interpret what does survive within an unintended perspective. I suspect Richard Walzer of doing that when he makes a very natural complaint: 'Every student of the *Nicomachean Ethics* is puzzled by the fact that Aristotle tacitly disowns Plato's divine *erōs* in his discussion of human relations and mentions associations founded on *erōs* only under the heading of pleasure and gain.'[2] 'Tacitly disown' is only an appropriate phrase if Aristotle had Plato's ideal in mind, and not just Athenian practice; then his remarks about pederasty would indeed be bizarrely disrespectful. As it is, they inhabit the world of Pausanias's speech in the *Symposium*, not of Diotima's teaching; also of Socrates' first speech in the *Phaedrus*, not of his second. What Aristotle thought of Plato's own high hopes, apart from his rejection of the transcendental metaphysic that they presuppose, we have no way of knowing; to compare Plato's prescriptions with Aristotle's descriptions must be misleading. It is difficult enough to try to infer from the fragmentary evidence we do possess what Aristotle took love to be; yet it seems worth while to attempt a kind of archaeological reconstruction.

A useful starting-point is a passage from al-Dailami, which, however dubiously Aristotelian, makes just the distinction that we need if we are to arrange remarks scattered through the corpus to form a coherent psychological pattern. Far from purporting to record anything that Aristotle actually wrote, it associates a purported piece of oral teaching with a pleasing anecdote more Arabian than Greek. The teaching is this:

---

[1] Of these, the 'Eroticus' is presumed to be an early dialogue; the 'Theses on Love' sounds like a workshop product.
[2] 'Platonism in Islamic Philosophy', in *Greek into Arabic* (Oxford, 1962), 241.

Love is an impulse which is generated in the heart; when it is once generated, it moves and grows; afterwards it becomes mature. When it has become mature it is joined by affections of appetite whenever the lover in the depth of his heart increases in his excitement, his perseverance, his desire, his concentrations, and his wishes. And that brings him to cupidity and urges him to demands, until it brings him to disquieting grief, continuous sleeplessness, and hopeless passion and sadness and destruction of mind (Barnes, ii. 2424).[3]

Implicit here is a partition of the soul, for ethical and not biological purposes, that owes much to Plato. Love in origin is an emotion, which may recruit appetite; it is the conjunction which yields all the symptoms that we subsume under being in love. (I cannot believe that Aristotle really held that love comes first.) So love is an emotion naturally accompanied by an appetite. Remarks in the corpus about the affection of friends, ranging there (and perhaps in time) from the *Topics* to the *Politics*, are more precisely reminiscent of Plato. The *Topics* speaks of 'the spirited part' (*to thūmoeides*, 2.7.113a36), the *Politics* of 'spirit' (*thūmos*) as a 'capacity' (*dunamis*) of the soul (7.7.1327b40–1328a1); that is all Platonic language. Affection is located within spirit on the basis of two inferences starting from the premiss, also Platonic, that it is the seat of anger: as anger follows hatred, this too must attach to spirit, and so also must its opposite, affection (*philiā*, *Top* 113a35–b3); evidence to the same effect is that we are more angry with friends than with strangers if we think that they have slighted us (*Pol* 1328a1–3). Similar in suggestion is a remark elsewhere that dogs are at once short-tempered and affectionate (*Hist an* 1.1.488b21–2). If the affection of friends belongs within spirit, so presumably does the emotion of lovers. What distinction between spirit and appetite does Aristotle have in mind? Most indicative is a contrast which he draws in the context of acrasia between the workings of anger and of appetite:

Reason or imagination informs us that we have been insulted or slighted, and anger, reasoning as it were that anything like this must be fought against, boils up straightway; while appetite, if reason or perception merely says that an object is pleasant, springs to the enjoyment of it. Therefore anger obeys reason in a sense, but appetite does not (*NE* 7.6.1149a32–b2).

---

[3] This is discussed by Walzer, 'Aristotle, Galen, and Palladius on Love', in *Greek into Arabic*. Late footnotes to that justify a more determinedly sceptical view than his of its ascription to Aristotle: the anecdote (translated in Barnes) contains a line of verse now known to be Arabic (ibid. 49, n. 1); and the teaching is variably ascribed elsewhere to Aristotle, (in a fuller version) to Hippocrates, to 'a physician', and even to Pythagoras (ibid. 49, n. 2). My use of it here is illustrative, not evidential.

Though in itself it lacks judgement and does not involve choice, anger is evaluative, indeed imperative, in its way, while appetite merely responds to the prospect of pleasure. This is still close to Plato: appetite aims at pleasure (*Rep* 4.436a10–11), but knows no good or evil (439a5–6); spirit has the evaluative function of admiring, honouring, and taking pride in things (8.553d4–6). Appetite and spirit can still work together, as when, corruptly, spirit only prizes the wealth that appetite needs (553d4–7); yet their roles are always distinct. Accordingly, in Aristotle, we shall find the two aspects of love interreacting without fusing: sexual appetite pursues pleasure, while erotic emotion adores its object. So long as we preserve that contrast, we may be able to accommodate remarks about love scattered through the corpus within a framework both consistent and, we may feel, true to life.

More or less illuminating points about love are made in passing in Aristotle's logical writings. The *Topics* touches twice on love in illustration of semantic points. One argument is to show that the verb 'to love' (*philein*) is used in more than one way: 'To love, used of the frame of mind, has to hate as its contrary, while as used of the physical activity it has none; clearly, therefore, to love is homonymous' (1.15.106b2–4).[4] So kissing (the one physical activity which *philein* can ordinarily signify) and loving cannot be the same; the point is valid but restricted, since 'to be in love' (*erān*) also lacks a contrary. The second argument, to show that being in love cannot be defined as desiring intercourse, is more interesting for us:

See if, while both of them [sc. *definiendum* and proposed *definiens*] admit of degrees, they yet do not both become greater together: e.g. suppose love to be the appetite for intercourse; now he who is more intensely in love has not a more intense appetite for intercourse, so that both do not become intensified at once; they certainly should, however, had they been the same thing (6.7.146a7–12).

The terms are *erōs* ('love'), and *epithūmiā* ('appetite'); the conclusion, reached with some ingenuity, is that love can never be identified with sexual desire. Significantly, the point does not depend on a variation between cases: even if the emotion is parasitic upon sexual appetite, it is still not itself an appetite, and its increase is not an

---

[4] Stephen Clark understands this differently, and more interestingly: 'Love is more than desire, for hatred is opposite to "mental friendship" while bodily desire has no opposite' (*Aristotle's Man*, 209). If so, this passage is arguing for the same distinction as the next one I shall discuss.

increase in appetite. A third passage, in the *Prior Analytics*, illustrating a point in the logic of preference, marks love off from appetite still more saliently:

If then every lover in virtue of his love (*erōs*) would prefer A, viz. that the beloved should be such as to grant his favours, and yet should not grant them (for which C stands), to the beloved's granting his favours (represented by D) without being such as to grant it (represented by B), it is clear that A (being of such a nature) is preferable to granting the favours. To receive affection (*phileisthai*) then is preferable in love to sexual intercourse. Love then aims at affection rather than at intercourse. And if it aims most at affection, then this is its end. Intercourse then either is not an end at all or is an end relative to the receiving of affection (2.22.68a39–b6).

The topic is again love with a sexual aspect, and the affection that it is said to prefer to intercourse has a sexual focus: it is the affection that, conventionally in default of any sexual reciprocity, makes the boy willing to consent (cf. K. J. Dover, *GH*, 53). Love so construed is at once sexual and mental; it is an emotion that accompanies appetite not to second it, but to attach to its goal (which is receiving gratification) a new goal (that of receiving a willingness to offer gratification) whose value it creates. While appetite welcomes willingness as a means to performance, love welcomes performance as an expression of willingness. The goal of appetite is presented not as part of love's goal, but as related to it; equally, appetite itself stands to love as precondition, not as part. The relation of the two is not antagonistic: if love did not respect appetite, it would not value affection under the aspect of a willingness to gratify it. The last sentence must mean not that making love is an end from no point of view, but that it is not in itself an end of love: its desirability is to love, as it were, not a conclusion, but a premiss; relative to love, it is ground, not focus. All this seems sensitive and human; it fits a love distinctive of men who are neither angels nor animals.

Relevant remarks in the *Eudemian Ethics* are for the most part rather less illuminating. Walzer takes them to be disparaging;[5] yet they cannot be pressed into assimilating love and appetite. Love (*erōs*) is first mentioned together with anger as an 'irrational feeling' which inspires a kind of courage (3.1.1229a20–5).[6] 'Irrational' no

---

[5] 'Aristotle, Galen, and Palladius on Love', in *Greek into Arabic*, 56.

[6] It is unclear how the passage relates love to spirit, as it applies the term *thūmos* not to spirit in general, but to the emotion of anger, which it also calls *orgē*. But, if we were to speak of spirit, the suggestion would be that love and anger belong together within it.

doubt conveys that deliberation and choice are not involved; hence this is not courage strictly so called (a30). The thought is not excluded that, in comparison with appetite, anger can be said to 'obey reason in a sense' (NE 7.6.1149b1, already quoted). The next two passages come in 7.1, where Aristotle is only, in his usual manner, raising various opinions and puzzles in order to set the scene for his own discussion. That 'the object of love and of appetite is dear to all' (1235a14–15) does not entail that love and appetite are the same. Also indecisive is this:

Another puzzle is whether the good or the pleasant is what is held dear. For if we hold dear what we have an appetite for—and love is specially of this kind, for 'none is a lover but one who ever holds dear'—and if appetite is for the pleasant, in this way what is held dear would be the pleasant; but if it is what we have a wish for, then it is the good—the good and the pleasant being different (1235b18–23).

Even if we punctuate so, with 'love is specially of this kind' asserted and not hypothesized, the passage is too provisional and loosely written to prove anything. It could mean that love is an appetite (though what then is the force of 'specially'?); it means more likely that appetite accompanies love more than it does any other emotion. It raises as a possibility not that only the pleasant is held dear (which would suggest that all desire is appetite), but that being an object of appetite is one way of being held dear. It does suggest that love is not a kind of wish, but that must be right: a wish is the desiderative aspect of a judgement about ends, while emotion (to quote again) only 'obeys reason in a sense'. A fourth passage is more concrete:

Love (erōs) seems to resemble friendship; for the lover desires a life together, although not in the most proper way but according to sensation (or perception, aisthēsis; 7.12.1245a24–6).

In this chapter friendship is being spoken of restrictively, as if the friend because of virtue is the only friend (1244b16–17). It is still allowed that some friends who live their lives together will share bodily pleasures, while others share artistic contemplation or philosophy (1245a19–22). The sentence quoted is doubly ambiguous, lexically because aisthēsis may be sensation (which is low-minded) or perception (which in the form of sight is relatively high-minded), syntactically because the qualification may be taken either with 'desires' or with 'a life together'. Accordingly, it could mean either that what the lover desires is not, as ideally it should be, to benefit the beloved, but to enjoy seeing or embracing him; or that the lover's desire for the company of the beloved is dictated not by choice, as ideally it should be, but by a desire for sight or contact. While leaving the ambiguities open, Aristotle could be contrasting true friends who in their life together choose to make love because that is the best that they can offer one another (a19–21), with the lover whose passion urges him to share the beloved's life because he wants to be with him (even if he will benefit him less by enjoying him physically than by doing philosophy with him). Put abstractly, the point is that love itself is not a virtue, and does not involve choice; it is not excluded that some choices may serve both love and virtue.

The relation between love (*erōs*) and affection (*philein*) is usefully raised in the course of Lysias's speech in the *Phaedrus*, when the non-lover mentions (without endorsing) this thought: 'It is right to put a high value on those in love, because they say they show the greatest degree of affection to those they love, and are ready to say and to do what will incur the enmity of everyone else, if it pleases the beloved' (231b7–c4). Essential to affection is precisely taking pleasure in pleasing the other, for his sake. (So this kind of *philein* belongs within that *philiā* singled out by Aristotle which involves wishing to benefit the other for his sake.) But then need it accompany love? An ambiguous example in the *Prior Analytics* of a 'probability', that is of a proposition known to be true only for the most part, is that lovers feel affection for those they love (if it is not that those who are loved feel affection for their lovers, 2.27.70a4–6). Plato proposes in the *Laws* that the feeling of friendship, whether towards someone like or unlike oneself, becomes love when it is intense (8.836a6–9). Of course that cannot be right: the *Lysis* recognized that intense affection may link parents to children (207d6), or friends of the same age (212a4). In the *Nicomachean Ethics* Aristotle remarks that love 'tends to be an excess of friendship', and exclusive for that reason; this indicates that one cannot enjoy an intense friendship with many (9.10.1171a10–13, cf. 8.5.1158a10–13). A tendency does not yield an identity (and friendship towards oneself, to which 'an excess of friendship' can be likened, 9.4.1166b1–2, is hardly a case of being in love); yet the connection suggests an affectionate side to friendship, and a benevolent side to love. Whatever may be said now and then about love itself, or the lover *qua* lover, there cannot be any incompatibility between love and even the best friendship.

Another valuable point made twice in the *Nicomachean Ethics* is that love is specially related to sight. Sight is both the beginning and the continuation of love: 'For lovers the sight of the beloved is the thing they love most, and they prefer this sense to the others because on it love depends most for its being and for its origin' (9.12.1171b29–31). More precisely, sight prepares the way for love: 'Goodwill seems to be a beginning of friendship, as the pleasure of the eye is the beginning of love. For no one loves if he has not first been delighted by the form of the beloved' (9.5.1167a3–4). But sight is not superseded once it has chosen an object for the other senses; falling in love is not like falling for a particularly rosy peach which one next only wants to taste.⁷ The focus of the lover's visual attention must be primarily the face, in which alone he can see the mind of the beloved (as Socrates finds beauty in Charmides' blush precisely because he can see in it the modesty that befits someone of his age, *Charm* 158c5–6). Beauty of soul is less easy to see than beauty of body (*Pol* 1.5.1254b38–1255a1); less easy, not impossible. Still more narrowly, it is in observing the other's eyes that the lover can best hope to detect the attitude of the beloved towards himself. That must be the psychological context of a piece of evidence in Athenaeus (more probably drawing on a lost work than was al-Dailami): 'Aristotle said that lovers look to no other part of the bodies of the beloved than their eyes, in which modesty dwells' (564b, Rose³ fr. 96).⁸ Modesty is the response of the beloved whose eyes betray that he has noticed, and accepts, that he is loved, but do not collusively encourage the lover to advance from looking to embracing.⁹ Though the kinds of love are rather different, this remark in Athenaeus is close to Aristotle's argument already quoted that 'love aims at affection rather than intercourse' (*Pr Anal* 2.22.68b4): it is the mental response of the beloved that most concerns the lover, whether or not he retains sexual goals. This again distinguishes love from any kind of appetite. The pleasures of sight can indeed be an object of appetite (though not

---

⁷ Psychoanalytically, falling in love is caused by the displacement of cathexis from a tactile interest (sometimes unconscious) to an aesthetic interest, limited to sight and hearing, that supplements or replaces sexual appetite aiming at its own relief by an erotic obsession which, knowing no satisfaction and unconnected with any organ-pleasure, attaches the lover faithfully to the person of the loved one.

⁸ The *Rhetoric* cites a possibly apposite proverb, 'Shame dwells in the eyes' (2.6.1384a34), but glosses it irrelevantly.

⁹ He contrasts with the boy complained of by Right in Aristophanes' *Clouds* who 'acts as his own procurer with his eyes' (980); cited in Dover, *GH*, 85.

of those appetites with which temperance is concerned, *NE* 3.10.1118a1–6). Yet the lover's desire to see the other's mind belongs with personal attitudes and emotions whose object is not the pleasure of the senses: it is not that he is so sophisticated that what he enjoys is catching sight of how people feel, not how they look, but that he cannot help attaching the greatest importance to how a certain person feels, especially towards him.

Even a concern with the other's attitude might be an occasional interest (like that which one resumes as one picks up a novel). Aristotle also notes that love depends upon an absence that is felt: 'He who delights in the form of another does not, for all that, love him, but only does so when he also longs for him when absent and craves for his presence' (9.5.1167a4–7). Above all, love is a collaboration between the heart and the visual imagination:

A lover enjoys talking or writing about his loved one, or doing any little thing connected with him; all these things recall him to memory and make him as it were present to perception. Indeed, it is always the beginning of love that, besides enjoying someone's presence, we remember him when he is gone and feel pain because he is there no longer (*Rhet* 1.11.1370b19–25).

The point in context is that pain can be accompanied by 'a kind of pleasure' (b25–6). This does not in itself differentiate love from appetite: 'A kind of pleasure accompanies most of our appetites: we are enjoying either the memory of a past experience or the expectation of a future one, just as persons down with fever, during their attacks of thirst, enjoy remembering the drinks they have had and looking forward to others to come' (b15–19). That imagining the beloved and imagining a feast are quite different becomes implicit if we take all these pieces of evidence together: the end of desire that it pains, but also pleases, the lover to dwell upon in his imagination is not so much seeing the affection of the other in his eyes as that he should indeed feel affection, even undetectedly. Just as the lover prefers a willingness to gratify to actual gratification, so, unless he is playing at being in love, he must prefer an affectionate heart to an appearance of affection. (That is not to imply that he may not keenly want all of these.) The goal of love that makes love what it is is not an experience.

Given the seclusion of women in Athens, especially among the upper classes (cf. Dover, *GPM*, 95–8, 209–13), love between the sexes must have flourished mostly within marriage, which is the grave (if with the hope of a happier resurrection) of the kind of love that we have been considering; hence passages in Aristotle about being in love are at least implicitly about pederasty also. So it is surprising if explicitly pederastic passages take a different view. Yet this appears to be the case: the recurrent pattern of a pederastic relationship is a 'mixed' friendship in which the lover pursues his own pleasure, the beloved his own profit. Even if (as I urged) we do not take Aristotle to be responding to Plato, such a view still seems ungenerous. If we look more closely, we find a divergence between the *Eudemian* and the *Nicomachean Ethics*: whereas the *Eudemian* only presents pederasty within the pattern (though without asserting that it always applies), the *Nicomachean* permits a development that escapes the rigidity of the classification.

The two relevant passages in the *Eudemian Ethics* ascribe to pederasty precisely its most convenient description within the model. The first cites a common cause of dissension (which may, but need not, mean a cause of common dissension) between lover and beloved:

With those who are friends through use or pleasure, some are related by equality, others by superiority or inferiority. Therefore those who suppose the former to hold find fault if the other is not equally useful to and a benefactor of them; and similarly with regard to pleasure. This is obvious in the case of love affairs, for this is frequently the cause of mutual strife. For the lover does not perceive that the readiness of each does not have the same reason; therefore . . . a lover would not say such things. But they [i.e. lovers] suppose that the reason is the same (7.3.1238b32–9, retaining Barnes's lacuna in the place of some corrupt text).

The scenario which is being rather awkwardly articulated seems to be this: *A* (the lover) supposes that he causes *B* (the beloved) as much pleasure as *B* causes him, and so expects *B* to be as useful to him as he is to *B*; but *B* expects to be rewarded for the greater pleasure he gives *A* by receiving greater benefits (and so, for example, always leaves *A* to pay the bill). This implies a more precise view than we have met before of what a lover naturally desires: that the beloved not only accept his love but return it, so receiving the same pleasure from the lover's company that that the lover receives from his. That makes pederasty problematic, for the beloved was expected to return not love but affection (cf. Dover, *GH*, 52–3). Aristotle is evidence of an upshot more interesting than surprising: with a general recognition of that, at least in the case of other people, there often coexisted a particular hope by the individual lover that his case would be different, a hope that the beloved might be too tactful to contradict. This could give rise in the beloved to a conflict between affection and prudence, affection reinforcing tact by wishing to preserve the illusion, prudence counselling a working arrangement based on an acceptance of the reality. (Alternatively, prudence may second affection, as when the lover is happy always to pay the bill so long as he can suppose that that is not what the beloved is after; then the dissension described by Aristotle will not occur.) All that is implicit in the passage; what is explicit is constrained by Aristotle's framework, and cruder. It remains open whether Aristotle makes no comment about the goals other than selfish pleasure or utility that govern such a relationship because they are irrelevant to the point that he is making, or because he holds them to be unreal.

Philosophically interesting, but equally ungenerous, is a second passage:

Recriminations are common in friendships not in the same direction, and it is not easy to see what is just; for it is hard to measure different directions by this one unit. We find this in the case of lovers; for the one seeks the other as a pleasant person, in order to share his life, while the latter seeks the other at times for his utility. When the love is over, one changes as the other changes, and then they calculate the *quid pro quo* (7.10.1243b15–20).

The retrospective balance sheet is less disconcerting than the behaviour of the ex-lover in Socrates' first speech in the *Phaedrus* who simply writes off his own debts (241a2–b5), but we are disagreeably close to the book-keeping alleged by Lysias: 'Those who are in love consider the damage they did to their own interests because of their love and the services they have performed, and adding in the labour they put in they think they have long since given return enough to the objects of their love' (231a6–b2). Aristotle discusses the problem of commensurability further, and resolves it rather rapidly, in the lines that follow. We cannot discount what he has said here as pure schematizing: there is too much bite in the qualification 'at times'. As before, it is left open how generally the description applies.

The *Nicomachean Ethics* again raises the problem of how to find a common measure in the case of friendship between parties who are dissimilar (and implicitly each out for what he can get) (9.1.1163b32–1164a2), before expatiating upon the problems that can arise within pederasty:

In erotic friendship sometimes the lover complains that his excess of friendship is not met by friendship in return (though perhaps there is nothing in him to merit it), while often the beloved complains that the lover who formerly promised everything now performs nothing. Such incidents happen when the lover befriends the beloved for the sake of pleasure while the beloved befriends the lover for the sake of utility, and they do not both possess the qualities expected of them. If these be the reasons for the friendship it is dissolved when they do not get the things that formed the motives of their friendship; for each did not treasure the other person himself but the qualities he had, and these were not enduring; that is why the friendships also are transient. But friendship of character, as has been said, endures because it is self-dependent (1164a2–13).[10]

In the theme of the lover who forgets his promises as he falls out of love this passage is close to the end of Socrates' first speech in the *Phaedrus* (241a2–b7). Yet it is now explicit that no universal generalization is possible about the nature of such friendship, and its perils: note 'sometimes', 'often', and 'such incidents happen when'.

Another passage curiously moots subsuming pederastic relationships within a friendship of utility between contraries:

Friendship because of utility seems especially to arise from contraries, e.g. between poor and rich, ignorant and learned; for what a man actually lacks he aims at, and he gives something in return. Under this head too one might drag in lover and beloved, and beautiful and ugly. This is why lovers sometimes seem ridiculous, when they demand to be loved as they love; if they are similarly lovable their claim can perhaps be justified, but when they have nothing lovable about them it is ridiculous (8.8.1159b12–19, with 'love' translating *philein*, 'lovable' *philētos*).

The term 'drag' conveys that this is not Aristotle's own position. Presumably he would see it as contrived partly, at least, because it counts pleasure as a kind of utility (which the beautiful can offer the ugly); also, perhaps, because it is not in fact distinctive of the ugly to fall for the beautiful.[11] Aristotle's comment ('This is why . . .') implies that, at least in some cases, lover and beloved are indeed pursuing quite different things, and expect a fair exchange. 'Similarly lovable' is equivalent in context to 'also useful': what fits the proposal

---

[10] I take the obscure 'self-dependent' (*kath' hautēn*) as equivalent to 'in respect of the parties themselves' (cf. *di' hautous*, 8.3.1156b10).

[11] Implicit in the proposal is a confusion between desiring the beautiful in the sense of taking pleasure in beautiful people, and in that of wishing to become beautiful; of course a love affair is not a course of plastic surgery. When Socrates described Eros as not 'soft and beautiful' but 'hard and dry' (*Symp* 203c6–d1), he was speaking of lovers *qua* lovers, and hence of their erotic way of life, not their physical appearance.

is that the beloved should provide pleasure, the lover utility properly so called. Which is precisely Aristotle's own model.

Finally, there is an earlier passage which makes pederasty a matter of contrary pleasures, out of which a better friendship may grow:

> Among men of these sorts too [viz. the pleasant or useful], friendships are most permanent when they get the same things from each other (e.g. pleasure), and not only that but also from the same source, as happens between ready-witted people, and not as happens between lover and beloved. For these do not take pleasure in the same things, but the one in seeing the other and the other in receiving attentions from the lover; and when the bloom of youth is passing the friendship sometimes passes too (for the one finds no pleasure in the sight of the other, and the other gets no attentions from the first); but many on the other hand are constant, if familiarity has led them to love each other's characters, these being alike (8.4.1157a3–12).

Aristotle here starts by presenting a pederastic relationship as a friendship mixed not out of pleasure for one and utility for the other, but out of different pleasures for each (and so preferable to any utility-friendship). His claim that such a friendship is less likely to last than one in which they are the same can at most be a 'probability' (which is what it ought to be, cf. 1.3.1094b11–27): even if the lover falls (like Echo) for a narcissist, their friendship will last no longer because of that when the boy grows a beard. Also no more than generally true would be a supposal that a friendship based on different pleasures for each is more likely to be brought to an end unilaterally: more dangerous might be common pleasures which one party will outgrow before the other (juvenile pleasures, say, if they are of slightly different ages). But the novelty here that matters is the acknowledgement that out of transient interests that set the two apart even as they bring them together may often develop a mutual affection for each other's character that will last. The initial interests are not a mistake to be regretted: they provide the opportunity for the affection that will outlive them. More ambiguous is the causal relation between familiarity, affinity, and affection.[12] The ambiguity is in part syntactical (or, in logical jargon, one of scope):

1. Because of the affinity of the two, familiarity brings affection;
2. Because of the familiarity of the two, there is an affinity to bring affection.

---

[12] This is pointed out in M. van Straaten and G. J. de Vries, 'Notes on the 8th and 9th Books of Aristotle's *Nicomachean Ethics*', 203–4.

In (1), there is a complex cause, affinity plus familiarity, of a single effect, affection; in (2), there is a causal chain from familiarity to affinity, and from affinity to affection. Correlated with the syntactical is a terminological ambiguity: does 'character' here mean the natural, or the fully developed, state of virtue or vice (cf. 6.13.1144b15–16)? Boys and young men are incapable of the second, because they lack experience (1.3.1095a2–8, 1.9.1100a2–3, 6.8.1142a12–19). So only two real possibilities result from these four variables (two syntactical, two terminological): in (1) that the affinity is natural (indeed innate, 6.13.1144b4–6); and in (2) that it is achieved through a personal familiarity drawing upon a natural predisposition.[13] Neither of these alternatives is quite satisfactory. Virtue can only be fully developed by the time that lover and beloved have become husbands and heads of a family, which seems too late; yet, while Aristotle allows a kind of character-friendship between or towards the morally immature, he emphasizes that it may not last once both parties are grown up (9.3.1165b13–31). The best solution seems the obvious compromise: the virtue is half-developed, so that its turning out wrongly is possible but unlikely. That fits (2): it is familiarity, of course exploiting nature, that creates the affinity. If this is right, Aristotle is here quite close to Plato (perhaps inconsciently): both see in the love of boys an opportunity for developing a similarity of character that will ground a mutual and enduring affection.[14]

That is their ideal; of course reality can fall far short. Plato recognizes a corrupt lover who tries to treat boys like women (*Phdr* 250e3–251a1), Aristotle a corrupting lover who risks turning boys into women (*NE* 7.5). He distinguishes two sources of sexual passivity: an innate bodily defect, and a disease-like deterioration. Female differentiae are a natural 'deficiency' or 'mutilation' (*De gen an* 4.6.775a15–16); a woman is like a eunuch (4.1.766a25–8). It is not idiomatically acrasia (literally, lack of self-control) if a man cannot help playing the female role from an equally innate defect; nor is it if the cause is some pathological state produced by habituation to sexual

---

[13] Strictly, there is also the possible coincidence that the affinity develops simultaneously with the familiarity, but independently of it; I set that aside.

[14] It presumably goes with Plato's theory of recollection that he takes the original innate affinity that is a precondition of the one emergent later to be more determinate than Aristotle takes it to be; for Plato, developing the affinity is a process of recovering it. That would be a real divergence; the apparent discrepancy in emphasis, which has one sentence in Aristotle (1157a10–12) answering to pages of Plato, signifies nothing in view of the lost works.

abuse from boyhood (*NE* 7.5.1148b29–34).[15] So Aristotle has a special concern, medical instead of metaphysical, that pederasty should keep to its higher forms, 'looking rather than loving', as Plato had put it (*Laws* 8.837c4–5).

As observers of love as it actually was, neither Plato nor Aristotle is a fully satisfactory guide: Plato is too idealistic, Aristotle too schematic. Both remain capable of real insights; of the relevant Aristotle so little remains that it is only speculatively that we can fit them within a psychological pattern which sets erotic love in relation to sexual appetite without confounding the two. More explicit, but less adequate, is an ethical pattern which associates erotic love, in the form of pederasty, with a lesser form of friendship. If we take that together with all the incidental evidence, we find a mismatch between a general theory which applies only to an egoistic lover in pursuit of his own pleasure, and particular concessions, implicit or explicit, to the effect that the lover's fundamental goal is no experience of his own, but that the beloved should reciprocate his affection or even his love. As the theory is presented in Aristotle's later ethical writings, while the crucial concession is only explicit in an earlier logical text (*Pr Anal* 2.22.68a39–b6), the need for a reconciliation may be clearer to us than it ever was to him.[16] What he does briefly allow is that being in love may generate a different kind of loving, less erotic but more faithful. Ultimately, both within the permanent inequalities of marriage and the transient inequalities of pederasty, Aristotle envisages the emergence of that reciprocal concern and respect which constitute the best kind of friendship, linking individuals not merely as satisfiers of one another's incidental needs, but as partners in a life of personal self-realization. The moral end of love is to transcend itself in friendship.

---

[15] There is no reason to suppose that Aristotle has in mind any particular sexual practice, as if 'safer sex' would avoid the danger; but it is an intelligible distortion that the author of the pseudo-Aristotelian *Problemata* spells out the two alternatives physiologically in relation to anal intercourse (4.26). Cf. Dover (*GH*, 168–70), who rightly stresses that Aristotle is thinking of sexual inversion in particular (which the Greeks disparaged), and not homosexuality in general (which they were far from conceiving as a unitary quasi-medical condition). It is striking that he is not concerned, as we might be, that a sexually abused boy may abuse other boys in his turn; it is habitual passivity, and not imitative activity, that he sees as the danger. At 1148b29 'paederasty' in the Oxford Translation is a misleading departure from a phrase that Terence Irwin renders literally as 'sexual intercourse between males'.

[16] Of course, one misses the 'Eroticus'; it is a reasonable guess that it was the source of the illustrative remarks about love in the *Topics* and *Prior Analytics*.

LIST OF MODERN WORKS CITED

(For translations used or cited, see 'Note to the Reader'.)

Ackrill, J. L., 'Aristotle on *Eudaimonia*', in Rorty (ed.) *Essays on Aristotle's Ethics*, 15–33.

Adam, J., *The Republic of Plato* (2 vols.; Cambridge, 1902).

Allan, D. J., 'Individual and State in the *Ethics* and *Politics*', in Fondation Hardt, *Entretiens 9, La 'Politique' d'Aristote* (Geneva, 1964), 55–95.

Allen, R. E., 'A Note on the Elenchus of Agathon: *Symposium* 199c–201c', *Monist* 50 (1966), 460–3.

Annas, J., *An Introduction to Plato's Republic* (Oxford, 1981).

Anscombe, G. E. M., 'You Can have Sex without Children: Christianity and the New Offer', in *Ethics, Religion and Politics* (Oxford, 1981), 82–96.

Archer-Hind, R. D., 'On Some Difficulties in the Platonic Psychology', *Journal of Philology* 10 (1882), 120–31.

Auden, W. H., *A Certain World* (London, 1971).

Auster, P., *The New York Trilogy* (London, 1987).

Barnes, J., 'Aristotle's Concept of Mind', in J. Barnes, M. Schofield, R. Sorabji (eds.) *Articles on Aristotle 4: Psychology and Aesthetics* (London, 1979), 32–41.

—— 'Aristotle and the Methods of Ethics', *Revue internationale de philosophie* 34 (1980), 490–511.

Barthes, R., *Fragments d'un discours amoureux* (Paris, 1977).

Baudelaire, C., *Œuvres complètes*, ed. C. Pichois (2 vols.; Paris, 1975–7).

Berti, E., 'Multiplicité et unité du bien selon *EE* 1.8', in P. Moraux and D. Harlfinger (eds.) *Untersuchungen zur Eudemischen Ethik* (Berlin, 1971), 157–84.

Bluck, R. S., 'The *Phaedrus* and Reincarnation', *American Journal of Philology* 79 (1958), 156–64, 405–14.

Bornemann, E., 'Aristoteles' Urteil über Platons politische Theorie', *Philologus* 79 (1923–4), 70–111, 113–58, 234–57.

Bosanquet, B., *The Principle of Individuality and Value* (London, 1912).

Bostock, D., *Plato's Phaedo* (Oxford, 1986).

Bradley, F. H., *Ethical Studies*, 2nd edn. (Oxford, 1927).

Brendel, A., *Musical Thoughts and Afterthoughts* (London, 1976).

Burnyeat, M. F., 'The Passion of Reason in Plato's *Phaedrus*' (unpublished).

Carpenter, H., *The Inklings* (London, 1978).

Calvert, B., 'Slavery in Plato's Republic', *Classical Quarterly* 37 (1987), 367–72.

Cherniss, H., Letter to the *Classical Review* NS 3 (1953), 131.

Chroust, A.-H., *Aristotle* (2 vols.; London, 1973).

Clark, S. R. L., *Aristotle's Man* (Oxford, 1975).

Cooper, J. M., 'The *Magna moralia* and Aristotle's Moral Philosophy', *American Journal of Philology* 94 (1973), 327–49.

—— 'Aristotle on the Forms of Friendship', *Review of Metaphysics* 30 (1976/7), 619–48.

—— 'Aristotle on Friendship', in Rorty (ed.) *Essays on Aristotle's Ethics*, 301–40.

Crombie, I. M., *An Examination of Plato's Doctrines* (2 vols.; London, 1962).

Denniston, J. D., *The Greek Particles*, 2nd edn. (Oxford, 1954).

Devereux, G., 'Greek Pseudo-homosexuality and the "Greek Miracle"', *Symbolae Osloenses* 52 (1967), 69–92.

Dover, K. J., 'Aristophanes' Speech in Plato's *Symposium*', *Journal of Hellenic Studies* 86 (1966), 41–50.

—— *Greek Popular Morality in the Time of Plato and Aristotle* (Oxford, 1974).

—— *Greek Homosexuality* (London, 1978).

—— *Plato: Symposium* (Cambridge, 1980).

Ferrari, G. R. F., *Listening to the Cicadas: A Study of Plato's Phaedrus* (Cambridge, 1987).

Fortenbaugh, W. W., 'Aristotle's Analysis of Friendship: Function and Analogy, Resemblance, and Focal Meaning', *Phronesis* 20 (1975), 51–62.

Foucault, M., *L'Usage des plaisirs* (Paris, 1984).

Freud, S., *The Pelican Freud Library*, ed. A. Richards (15 vols.; Harmondsworth, 1973–86).

Gallop, D., *Plato: Phaedo* (Oxford, 1975).

Geach, P. T., 'Good and Evil', in P. Foot (ed.) *Theories of Ethics* (London, 1967), 64–73.

Gill, C., 'Plato and the Education of Character', *Archiv für Geschichte der Philosophie* 67 (1985), 1–26.

—— 'Platonic Love and Individuality', in H. Lesser and A. Loizon (eds.) *The Good of Community* (Gower, forthcoming).

Gomperz, T., *Greek Thinkers: A History of Ancient Philosophy*, tr. L. Magnus and C. G. Berry (4 vols.; London, 1901–12).

Griffin, J., *Well-Being* (Oxford, 1986).

Groag, E., 'Zur Lehre vom Wesen der Seele in Platons *Phaidrus* und im zehnten Buch der *Republik*', *Wiener Studien* 37 (1915), 189–222.

Grote, G., *Plato, and the Other Companions of Sokrates*, 2nd edn. (3 vols.; London, 1867).

Guthrie, W. K. C., *A History of Greek Philosophy* (6 vols.; Cambridge, 1962–81).

—— 'Plato's Views on the Nature of the Soul', in G. Vlastos (ed.) *Plato II* (New York, 1971), 230–43.

Guyau, M., *Esquisse d'une morale sans obligation ni sanction*, 4th edn. (Paris, 1896).

Hackforth, R., 'Immortality in Plato's *Symposium*', *Classical Review* 64 (1950), 43–5.

—— *Plato's Phaedrus* (Cambridge, 1952).

Hare, R. M., *Moral Thinking* (Oxford, 1981).

Horn, F., *Platonstudien* (Vienna, 1893).

Housman, A. E., *The Letters of A. E. Housman*, ed. H. Maas (London, 1971).

Huxley, G., *On Aristotle and Greek Society* (Belfast, 1979).

Irwin, T. H., *Plato's Moral Theory* (Oxford, 1977).

—— 'Homonymy in Aristotle', *Review of Metaphysics* 34 (1980/1), 523–44.

—— *Aristotle: Nicomachean Ethics* (Indianapolis, 1985).

Jaeger, W., *Paideia*, tr. G. Highet (3 vols.; Oxford, 1939–45).

Jenkyns, R., *The Victorians and Ancient Greece* (Oxford, 1980).

Kenny, A., *The Aristotelian Ethics* (Oxford, 1978).

Klein, M., 'Some Theoretical Conclusions Regarding the Emotional Life of the Infant', in *Envy and Gratitude and Other Works: 1946–1963*, ed. R. Money-Kyrle (London, 1975), 61–93.

—— 'On Identification', in *Envy and Gratitude*, 141–75.

Klein, M., 'Envy and Gratitude', in *Envy and Gratitude*, 176–235.

Kosman, L. A., 'Platonic Love', in W. H. Werkmeister (ed.) *Facets of Plato's Philosophy* (Assen, 1976), 53–69.

Kraut, R., 'Egoism, Love, and Political Office in Plato', *Philosophical Review* 82 (1973), 330–44.

—— 'Aristotle on Choosing Virtue for Itself', *Archiv für Geschichte der Philosophie* 58 (1976), 223–39.

Lebeck, A., 'The Central Myth of Plato's *Phaedrus*', *Greek, Roman, and Byzantine Studies* 13 (1972), 267–90.

Le Guin, U. K., *The Left Hand of Darkness* (London, 1969).

Lewis, C. S., *The Four Loves* (London, 1960).

Lloyd, A. C., 'Genus, Species, and Ordered Series in Aristotle', *Phronesis* 6 (1962), 67–90.

McGibbon, D. D., 'The Fall of the Soul in Plato's *Phaedrus*', *Classical Quarterly* NS 14 (1964), 56–63.

Montaigne, M. de, *Essays*, tr. J. Florio (London, 1632).

Montherlant, H. de, *Les Garçons*, in *Romans II*, ed. M. Raimond (Paris, 1982).

Moravcsik, J. M. E., 'Reason and Eros in the "Ascent"-passage of the *Symposium*', in J. P. Anton and G. L. Kustas (eds.) *Essays in Ancient Greek Philosophy* (Albany, 1971), 285–302.

Müller, A. W., 'Radical Subjectivity: Morality versus Utilitarianism', *Ratio* 19 (1977), 115–32.

Murdoch, I., *The Fire and the Sun* (Oxford, 1977).

Napier, C., 'The Design of the Creator: A Guide to Humanae Vitae' (London, 1969).

Newman, W. L., *The Politics of Aristotle* (4 vols.; Oxford, 1887–1902).

Nietzsche, F., *Twilight of the Idols*, tr. R. J. Hollingdale (Harmondsworth, 1968).

—— *The Will to Power*, tr. W. Kaufmann (New York, 1968).

—— *The Gay Science*, tr. Kaufmann (New York, 1974).

—— *Daybreak*, tr. Hollingdale (Cambridge, 1982).

—— *Human, All Too Human*, tr. Hollingdale (Cambridge, 1986).

Novalis, *Werke und Briefe*, ed. A. Kelletat (Munich, 1962).

Nussbaum, M. C., 'Shame, Separateness, and Political Unity: Aristotle's Criticism of Plato', in Rorty (ed.) *Essays on Aristotle's Ethics*, 395–435.

—— 'Plato on Commensurability and Desire', *Proceedings of the Aristotelian Society* Supp. Vol. 58 (1984), 55–80.

—— *The Fragility of Goodness* (Cambridge, 1986).

Ogden, T. H., 'On Projective Identification', *International Journal of Psycho-analysis* 60 (1979), 357–73.

Owen, G. E. L., 'Logic and Metaphysics in some Earlier Works of Aristotle', in *Logic, Science and Dialectic*, ed. M. C. Nussbaum (London, 1986), 180–99.

Parfit, D., *Reasons and Persons* (Oxford, 1984).

Pater, W., *Plato and Platonism* (London, 1893).

Percival, G., 'Notes on Three Passages from the *Nicomachean Ethics*, Book 8', *Classical Quarterly* 29 (1935), 171–6.

Price, A. W., 'Aristotle's Ethical Holism', *Mind* 89 (1980), 338–52.

—— 'Loving Persons Platonically', *Phronesis* 26 (1981), 25–34.

—— 'Plato and Freud', in C. Gill (ed.) *The Person and the Human Mind: Issues in Ancient and Modern Philosophy* (Oxford, 1990), 247–70.

Proust, M., *A la recherche du temps perdu*, ed. P. Clarac and A. Ferré (3 vols.; Paris, 1954).

Reeve, M. D., 'Eleven Notes', *Classical Review* NS 21 (1971), 324–9.

Robin, L., *Platon: Le Banquet* (Paris, 1929).

—— *Platon: Phèdre* (Paris, 1933).

Robinson, D. B., 'Plato's *Lysis*', B.Litt. thesis (Oxford, 1961).

—— 'Plato's *Lysis*: The Structural Problem', *Illinois Classical Studies* 11 (1986), 63–83.

Rorty, A. O. (ed.), *Essays on Aristotle's Ethics* (University of California, 1980).

Ross, W. D., *Aristotle's Metaphysics* (2 vols.; Oxford, 1924).

Rougemont, D. de, *The Myths of Love*, tr. R. Howard (London, 1964).

Rowe, C. J., *Plato* (Brighton, 1984).

—— *Plato: Phaedrus* (Warminster, 1986).

—— 'The Argument and Structure of Plato's *Phaedrus*', *Proceedings of the Cambridge Philological Society* NS 32 (1986), 106–25.

Russell, B., *The Autobiography of Bertrand Russell: 1872–1914* (London, 1967).

Schiffer, S., 'A Paradox of Desire', *American Philosophical Quarterly* 13 (1976), 195–203.

Schirlitz, K., *Beiträge zur Erklärung der Rede des Sokrates in Platons Symposion* (Neustettin, 1890).

Scruton, R., *Sexual Desire* (London, 1986).

Seth, V., *The Golden Gate* (New York, 1986).

Stewart, J. A., *Notes on the Nicomachean Ethics of Aristotle* (2 vols.; Oxford, 1892).

—— *The Myths of Plato*, 2nd edn. (Fontwell, 1960).

Stokes, M. C., *Plato's Socratic Conversations* (London, 1986).

Straaten, M. van and Vries, G. J. de, 'Notes on the 8th and 9th Books of Aristotle's *Nicomachean Ethics*', *Mnemosyne* 13 (1960), 193–228.

Thompson, W. H., *The Phaedrus of Plato* (London, 1868).

Tournier, M., *Les Météores* (Paris, 1975).

Verdenius, W. J., 'Notes on Plato's *Phaedrus*', *Mnemosyne* 8 (1955), 265–89.

Vlastos, G., 'The Individual as Object of Love in Plato', in *Platonic Studies*, 2nd edn. (Princeton, 1981), 3–42.

—— 'Justice and Happiness in the *Republic*', in *Platonic Studies*, 111–39.

—— 'Does Slavery Exist in Plato's *Republic*?', in *Platonic Studies*, 140–6.

—— 'The Unity of the Virtues in the *Protagoras*', in *Platonic Studies*, 221–69.

Vries, G. J. de, *A Commentary on the Phaedrus of Plato* (Amsterdam, 1969).

Walker, A. D. M., 'Aristotle's Account of Friendship in the *Nicomachean Ethics*', *Phronesis* 24 (1979), 180–96.

Walzer, R., 'Aristotle, Galen, and Palladius on Love', in *Greek into Arabic* (Oxford, 1962), 48–59.

—— 'Platonism in Islamic Philosophy', in *Greek into Arabic*, 236–52.

Warner, M., 'Love, Self, and Plato's *Symposium*', *Philosophical Quarterly* 29 (1979), 329–39.

Wenzig, C., *Die Conception der Ideenlehre im Phaedrus bildet den einheitlichen Grundgedanken dieses Dialoges und liefert den Schlüssel zur Verständnis der Platonischen Ideenlehre überhaupt* (Breslau, 1883).

Wiggins, D., 'Truth, Invention and the Meaning of Life', in *Needs, Values, Truth* (Oxford, 1987), 87–137.

Wilamowitz-Möllendorf, U. von, *Platon* (2 vols.; Berlin, 1919).

Williams, B., *Ethics and the Limits of Philosophy* (London, 1985).

Wippern, J., 'Eros und Unsterblichkeit in der Diotima-Rede des *Symposions*', in H. Flashar and K. Gaiser (eds.) *Synusia* (Pfullingen, 1965), 123–59.

Wittgenstein, L., *Philosophical Investigations*, 2nd edn. (Oxford, 1958).

Wollheim, R., 'The Sheep and the Ceremony' (Cambridge, 1979).

—— *Art and its Objects*, 2nd edn. (Cambridge, 1980).

—— *The Thread of Life* (Cambridge, 1984).

Woods, M., *Aristotle's Eudemian Ethics: Books 1, 2, and 8* (Oxford, 1982).

Zeller, E., *Plato and the Older Academy*, tr. S. F. Alleyne and A. Goodwin (London, 1876).

INDEX